A Concise Introduction to International Law

The painting on the cover is *The Last Day of Pompeii* (1830-1833) by Karl Pavlovich Bryullov (St. Petersburg, Russia, 12 December 1799 – Manziana, Italy, 11 June 1852).

Attila M. Tanzi

A Concise Introduction to International Law

Second edition

G. Giappichelli Torino

eleven

Published by Eleven International Publishing and G. Giappichelli Editore

ISBN 978-94-6236-339-7 (hbk)
ISBN 978-94-0011-219-3 (ebk)

http://www.elevenpub.com

ISBN/EAN 978-88-921-4533-7

http://www.giappichelli.it

Sold and distributed
by Eleven International Publishing

P.O. Box 85576
2508 CG The Hague
The Netherlands
Tel.: +31 70 33 070 33
Fax: +31 70 33 070 30
e-mail: sales@elevenpub.nl
www.elevenpub.com

Sold and distributed in USA and Canada
Independent Publishers Group

814 N. Franklin Street
Chicago, IL 60610, USA
Order Placement: +1 800 888 4741
Fax: +1 312 337 5985
orders@ipgbook.com
www.ipgbook.com

Eleven International Publishing is an imprint of Boom uitgevers Den Haag.

Printed by Stampatre s.r.l. - Torino (Italy)

To Alvise, Ruben and Maxi

... But if we with our evidence we can transmit out of the decaying structure only one grain of truth to the next generation, we shall not have laboured entirely in vain.

(S Zweig, *The World of Yesterday. An Autobiography*, Viking Press, 1943, p 8)

Contents

Chapter 3
Making and changing international rules

Chapter 4
International law and domestic jurisdictions

The law as I see it has two great objects: to preserve order and to do justice; and the two do not always coincide. Those whose training lies towards order, put certainty before justice; whereas those whose training lies toward the redress of grievances, put justice before certainty. The right solution lies in keeping the proper balance between the two.

(A Denning, *The Need for a New Equity* (1952) 5 *Current Legal Problems* 1, 9)

Preface to the second edition

This edition aims to remain faithful to the practical and minimalist approach of the first one. It remains a slim book. But, next to minor changes and corrections, few additions were necessary.

First, the previous narrative has been brought up to date – even though to the bare minimum – with new developments on the international scene occurred over the last three years, including the dramatic ones in Ukraine. Second, few gaps in the illustration of fundamental international legal institutions, with special regard to treaty law, have been duly filled.

My grateful thanks go to Niccolò Lanzoni for his competent support in the updating effort and his valuable contribution to the overall endeavour.

Attila M. Tanzi
Campione d'Italia – Bologna
September 2022

Preface to the first edition

This textbook visibly differs from the many others on the same subject, at least in size. A textbook as slim to the extreme as the present one may seem an oddity in light of the immense developments of international law of the last decades. Such developments pervade the main body of international law concerning the regulation of its subjects, sources, state responsibility, the means of dispute settlement and the ever increasingly problematic relation to domestic jurisdictions. And they also involve the numerous branches of substantive international law, such as the law of the sea, environmental law, human rights law, investment and trade law, international criminal law, and jurisdictional immunities, amongst others.

There is no denying that the idea of producing an extremely concise textbook, nonetheless, aims to provide an incentive for the students at first degree level to study the subject; however, it also purports to complement the individual teachers' choice of a more particularised syllabus which may build on a very basic overview of the dynamics of international law.

The high degree of concision and generality of the book is also meant to embolden domestic attorneys to skim through the book and realise how much embedded in international law are most of the rules they use, and how many more arguments they could plead before a domestic court if they were aware of this. Whether in criminal, commercial or public law cases, there are increasing instances in which one's client's rights which flow from international law are not invoked, nor applied, which should be invoked and applied.

It is against this backdrop that the broad-brush overview presented in the book aims to promote a basic understanding of the functioning international law rather than the full knowledge of its institutions. This accounts for the fact that the book addresses more the question 'why' and 'how', rather than 'what.'

My grateful thanks go to Gian Maria Farnelli for his generous and tactful research assistance and to Ludovica Chiussi, Niccolò Lanzoni and Guglielmo Roversi Monaco for the bibliographical and related research.

Attila M. Tanzi
Department of Legal Studies 'Antonio Cicu'
Alma Mater Studiorum University of Bologna
January 2019

List of abbreviations

ACHPR African Charter on Human and Peoples' Rights
ACtHPR: African Court on Human and Peoples' Rights
ASEAN: Association of South-East Asian Nations
ASR: Draft Articles on State Responsibility for Internationally Wrongful Acts
BINGO: Business-Interest NGOs
BIT: Bilateral Investment Treaty
CoE: Council of Europe
CoP: Conference of the Parties
EC: European Community
ECHR: European Convention on Human Rights
ECOSOC: Economic and Social Council
ECtHR: European Court of Human Rights
EIA: Environmental Impact Assessment
EU: European Union
GAOR: General Assembly Official Records
GATT: General Agreement on Tariffs and Trade
IACtHR: Inter-American Court of Human Rights
ICAO: International Civil Aviation Organisation
ICC: International Criminal Court
ICJ: International Court of Justice
ICSID: International Centre for Settlement of Investment Disputes
ICTY: International Criminal Tribunal for the former Yugoslavia
ICTR: International Criminal Tribunal for Rwanda
ILA: International Law Association
ILC: International Law Commission
ILM: International Legal Materials

ILR: International Law Reports
IMF: International Monetary Fund
IMO: International Maritime Organisation
ITLOS: International Tribunal for the Law of the Sea
MEA: Multilateral Environmental Agreement
Mercosur: Mercado Común del Sur
MoP: Meeting of the Parties
MoU: Memorandum of Understanding
NATO: North Atlantic Treaty Organisation
NGO: Non-Governmental Organisation
OAS: Organisation of American States
OAU: Organisation of African Unity
OECD: Organisation for Economic Cooperation and Development
OIC: Organisation of Islamic Cooperation
OSCE: Organisation for Security and Cooperation in Europe
PCA: Permanent Court of Arbitration
PCIJ: Permanent Court of International Justice
PINGO: Public-Interest NGOs
PRC: People's Republic of China
TEU: Treaty on European Union
TFEU: Treaty on the Functioning of the European Union
UK: United Kingdom
UN: United Nations
UNCITRAL: United Nations Commission on International Trade Law
UNCLOS: United Nations Convention on the Law of the Sea
UNCTAD: United Nations Conference on Trade and Development
UNECE: United Nations Economic Commission for Europe
UNRIAA: United Nations Reports of International Arbitral Awards
US: United States of America
USSR: Union of Soviet Socialist Republics
USR: United States Reports
VCLT: Vienna Convention on the Law of Treaties
WB: World Bank
WEF: World Economic Forum
WTO: World Trade Organisation

Chapter 1

What is international law

1. Who needs a basic knowledge of international law and why

A basic knowledge of international law, as with any body of the law, is necessary, in the first place, for legal practitioners.

Because of its primarily international and public law configuration, one would assume that a purely domestic lawyer would be spared of the need to know international law. That is a wrong assumption, as there is hardly a domestic legal issue – be it of a commercial, criminal or labour law nature, let alone of a constitutional law character – which is not connected with a rule of international law whose interpretation is relevant to the application of a domestic rule, or the settlement of a domestic dispute in such matters.

The point has been addressed in impassionate terms by Professor Shabtai Rosenne, one of the most thorough international legal scholars and practitioners of recent times. His acceptance speech at the presentation of The Hague Prize, which he received in 2004, precisely revolved around the importance of international law for the legal practice. Professor Rosenne lamented that the average practitioner of our time is often hardly qualified to identify an international law problem when professional advice would so require.[1] He observed that:

> '[A]n attorney can[not] be fully qualified if he or she is unable to identify an international law element in a client's problem. I do not expect every attorney to be able to solve that international law prob-

---

[1] 'The Hague Prize for International Law 2004 Awarded to Professor Shabtai Rosenne' (2004) 51 Netherlands International Law Review 475, especially at 482-485.

> lem (…). But the least that can be expected is that the attorney will identify that the international law problem is part of the complex to be resolved (…).'[2]

Within the domestic legal community, the prominence of the judiciary should not be lost sight of, since domestic courts and tribunals play a significant role in the application, or violation, as well as in the making and changing of international law. Notice should also be taken of the increasing legal representation of the Government before international courts and tribunals by the Office of the Attorney General, due to international litigation involving sovereign parties, which is developing to an extent unknown in the past.[3]

The increasing global interdependence in time of economic growth, and, paradoxically all the more so, in time of economic and environmental crisis, has added an international dimension to the work of a wider spectrum of governmental administrations traditionally devoted to domestic affairs, such as Treasury, Health, Environment and even the Interior.

Much the same applies to members of the civil society organised within NGOs, which, as we shall also see, are taking an increasingly prominent stand in promoting the making and enforcement of international law on the domestic and transboundary levels. That is especially the case in the field of environmental and human rights law. At the same time, we are witnessing a new corporate role in the promotion of new international economic law standards through BINGOs. In both areas, lawyers who are knowledgeable of the basics of international law are in demand.

Lastly, a basic knowledge of international law is required for those who want to work in media communication and journalism, given the ever-increasing international interdependence of the great and dramatic challenges confronting our societies. From climate

---

[2] *Ibidem*, 482.

[3] See Chapter 6.

change to military or digital security, access to essential natural resources, demographic growth, pandemics, finance and economics, or the use and management of artificial intelligence and neuro-sciences, all such challenges cannot be effectively tackled by individual nation-states, without internationally regulated cooperation. The related international law-making, and implementation, policies, while involving national and transnational civil societies, require highly competent media, including in the field of international law.

2. Regulating the relations between states and constraining their external sovereignty…

One can say that international law consists of a set of rules made by states in order to regulate the legal relations between them. Such rules belong to one legal order shared by each and all members of the international community of states, even if a state may differ from another with regard to the interpretation and application of these rules. That is to say that international law is not to be confused with anything to do with foreign laws, as is sometimes the case with beginners to the subject. The study of foreign laws pertains to the subject of comparative law, public or private.

Nor should international law be confused with **private international law**, more properly known as ***conflict of laws***. This body of law is to be found in each national legal system, each with its own differences, with a view to guiding the domestic judge in deciding *a*) whether it has jurisdiction, and if so, *b*) which law – domestic or foreign – to apply to any given legal case between private individuals, or companies, containing a foreign element. Such foreign element may pertain to issues of contract law, when one of the parties is a foreigner and/or the contract is to be performed abroad; to tort law, when the damage is suffered or caused by conduct carried out abroad; to marital law, when one of the spouses is a foreign national, or the marriage was celebrated abroad; or in cases of cross-border inheritance. Namely, if you have connections, in terms of nationality or residence, with more than one country, you need to know which country's law will govern who inherits your assets when you pass away.

Each national legal system, through its body of rules on conflict of laws, provides for connecting factors – *e.g.* citizenship or habitual residence of either parties, the place of conclusion, or of performance, of the contract, the place where the damage was caused, or suffered – in order for the domestic judge to choose the applicable legal order among those connected to a given case, including its national law. Given the uncertainties and complications deriving from the fact that each national law may provide different connecting patterns in relation to the same legal relationships, states and international organisations, including the EU, have promoted the adoption of international conventions on uniform domestic rules of private international law.

Defining international law – or any other legal order – as a set of rules is a useful simplification. But an incomplete one. Next to its rules, a legal system is defined by the process which produces, uses and applies such rules, as well as by the social, political, economic factors which underlie such process. That inevitably requires a degree of interdisciplinary approach to the law,[4] even by black-letter practitioners, as no persuasive legal argument may be made without

---

[4] The New Haven School of legal thinking, gathered around the Yale School of Law, has been a precursor to this approach, see MS McDougal, HD Lasswell and WM Reisman, 'The World Constitutive Process of Authoritative Decision' (1967) 19 Journal of Legal Education 253. For a clear illustration of international law as a process of authoritative decisions, see, by Dame Rosalyn Higgins – an epigone of the New Haven School on the British legal scene and former President of the ICJ – *Problems and Process: International Law and How We Use It* (Clarendon Press 1994). See also JL Dunoff and MA Pollack (eds), *Interdisciplinary Perspectives on International Law and International Relations: The State of the Art* (CUP 2013). See also, more recently, P Palchetti, 'An Interdisciplinary Approach to International Law? Some Cursory Remarks' in M Meccarelli (ed), *Reading the Crisis: Legal, Philosophical and Literary Perspectives* (Editorial Dykinson 2017), 199ff.

a sufficient grasp of the social, economic, policy, technical or scientific aspects underlying the making or application of the law.

The prevailing **inter-state nature** of international law is apparent from the diplomatic settings in which inter-state agreements are negotiated and entered into by state organs in charge of foreign relations. Its international character is evidenced by the international scope of application of most rules of international law. One may consider the rules governing the terrestrial and maritime delimitation of sovereignty between states; those on the use, management and conservation of shared natural resources, such as transboundary watercourses and aquifers, or oil and gas. The same applies to the currently much debated rule banning the use of force, or acts of aggression, 'against the territorial integrity and political independence' of other states as enshrined in Article 2(4) of the *UN Charter*.

The above may lead one to think of international law as a body of law merely confined to diplomatic and transboundary relations. Namely, one regulating only the **external sovereignty** of states. However, one ought to consider that most rules of international law are applied, misapplied, or infringed upon, within the domestic legal orders of the recipient states, hence, by state officials in charge of domestic affairs, either legislative, executive or judicial. As it will be illustrated in the next section, this naturally flows from the contents of most international rules which impinge upon domestic sovereignty, on a daily basis.

3. …And internal sovereignty

In fact, a large number of international rules provide, through their obligations, constraints over the internal sovereignty of the recipient states, whether this is in relation to the jurisdiction to prescribe, to adjudicate, or to enforce. That is corroborated by most of the bodies of international law illustrated in a summary fashion in Chapter 7.

By way of anticipation, apart from the self-evident case of the international body of human rights rules, one may single out the traditional international rules on the treatment of aliens, according to which states cannot treat foreign individuals and companies in an arbitrary or discriminatory way; similarly, one may point to the rules on the treatment of foreign states and intergovernmental organisations, whose standards, given the superior need to protect the state functions exercised by foreign officials, are higher than those applicable to foreign private individuals and companies. To that end, for example, foreign Heads of state and of Governments, foreign Ministers and accredited diplomatic envoys enjoy jurisdictional immunities from the domestic courts and tribunals of foreign countries.

One may also look at most international environmental rules. They usually require the passing of domestic legislation and administrative conduct, to be taken by state agencies in charge, and local entities, with special regard to authorisation procedures, including EIA. International trade law is made up of international obligations on tariffs and non-tariff barriers that require domestic legislative and administrative regulatory action on the importation and treatment of foreign goods and services that, even when appropriately adopted, further requires application by custom, or other, officers. When such legislative and/or administrative action is deemed to be in contrast with international legal standards by the private beneficiaries of the rules in question – *i.e.* domestic import companies, as well as foreign export, industrial or service corporations – the latter may resort to the local domestic judiciary asking for redress. When redress is accorded to the claimant by a domestic court in such a case – usually brought against a branch of the public administration – the domestic judiciary would be mending state conduct inconsistent with an international obligation by other state organs, eventually bringing the state in compliance with such obligation before an internationally wrongful act is completed.

This aspect will be taken up and elaborated upon in Chapter 4 on the relationship between international law and domestic jurisdictions.

4. Why do states undertake international obligations?

As much as **the 'duty' side of international rules** is usually emphasised, generally legal obligations are created by such rules as a consequence and **a mirror of the rights** they produce by way of reciprocity. That is to say that, generally, states produce international rules providing for self-constraints in exchange for a corresponding advantage deriving from reciprocity. Formally, this is reflected on the **bilateral obligations** based on reciprocity – so-called *synallagmatic* (*quid pro quo*) – stemming from most of the rules of international law producing rights for the recipient states that are symmetrically corresponding to their international obligations. This corresponds to the traditional civil law like approach followed unswervingly by international law – *i.e.* by the states making up the international community – for about three centuries since its inception in the 17th century. We shall see in due course that, particularly after the scourge of the crimes committed during the Second World War, new rules have been brought about that provide for obligations that each state owes towards the international community of states, as a whole. They are so-called *erga omnes* obligations, which in Latin translates to 'towards everyone.'

Reverting to the traditional bilateralism of international law, the *quid pro quo* nature of the rules on the treatment of aliens is evident from the fact that they have been created by the practice of states engaging in a number of obligations to abstain from treating foreign nationals below certain international standards both for the purpose and following the condition that the same treatment is ensured to their nationals abroad.

Likewise, states accept their obligation not to use military force in their international relations as an immediate consequence of their right that their territorial integrity and political independence be respected by other states.

4.1. *The example of the Rio Grande Agreement*

It is a well-known fact that, in the not-so-distant past, riparian states involved in disputes with their neighbours over transboundary waters used to take rigid stances, to the extreme, with respect to the use of disputed shared waters. Similar attitudes were based on extreme interpretations of the concept of state sovereignty over the portion of the transboundary waters flowing or lying in the national territory, which held that watercourses were part of the territory of the state, and hence, subject to the exclusive territorial sovereignty of that state.

Upstream countries claimed absolute freedom to use transboundary waters regardless of downstream impact according to the so-called *absolute territorial sovereignty theory*. This approach is best expressed in the notorious opinion rendered in 1895 by the Attorney-General Judson Harmon in the dispute between Mexico and US over the use of the Rio Grande River.[5] Conversely, downstream countries claimed the right to receive perfectly unaffected waters from upper countries, following the so-called *absolute territorial integrity theory*.[6]

One of the factors behind such irreconcilable claims, apart from the political lack of good will and the wrong perception by both parties of the means to pursue their best interest, was to be found in the underdeveloped and unclear state of international water law un-

---

[5] 'The fact that the Rio Grande lacks sufficient water to permit its use by the inhabitants of both countries does not entitle Mexico to impose restrictions on the United States which would hamper the development of the latter's territory or deprive its inhabitants of an advantage with which nature has endowed it and which is situated entirely within its territory. To admit such a principle would be completely contrary to the principle that the United States exercise full sovereignty over its national territory' quoted in A Boyle and C Redgwell, *Birnie, Boyle, and Redgwell's International Law and the Environment* (4th edn, OUP 2021), 576.

[6] See *Ibidem*, 576-577.

til the early 1900s. Emphasising how similar situations of non-co-operation led to the worse-off scenario for all the states involved, the former President of the ICJ, Judge Jiménez de Aréchaga recalled how such absolute claims 'may operate to the detriment of the State invoking [them] and, carried to an extreme, would lead to reciprocal reprisals whereby States would injure each other and use a watercourse uneconomically, instead of seeking an integral and co-ordinated utilization of the whole basin.' [7] This was the situation that could characterise the relations between Mexico and the US over their conflict of interests concerning the use of the Rio Grande at the end of the 19th century.

Starting from the most extreme situation of disagreement, based on mutually irreconcilable claims – as it emerged from diplomatic exchanges in 1895 – the representatives from the two countries gradually realised that they would only have to lose from insisting their positions based on absolute sovereignty claims. Therefore, they eventually engaged in negotiations on how to best allocate to each other the quantity of water flowing through the shared river culminating ultimately, eleven years after, on 21 May 1906, in the conclusion of the *Convention concerning the Equitable Distribution of the Waters of the Rio Grande for Irrigation Purposes*. This treaty, by recognizing the rights of both parties to the use of the waters of the Rio Grande, settled an age-old dispute creating new obligations formally constraining the sovereignty of the parties with a view to pursuing substantive mutual benefits.

One can say that the history of international law, not just international water law, is characterised by states **promoting and accepting constraints over their sovereignty in exchange for comparable benefits**. This applies *inter alia* to the freedom of navigation and trade, to the treatment of aliens, or the prohibition on the use of force.

---

[7] E Jiménez de Aréchaga, 'International Law in the Past Third of a Century' (1978) 159 Collected Courses of the Hague Academy of International Law 3, 191.

5. Why do states comply with and breach international law?

The large majority of international rules are silently complied with every day. That is to say that states exercise their rights under international law as a matter of course without much notice being given by the public to this matter of fact. It is mostly when a rule is breached that international law comes to the fore and its effectiveness is questioned. This accounts for the fact that it is the **'duty' side**, rather than the 'rights' aspect, of international rules that is usually emphasised, while it is the **'right' side** that lies behind the utilitarian motives why states enter into international rules and generally comply with them.

As already alluded, the international community of nation-states have not provided their legal system with a centralised law-enforcement mechanism. However, given **the participatory nature of the sources of international legal rules**, the high degree of compliance is spontaneous and not induced by the prospect of legal sanctions. Despite the major structural differences between international law and domestic jurisdictions, provided with centralised enforcement, it is fair to say that also in domestic legal systems, generally, individuals spontaneously comply with the law, not so much because of fear of legal sanctions, as much as because the legal rules in question reflect the interest and social values of the subjects involved.

As observed by a great lawyer of the last century, Professor Louis Henkin:

> 'The preoccupation with "sanctions" seems largely misplaced. The threat of such sanctions is not the principal inducement to observe international obligations. At least, the absence of sanctions does not necessarily make it likely that nations will violate law. There are other forces which induce nations to observe law.' [8]

---

[8] L Henkin, *How Nations Behave* (2nd edn, Columbia UP 1979), 49.

There is no denying that also in international law we are confronted with breaches of the law, some of which are egregious, and even dramatic. Two brief general considerations are called for on the point at issue.

The first one, ties in with the above-mentioned twofold dimension of international legal rules. Namely, their 'right' side and the 'duty' side. It appears that, when negotiating and adopting treaties – as well as when carrying out implementation practice which may result in the formation of customary rules – the political and administrative apparatus of states involved in such law-making processes have mostly in mind the creation of rights for their country and their nationals, while at a later stage, different state organs involved in the implementation of the rules in question are confronted with the obligations stemming from the same rules, and see them through a lens different from the one of the officials involved in the making of same rules.

This accounts for the first of the two general answers to the question of why states sometimes find themselves infringing the obligations stemming from rules of their own making, or even rejecting the same rules altogether, as we shall see more in detail in Chapter 5. The risk of this apparent political and administrative contradiction is ever-increasing with the widening of the subject matters falling under international regulation, which were once exclusively of domestic relevance. This has the implication of requiring Ministries (such as the Ministries of the Interior, Health, Justice, Environment, Finance, or Culture) to increasingly involve themselves with international affairs concerns, in a manner which, until recently, they were seldom called upon to do so. This requires a level of **administrative coordination** within states that is often difficult to attain.

One should add the often complex scientific, technological or financial nature of certain international obligations. The combination of the above factors may produce state conduct which is only inadvertently in breach of certain international obligations.

As we shall see in Chapter 5, this is particularly the case in the field of environmental law. MEAs address cases of state conduct at variance with their standards through so-called non-compliance mechanisms in preference to the hard and fast rules of the law state responsibility for internationally wrongful acts. Compliance mechanisms may even result in scientific, legal and financial assistance to the non-complying state, whilst the law of state responsibility would apply on a subsidiary basis. Namely, in case of lack of cooperation with the treaty body in charge of the mechanism in point by the state which is in non-compliance.

The second general consideration about the reasons why states may breach international law is one which applies to infringements of the law in any legal system. And it consists of the tension which may arise at any point in time between the perception of one's self-interest and the obligations stemming from the law.

Under such circumstances, two sceneries may alternatively present themselves which concern the attitude of the wrongdoing state.

Under one scenery, a given state may infringe a certain rule relying on a wrong interpretation of it, or by justifying its conduct invoking a circumstance precluding wrongfulness. [9] A recent egregious example of this attitude is given by the armed attack on Ukraine by the Russian Federation. Russia has not waged the attack in denial of the validity of the ban on 'the use of force against the territorial integrity and political independence' of other nation-states, under customary law and Article 2(4) of the *UN Charter*. [10] On the contrary, Russia has tried to justify its conduct by putting forward two arguments which fully acknowledge the validity of the rules in question. Namely, self-defence under Article 51 of the *UN Charter* [11]

---

[9] On internationally wrongful acts and circumstances precluding wrongfulness, see Chapter 5, Section 2.1 (especially 2.1.2).

[10] Article 2(4) of the *UN Charter* reads as follows: 'All Members [of the UN] shall refrain in their international relations from the threat or use of force against the territorial integrity or political independence of any State, on in any other manner inconsistent with the Purposes of the United Nations.'

[11] Article 51 of the *UN Charter* reads as follows: 'Nothing in the present

and humanitarian intervention for the protection of Russian nationals from acts of genocide allegedly attributable to Ukraine. [12]

The ensuing dispute is one over the assessment of the facts invoked, rather than about the existence of the ban on the use of force or the obligation to prevent and punish genocide. So far, the UN General Assembly has firmly rejected these arguments and condemned, by a large majority, the Russian attack. [13]

The legitimacy of the Russian conduct is currently under scrutiny in different international fora. With regard to the latter aspect of the dispute on the alleged genocide carried out by Ukrainian authorities against ethnic Russians, Ukraine has sued Russia before the ICJ under the 1948 *Genocide Convention* invoking the abuse of the Convention by Russia. [14] While the latter has not taken part in the proceeding, at the time of printing of the present book, 43 states have made a joint statement declaring their intention to intervene in the proceedings before the ICJ under Article 63 of the *ICJ Statute*, which provides for intervention in the proceedings by third parties

---

Charter shall impair the inherent right of individual or collective self-defence if an armed attack occurs against a Member of the United Nations, until the Security Council has taken measures necessary to maintain international peace and security (…).'

[12] See the English translation of Putin's declaration of war on Ukraine on the webpage of *The Spectator* (24 February 2022). See also M Milanović, 'What is Russia's Legal Justification for Using Force against Ukraine?' in *EJIL:Talk!* (24 February 2022).

[13] UN General Assembly, Res ES-11/1 of 2 March 2022. 141 states voted in favour of the resolution, while only 5 (Belarus, Eritrea, North Korea, Syria and obviously Russia) voted against. More interestingly, 35 states abstained from voting, including China, India and Iran.

[14] So far, the ICJ has issued an order of provisional measures see *Allegations of Genocide under the Convention on the Prevention and Punishment of the Crime of Genocide* (Ukraine v Russian Federation) (Provisional Measures) (Order) [2022] urging Russia to immediately suspend the military operations and to refrain from any action which might aggravate or extend the dispute before the Court.

who deem to have an interest in the interpretation of rules applicable to the dispute between applicant and defendant. [15]

Ukraine has also filed a lawsuit against Russia before the ECtHR and requested interim measures in relation to 'massive human rights violations being committed by the Russian troops in the course of the military aggression.' [16] The ECtHR has promptly upheld the Ukrainian request and urged Russia to refrain from military attacks against civilians and civilian objects and to ensure the safety of the medical establishments and personnel within the territory under siege. [17] The case, involving, among others, alleged violations of the right to life, prohibition of torture, slavery and forced labour is currently pending before the ECtHR. [18] In the meantime, Russia has been expulsed from the CoE, under whose auspices the ECtHR works, and, as a consequence, the Committee of Ministers of the Organisation has decided that it will cease to be a party to the ECHR from September 2022. [19]

---

[15] The statement is available on the webpage of the UK Government (<www.gov.uk>). See also B McGarry, 'Mass Intervention? The Joint Statement of 41 States on Ukraine v. Russia' in *EJIL:Talk!* (30 May 2022).

[16] 'The European Court Grants Urgent Measures In Application Concerning Russian Military Operations On Ukrainian Territory' (1 March 2022).

[17] *Ibidem*. The ECtHR had already issued a number of interim measures in connection with the then ongoing 2014 conflict in the Donetsk and Lugansk regions, see *Case of Ukraine and the Netherlands v Russia*, App Nos 8019/16, 43800/14 and 28525/20. The ECtHR has also ascertained its jurisdiction to assess the numerous alleged violations of the ECHR carried out by Russian authorities in occupied Crimea, See *Case of Ukraine v Russia (re Crimea)* [GC], Apps Nos 20958/14 and 38334/18, Decision (14 January 2021). Another dispute established under Annex VII to the UNCLOS concerning the 2018 detention of Ukrainian naval vessels and servicemen at the hand of Russian authorities has been recently ruled to be admissible by the PCA, *Dispute Concerning the Detention of Ukrainian Naval Vessels and Servicemen* (Ukraine v the Russian Federation) (Preliminary Objections) (Award) [2022] Case No 2019-28.

[18] *Case of Ukraine v Russia (X)*, App No 1055/22.

[19] Res CM/Res(2022)3 of 23 March 2022.

In passing, we can also add here that the legitimacy, under international law, of the armed operation in Ukraine has been challenged not only at the level of state responsibility, but also at that of individual (criminal) responsibility.[20] In fact, as of August 2022, 43 states parties to the *Rome Statute* have referred, pursuant to Articles 13(a) and 14(1) thereof, the situation in Ukraine to the Prosecutor of the ICC for the alleged commission of international crimes falling within the jurisdiction of the Court.[21]

The second scenery concerning the attitude of the wrongdoing state is the one in which a state may decide to breach a rule of international law with the view to trying to change it. This attitude was epitomised by the 1945 *Truman Proclamation* on the extension of the national exclusive jurisdiction over and under the seabed of the continental shelf adjacent to the US coasts. In fact, the geological configuration of the continental platform – which is often rich of natural gas and oil – may extend hundreds of miles from the shore. Therefore, such Proclamation, being contained in an Executive Order having legislative and executive nature,[22] represented a conduct in patent contrast with the international freedom of the high seas in force under the law of the sea at the time.

Such departure from the law was first met with the absence of significant protests – properly defined in law as acquiescence – and later even with the emulation by numerous coastal states from different regions of the world. Accordingly, in that particular instance, conduct in breach of the law has promoted the formation of new customary law, which was soon codified by the 1958 *Convention on the Continental Shelf*.

---

[20] See Chapter 7, Section 6.

[21] The referral is available at *Situation in Ukraine* (ICC-01/22) (<www.icc-cpi.int/ukraine>).

[22] Executive Order No 9633 of 28 September 1945.

6. Can we speak of a Constitution of the international society of states? A brief history

As put by renowned international French lawyer Georges Scelle, at the beginning of the last century:

> 'There is a constitution and constitutional rules insofar as one is confronted with the making of normative rules aimed at meeting the essential needs of social relations and at providing, even though in a rudimentary fashion, the means for the enforcement of such fundamental rules.' [23]

This passage complements the old tag *ubi societas, ibi ius* with the corollary assumption that ***ubi ius, ibi constitutio***. Namely, if there is a set of rules governing the relations among the actors of a given society, there must be some basic rules, generally recognised, that govern both the structural distribution of power between them and the procedures by which legal rules are brought about. In international law one would be at pains to find one comprehensive constitutional instrument. Over the last seventy years, the ***UN Charter*** can rightly be said to have been an important component of the constitutional principles of contemporary international law. However, the former cannot be considered to be exhaustively representative of the latter, if only for the fact that the founding principles of contemporary international law date back to a much earlier period than 1945, namely, to the 17th century in an unwritten form, like most international rules prior to the codifications of the 20th century. The unwritten character of the founding rules of interna-

---

[23] English translation by the author. The original text goes as follows: '[I]l y a constitution et normes constitutionnelles toutes les fois qu'il y a élaboration de règles normatives destinées à traduire les nécessités essentielles des rapports sociaux et à fournir, fut-ce de façon rudimentaire, les moyens de mise en œuvre de ces règles fondamentales,' G Scelle, 'Le droit constitutionnel international' in J Duquesne (ed), *Melanges R. Carré de Malberg* (Sirey 1933), 505.

tional law would not be a sufficient argument to deny the existence of an international constitution. It is sufficient to consider the example of the uncodified UK Constitution made up of a variety of written and unwritten sources of law.

The question of the existence, or not, of a constitution of international law is not regarded here as a theoretical statement, even though there is indeed an intensive ongoing theoretical debate on the subject.[24] Whilst international law is regarded here as a matter of social fact, looking for its constitution means looking for its basic constituent features. In any legal system, the constitutional ones are the rules and principles that are most directly connected with the underlying social and political process that produces them. Accordingly, the identification of such rules also serves the purpose of identifying the basic features of the organisation of power in a given society at any given point in time of history. This is particularly true given the 'living' nature of constitutions.

In empirical terms, as they emerge from history – hence, aside from the most formalistic and theoretical Kelsenian international law constructions[25] – it appears that the basic principle underlying the structure of the international society is that of the sovereign **equality of states**.

This *Grundnorm* of international law, since its inception in the mid-17th century, implies its low level of institutionalisation. It accounts for the **lack of a centralised power** with regard to law-

---

[24] On this topic, see J Klabbers, A Peters and G Ulfstein, *The Constitutionalization of International Law* (OUP 2009), K Zemanek, 'The Metamorphosis of Jus Cogens: From an Institution of Treaty Law to the Bedrock of the International Legal Order?' in E Cannizzaro (ed), *The Law of Treaties Beyond the Vienna Convention* (OUP 2011), 398ff and J Vidmar, 'Norm Conflict and Hierarchy in International Law: Towards a Vertical International Legal System?' in E de Wet and J Vidmar (eds), *Hierarchy in International Law: The Place of Human Rights* (OUP 2012), 18ff.

[25] See H Kelsen, *Principles of International Law* (re-edited, 2nd edn, The Lawbook Exchange 2003).

making, adjudication and enforcement. In fact, the principle of sovereign equality has determined the initial and long-lasting horizontal dimension of modern international society and relations, moulding accordingly the three main functions of international law. Namely, *a*) the consensual and participatory mode of the making of international rules, respectively, through agreements and custom under the constitutional rules *consuetudo est servanda* and *pacta sunt servanda*; *b*) the consensual nature of dispute settlement, with a prevailing relevance of self-assessment of legality; *c*) self-help in the ultimate law-enforcement function.

While the above shows how sovereignty as the constitutional principle of international law applies to the **structural dimension** of the international society of states, it should be stressed how the same principle also has a constituent impact at the level of **substantive law**. In fact, a basic corollary of the constituent principle of the formal sovereign equality of states is the absolute **political independence** of each sovereign state from any other state, or any other outside authority, unless and to the extent that it accepts it of its own free will. As already indicated, the making of international law rules by states is precisely an example of how states freely accept constraints on their sovereignty in exchange for the advantages accrued through the corresponding self-limitations adopted by other states.

It is precisely the participatory nature of the sources of international law that allows to reconcile the principle of independence of sovereign states with the idea of a system of international legal rules that provide constraints on their freedom. To put it as observed by Oscar Schachter, based on empirical data,

> 'No state (…) nor its autonomy (or sovereignty) is absolute in law. It is limited by international law which in the prevalent positivist conception is viewed as the collective expression of sovereign wills.' [26]

---

[26] O Schachter, 'The Decline of the Nation-State and Its Implications for International Law' (1997) 36 Columbia Journal of Transnational Law 7, 7.

The paradigm of the sovereign independence of states is matched by the principle of **non-intervention** in the internal affairs of other states. Needless to say, the principle of the political independence of states is to be taken in strictly legal terms and should therefore not be taken as being inconsistent with economic, financial, environmental or cultural interdependence between states globally.

After a period of anarchy during the Barbarian invasions, by the 17th century, neither the Pope, nor any prince, or king, got the upper hand in what can be considered as a centuries-old strife, a revolutionary clash between peoples, to inherit the hegemonic organisation of power of the Roman Empire. From the crystallization of such a stalemate, sanctioned by the 1648 Peace of Westphalia, a **horizontal legal setting** emerged which produced a new world order based on formal equality, mutual independence and competitive freedom between sovereign states. Just like in the bourgeois constitutional democracies of the 19th century, and long before them, in international law such equality was of a formal nature, leaving substantively more powerful states able to prevail over weaker ones. Such a horizontal legal setting is to be appreciated as the alternative model to a vertical one based on the hegemonic, imperial, distribution and organisation of power at the international level, as it was under the Roman Empire.

It is to be noted that the principle of sovereign equality in its original form applied only to Christian states making up a purely European international community. This paved the way for the **colonisation** of a large part of non-Christian peoples. In fact, the constituent principle in question has for a long time provided the basis for a minimal regulatory regime of co-existence within a minimal regulatory setting of free competition – from the economic to the military dimensions – among technologically advanced Christian European sovereign states and, later, Christian sovereign states of European descent.[27]

---

[27] See, in general, M Koskenniemi, W Rech and M Jiménez Fonseca (eds), *International Law and Empire: Historical Exploration* (OUP 2017).

The constitutional principle in question and its corollaries, not only have allowed for the growth of significant material inequalities at the international and domestic levels alike, they have also allowed for **revolutionary attempts** to reverse the international constitutional system from its horizontal setting into a hegemonic one. One may recall the Napoleonic project, as well as Bolshevik internationalism and Nazism. More recently, the unilateralist attitude characterising the US foreign policy at the beginning of the new century, under George Bush Jr, was an attempt to enforce a long-term hegemonic strategy. It now remains to be seen whether emerging powerhouses, such as the PRC, will venture in similar hegemonic project, at least at the regional level.

The common thread through all the above-mentioned **hegemonic attempts** is precisely the design to abolish the principle of sovereign equality through the breach of the corollary principles of non-intervention, political independence and territorial integrity of states.

Against this background, the constitutional evolution of the international law of coexistence among nation-states may be seen to have proceeded along the path of the growing regulatory limitation of state sovereignty – both internal and external – paradoxically through the exercise of the external sovereignty by the members of the international community through the participatory (custom) and consensual (treaties) sources of international law. Such an evolutionary process of self-reduction of state sovereignty has been two-pronged: on the one hand, it has promoted the growth of the organisational side of the international community through the development of international institutions; on the other, it has involved major developments in the field of the substantive rights and duties of states and, partly, also of non-state actors.

On the organisational side, it is to be stressed that **international institutions**, or organisations – *e.g.*, the UN, IMF, WB, WTO – have developed throughout the second half of the 20th century remaining prevailingly intergovernmental in their essence. Indeed, they do not involve full transfers, hence waiver, of state sovereignty on the part of their members: *a*) in international institutions, being of an intergovernmental nature, Member states still exercise elements of foreign policy, *i.e.* external sovereignty; *b*) usually, the typical acts of international institutions are *per se* not legally binding, and, even when they are binding, their enforcement depends on the exercise of domestic sovereignty by the Member states; *c*) even when the establishing instrument of a given international organisation does not provide expressly for denunciation or recess, it is generally agreeable that Member states may well exercise their foreign sovereignty to the full extent of quitting the organisation; *d*) accordingly, even when Member states introduce some kind of limitation on their sovereignty in relation to their membership in intergovernmental organisations, they are far from relinquishing their sovereignty.

On the substantive law side, the second half of the 20th century has produced gradual constitutional changes and a shift in the normative quality of their material obligations – although still far from being completed, if ever – from the law of co-existence into one of cooperation. This has been associated to the existing net of bilateral legal relations, one based on multilateral sources of international law, particularly.

This trend, in its most extensive expression, has reached an attempt at providing legal protection to indivisible general interests of the international community of states as a whole. While all developments consisting in the making of material international rules automatically result in some constraints on state sovereignty, this is especially so with regard to those among such rules that are of a solidarity nature and provide for so-called ***erga omnes* obligations** – *i.e.*, obligations owed to all the states of the international community – ranging from those on the use of force to those on human rights.

Such developments have been so qualitatively intense as to affect also the sovereign law-making power of states through a major constitutional change, to the effect that a treaty in contrast with such solidarity obligations is to be considered null and void. Indeed, in its most advanced expression, such developments have introduced in the second half of the last century the category of the so-called **peremptory norms**, or **rules of *jus cogens*** indicating an international rule, derogation from which is not permitted.

The idea of a set of rules that, because of their contents, may not be derogated from by the free will of states through mutual consent may seem to run contrary to the traditional concept of state sovereignty. However, such developments have been themselves the result of the exercise of the external sovereignty of the generality of nation states, particularly in the negotiations that have led to the VCLT.[28]

One ought to consider that such developments have been produced in a period of social, economic and ethical expansion following the horrors of the Second World War. Such an expansive trend towards the **internationalisation** of national policies occurred despite the Cold War. Actually, the aim of defeating the totalitarian regimes of the Soviet bloc represented in itself a boost towards such expansive trends. The fight for human rights in those regimes, as well as against racial discrimination in the US, combined with the need to comply with the international rules on the prohibition on the use of force against territorial integrity and political independence in the context of nuclear deterrence contributed to a widespread sense of the rule of law and spontaneous compliance with international law. The vivid memory of the humanitarian horrors and deprivations of the Second World War, combined with an era of overall economic expansion, added to the diffusion of such an attitude.

The end of the Cold War with the fall of the Soviet Union and of the Communist regime in the satellite countries across Eastern Europe in 1989, and the following years of transition towards constitutional regimes and a free-market economy worldwide, marked the climax of the internationalisation trends. A sense of achievement and fulfilment was globally diffused through the early '90s with the

---

[28] See, in general, W Czaplinski, '*Jus Cogens* and the Law of Treaties' in C Tomuschat and JM Thouvenin (eds), *The Fundamental Rules of the International Legal Order* (Brill-Nijhoff 2006), 83ff.

promotion of the full liberalisation of international trade and foreign direct investments, the development of environmental protection and the strategic-military harmony between the five permanent Members of the Security Council. This was evidenced by the unanimous reaction adopted by the latter against the Iraqi invasion of Kuwait in 1990 and 1991.

A number of factors in international politics broke the spell soon after. Amongst others, one can recall the failure of peace-keeping operations by the UN, particularly those in Somalia, the resurgence in the mid-'90s of disagreements between NATO and Russia over the former Yugoslavia, with special regard to the repressive policy by the then Serbian President Slobodan Milošević over ethnic minorities, the ensuing NATO bombing of Serbia in 1999 without the authorisation of the Security Council due to the anticipation of the Russian veto, the advent of the George Bush Jr Presidency in the US, with the bombing of Iraq by the US and the UK in 2003.

The international financial and economic crises since 2008 to date, Islamic terrorism, the Syrian and Libyan crises with the ensuing massive migration trends boosted a sense of insecurity, lack of confidence in international cooperation and rule of law, with an increasingly diffused revival of nationalism. This is the basis of the new 'sovereigntist movements,' which have been on rise over the last few years in Western countries, particularly EU countries and the US. Former US President Trump's statement concerning the withdrawal from the 2015 *Paris Agreement on Climate Change*, stressing that it represented a 'reassertion of America's sovereignty,' [29] the UK withdrawal from the EU (so-called 'Brexit'), and the Swiss referendum on the proposal to put the Swiss Constitution above international law, though rejected, [30] are just few examples of this tendency. This is in stark contrast with the opening to multilat-

[29] See 'Statement by President Trump on the Paris Climate Accord' (1 June 2017), available on the webpage of the US Government (<www.whitehouse.gov>).

[30] See R Kunz, 'Voting Down International Law? Lessons from Switzerland for Compensatory Constitutionalism' in *Völkerrechtsblog* (3 December 2018).

eralism by emerging powers, with special regard to the PRC. This may seem paradoxical to those who were used to the protectionist attitude of China, which resisted liberalisation until it joined the WTO in 2001. This definitely confirms that the wheels of history keep turning, even when certain clogs get blocked.

Indeed, history proceeds through cycles, between expansion and contraction, be it of economic, social or legal values. From a public international law perspective, particularly relevant is the **pendulum between internationalism and nationalism**, liberalism and protectionism. Inevitably, such historical perspective provides the lenses through which much of the overview of international law is presented in the following pages.

7. Differences and similarities between international law and domestic jurisdictions

In light of the above constitutional features of the international legal order, its main structural difference from the generality of domestic legal orders is to be found in the lack of a central and institutional exercise of the three main functions of a legal system: namely, law-making, law-assessment and law-enforcement.

As we shall see in Chapter 3, international law lacks a parliamentary authority that legislates, hence, prescribing international rules that are binding on all the subjects of the international community irrespective of their participation in the law-making process, differently from what we see in domestic legal orders. Nor is there an international kind of compulsory adjudication as we are used to in relation to domestic civil, administrative, or criminal cases where the respondent, or accused, is bound by the judicial proceedings irrespective of his, or her, voluntary recognition of the jurisdiction of the judges in question.

As we shall see in Chapter 6, international adjudication over inter-state disputes is always of a voluntary, or arbitral, nature, including by permanent adjudicative bodies, such as the ICJ, or IT-

LOS. Likewise, there is in principle no international centralised police that enforces international law or international judgements over states, unless this function is entrusted to an international body by the states concerned through a treaty before the problem calling for enforcement arises. This is the case of the UN Security Council which has been entrusted with enforcement decisions by the states parties to the *UN Charter*, which is the constituent treaty of the UN. Under the latter, it is unlikely that this body would adopt enforcement decisions against any of the permanent Members of the Security Council, since decisions of this kind may be adopted under a procedure providing for the so-called right of veto by each of the permanent Members. Institutional enforcement functions can be found to be exercised in a decentralised way by CoPs or MoPs to MEAs.

The above features may ground scepticism over the legal force of international law, also due to the assumedly low degree of its effectiveness. However, allusion has already been made to the consideration that the large part of international rules is daily complied with without any publicity. That is, for example, at the customs in ports and airports where goods are imported; when individuals cross borders; in the Ministries of justice when a letter rogatory from the courts of a foreign country requesting a given testimony, or other documents, is appropriately responded to; when a foreign student enrols in a local university, or when a foreign company does business in your country; when a municipality requires an EIA study by a company, local or foreign alike, or when it applies the polluter-pays principle.

Apart from those considerations, as a matter of social fact, one is to consider that the degree of effectiveness – in terms of compliance with the law – of the domestic legal orders is not extraordinarily superior to that of international law.

As to the lack of an international legislator, that is a major structural difference with respect to the domestic means of law-making. The direct, or indirect, participation of all the states concerned in the making of a given international custom, or treaty, accounts for the greater complexity of the international law-making process as opposed to negotiations to legislate in municipal parliaments.

At the same time, such a fully participatory aspect in international law-making, whereby the lawmakers coincide with the recipients of the obligations stemming therefrom, would in principle enhance the degree of spontaneous compliance with international law with respect to the attitude of the addressees of domestic law. This statement should be complemented by the qualification made above to the effect that the political and administrative facets of the state engaged in the law-making process, particularly treaty law, are different, at least at different points in time, from the components of the state apparatus vested with compliance.

As to the lack of compulsory international adjudication, one is to consider how cumbersome, costly, slow and unpredictable litigation is in domestic legal systems. This accounts for the fact that the majority of domestic disputes remain unsettled, or are settled out of court. This requires the same kind of negotiations between different interpretations of the respective substantive interests and the legal rights and obligations of the disputing parties in international law.

As to the weak form of institutionalisation of enforcement of international law, one is to consider that in domestic legal orders in a great number of cases important domestic rules remain unenforced. This does not apply only with regard to minor breaches of contract, but also to domestic rules of major importance, such as those on murder, or organised crime. Nonetheless, a high record of breaches of the law and the ineffectiveness of the domestic legal order is not a sufficient ground to do away with the domestic legal system in question altogether.

7.1. *Predictability*

Another ground for the arguments used to question the effectiveness and legal force of international law is the alleged indeterminacy of international rules. Customary law and general principles of international law would be inherently indeterminate due to their unwritten nature. The same would apply to treaty law despite its written nature, due to the fact that treaty rules always represent the compromise result following diplomatic and political negotiations. As to customary law, one should consider that, precisely because of the required diffused practice and recognition of the generality of states, the contents of customary rules are no more contested than in domestic legal systems and much the same applies to written domestic rules which are also the end-product of negotiations, either in parliament, or between parliament and Government, or between the parties to a contract.

In fact, as clearly put by James Crawford in his general course at The Hague Academy of International Law, indeterminacy is a problem inherent within all legal systems, domestic or international, alike:

> 'All lawyers in all legal systems know that law is indeterminate, at least to some degree. The result of any case taken to judgment is to some degree uncertain; the facts are disputed; a witness may perform badly on the day; the key documents are really capable of alternative readings, the appeal court's jurisprudence on point is conflicting and so on (…). So lawyers worry and (if they are sensible, or experienced) they will not tell their client that a win is certain.' [31]

Accordingly, it is wrong to say that **certainty, or predictability**, are constituent elements of a legal system. Were this to be the case, there would be hardly any legal system around the globe. As remarked nearly a century ago by the American legal philosopher, barrister and late judge, Benjamin Cardozo, '[w]e need not wonder that there is disappointment (…) when the effort is made to deduce

---

[31] J Crawford, 'Chance, Order, Change: The Course of International Law' (2013) 365 Collected Courses of the Hague Academy of International Law 13, 147.

the absolute and eternal from premises which in their origin were relative and transitory.' [32]

The aim of the law is certainly that to confer the highest possible degree of predictability, or minimum degree of uncertainty in the social interactions falling within the scope of the relevant substantive rules. Such a prescriptive function of the law is supported by adjudication and enforcement. However, this should not lead one to forget the **goal-oriented**, or aspirational, nature of the law. Entering into a contract is certainly aimed to enhance, with respect to a handshake, the predictability that the agreed terms and conditions will be respected, but there is no absolute guarantee that they will be respected. Different interpretations of the relevant facts and the applicable law will bear on the circumstances of a given dispute more significantly than the applicable rules as they were conceived *in abstracto*.

As put, again by Cardozo,

> '[We] tend sometimes, in determining the growth of a principle or a precedent, to treat it as if it represented the outcome of a quest for certainty. That is to mistake its origin. Only in the rarest instances, if ever, was certainty either possible or expected. The principle or the precedent was the outcome of a quest for probabilities.' [33]

At the same time, it would be fair to say that, even where a given rule is not fully complied with, or is even breached, often the following negotiations leading to a settlement falling short of the conduct required by the original rule are undertaken by using the rule as a term of reference in order to reach the settlement.

---

[32] BN Cardozo, *The Growth of the Law* (4th edn, Yale UP 1931), 70.

[33] *Ibidem*, 69.

8. Concluding remarks

International law, like any legal system, is the expression of the social and political process from which it stems. In the words of Professor Louis Henkin, '[t]he health of the law (…) will depend largely on the health of the society, on its ability to contain explosive forces and mobilize creative ones for general welfare.'[34] Accordingly, the assessment of the state of health of international law and its effectiveness are to be tested, at any point in time, against the degree of support for its basic legal tenets by its main social actors, who are still the nation-states. The degree of such support is proportional to the degree of support for the rule of law within the states themselves, hence, to the 'state of health' of their own legal systems.

As we have seen, history proceeds in cycles like the rhythm of a pendulum between expansion and contraction, liberalism and protectionism, internationalism and nationalism, in a multifarious combination of vectors between change and stability. Therefore, international law is to be considered as a legal process subject to the expansions and contractions with respect to the rule of law within itself, as well as within nation-states.

As stated more than a century ago by the then famous Russian international lawyer and diplomat, Friedrich Martens,

> 'It must necessarily be recognised that the flaws of international law and the lack of precision of its rules are only the inevitable consequence of the imperfections and instability that characterise the domestic legal system that has prevailed in all states to date.'[35]

---

[34] Henkin (n 8) 314.

[35] F de Martens, *Traité de droit international* (Vol I, Libraire Marescq 1883), 287, English translation by the author. The original text goes as follows: 'On doit nécessairement reconnaître que les défectuosités du droit international et le manque de précision de ses règles ne sont que la conséquence inévitable des

This certainly applies no less than to the present state of international law, particularly at a time of a revival in nationalism, also in its legal form, as we shall see in Chapter 4 concerning international law in domestic legal systems.

The late Sir Robert Jennings, a learned scholar of international law, Judge at the ICJ between 1982 and 1995, and President of the Court between 1991 and 1992, in the mid-'80s wrote an interesting definition of international law as a 'vocabulary of ideas' common to the then different components of international society:

> 'In a society of states much divided by ideologies, by religion, by poverty and wealth, by power and weakness, by size, by history, and by geography, it is well never to lose sight of the fact that the one vocabulary of ideas that they have in common is public international law.' [36]

Against such a potentially, or actually, conflicting background, international law has stood out during the Cold War as the one common language with which to argue – *i.e.*, engaging in peaceful conflict – about the interpretation and application of old rules and the making of new ones from different positions and in the pursuit of different goals.

Throughout more than half a century following the Second World War, international law has been a **common language** for the interaction between the different components of the international society and it has allowed to engage in some kind of *autopoiesis*, *i.e.* a process of self-generation, maintenance and transformation of the system. There was then in the international community a widely held interest, indeed, in relying on international law as the one common language. That feeling was shared both by those who wanted to en-

---

imperfections et de l'instabilité qui caractérisent l'ordre intérieur ayant prévalu jusqu'à ce jour dans tous les Etats.'

[36] R Jennings, 'Gerald Gray Fitzmaurice' (1984) 55 British Yearbook of International Law 1, 61.

gage in a process of change of the rules, particularly in the field of economic relations, and by those who wanted to conserve them, eventually, with a view to reaching agreement on compromise formulas which would permit peaceful international coexistence, if not cooperation.

Such a diffused attitude was based on the interest in reinforcing reliance on the international rule of law as basically shared by both the East and the West for pragmatic purposes. Namely, this was in order to complement the peaceful result deriving from nuclear deterrence with the confidence in the mutual compliance with strategic arms limitation treaties and the customary rules of non-intervention and the prohibition on the use of force.

As to the North-South level, the UN General Assembly resolutions promoting the so-called New International Economic Order were sponsored by developing countries and objected to by a large number of industrialised countries with a degree of mutual self-constraint that would allow pursuing change in the customary law to prevent disrupting the basic rules of the game. On the contrary, such rules – together with those ranging from diplomatic law to treaty law, or the law of state responsibility – were then being codified in famous UN codification conventions, or their codification was still under way.

In sum, during the Cold War the preservation of the basic international rules of the game was generally perceived to be in the interest of all states, rich and poor, mighty and weak, liberal and Soviet, in order to ensure the peaceful coexistence and, possibly, cooperation between them. From a military-strategic point of view, bipolarism simplified matters, as the two superpowers realised that neither of them could have the upper hand, while the state of the alliances around NATO, on the one hand, and the Warsaw Pact, on the other, had sufficiently crystallised not to alter that balance. Faith in the common language provided by international law and the mutual compliance with its rules would only corroborate the necessary confidence by both sides in order to maintain such a balance. From an economic standpoint, the former colonial powers used international treaties and customs to extend as much and for as long as possible their privileges, while the newly formed countries emerging from the decolonisation process would wield international law concepts with a view to changing or preserving the rules that they would find useful to change, or preserve. Obviously, with mixed success for all parties involved.

In the present state of the international society, the configuration of international law as one common language between the multiply divided components of that society, as expressed in the above quoted statement by Judge Jennings, is under threat. Under the international and domestic conundrum of today which is characterised by an upsurge of nationalism, not only among superpowers, but also among medium-sized states, the unity of the language of international law is challenged by the diffused sense of the diminished importance of cultural values, including those making up a possibly shared legal culture. Indeed, these are days which, in many countries, are reminiscent of those days, a little less than a century ago, disturbingly epitomised by the quip '[w]hen I hear "Culture"... I release the safety catch on my Browning! [a pistol gun].' [37]

It is worth noting that, while on the **public affairs** level the vision and practice of international law as a unique language is splitting up into many different unilateral visions, or incurring oblivion, on the **transnational business** level one may infer a diffused trend towards reliance on increasingly homogeneous legal parameters and on international mechanisms of alternative dispute resolution, *i.e.*, alternative to domestic jurisdictions. This trend is epitomised by the sprouting of international centres around the world offering arbitration or mediation services for international commercial disputes.

---

[37] This often-quoted line is originally from the first Act of Hanns Jhost's 1933 nazi-drama *Schlageter* on the life and death of the German far-right militant Albert Leo Schlageter.

Further reading

Abi-Saab G, 'Cours général de droit international public' (1987) 207 Collected Courses of the Hague Academy of International Law 15ff;

Carrillo-Salcedo A, 'Droit international et souveraineté des États: cours général de droit international public' (1996) 257 Collected Courses of the Hague Academy of International Law 35ff;

Focarelli C, 'The Construction of International Law' in Id, *International Law as a Social Construct* (OUP 2012), 89ff;

Jenks WG, 'Interdependence as the Basic Concept of Contemporary International Law' in JA Salmon (ed), *Mélanges offerts à Henri Rolin. Problèmes de droit de gens* (Pedone 1964), 147ff;

Lauterpacht H, *The Function of Law in the International Community* (reprinted, OUP 2011);

Lowe V, *International Law: A Very Short Introduction* (OUP 2015);

Mégret F, 'International Law as Law' in J Crawford and M Koskenniemi (eds), *The Cambridge Companion to International Law* (CUP 2012), 64ff;

Tanzi A, *Introduzione al diritto internazionale contemporaneo* (7th edn, CEDAM 2022);

Watts A, 'The Importance of International Law' in M Byers (ed), *The Role of Law in International Politics* (OUP 2001), 6ff.

Chapter 2

Who makes international law and its recipients

1. The subjects and actors of international law. Introductory remarks

Any given legal order provides for the rules which designate its own legal subjects, or **subjects of law**. Especially in international law, they are recognised by the law with having the **legal capacity** to create and/or transfer rights, duties and powers. As we shall see in Chapter 3, this may occur by entering into agreements or by undertaking conduct making up the practice and *opinio juris* instrumental in the formation of customary law.

At the same time, and consequently, legal subjects are the addressees of the rules of the international legal system. That is to say that they become the recipients of the legal rights, duties and powers which stem from such rules.

As it is illustrated in Chapter 5, insofar as recipients of rights and obligations, legal subjects are by definition entitled to invoke the responsibility of other subjects for the violation of their rights and, and in their turn, incur **international responsibility** for breaches of their legal obligations.

In domestic jurisdictions the attribution of legal personality to individuals, as **natural persons**, and to entities, as **juristic persons**, is strictly regulated, so as to enjoy universal application and recognition. Natural persons are individuals who acquire legal personality at birth under the law of any state. Juristic persons are non-living entities, such as corporations or cooperatives, that attain legal personality through incorporation under the laws of any given country. A legal subject, as a recipient of rights, obligations and powers, is entitled to lodge claims and may incur liability; therefore, can sue and be sued before domestic courts.

In international law – in line with the constitutional principle of sovereign equality, as illustrated in Chapter 1 – **states** are the traditional legal subjects, followed by **intergovernmental organisations**. Both are juristic persons. However, differently from domestic jurisdictions, the attribution of juristic personality in international law is far from being objectively attributed. This is an area of international law where the lack of institutional centralisation, of the kind which we find in advanced municipal legal systems, affects its legal process most. And here it is where international law shows most clearly the high degree of **relativism** of its functioning.

If that is so with regard to the legal personality of states and intergovernmental organisations, as we shall see, the position of **non-state actors** under international law is even more nuanced and complex.

By way of conclusion of these introductory remarks, one is to note that international legal subjects also enjoy **domestic legal personality** under the national jurisdictions in which they operate. For example, foreign states enter into contracts of purchase or lease in order to buy or rent the real estate where they establish their diplomatic and consular missions, or contracts for the running and maintenance of such missions, including the employment of administrative or service personnel, or the provision of electricity, gas, water and telephone services. The same applies to intergovernmental organisations in their relations with the states that host their headquarters.

We are not directly concerned here with the domestic legal personality of international legal subjects, because their domestic legal capacity and the legal relations they enter into in the exercise of such legal capacity are governed by the domestic law of the host state. However, international customary law and treaty law, with special regard to the so-called *headquarters agreements*, provide international legal standards on the treatment of foreign states and international organisations. Such standards basically consist of tax privileges and immunities for foreign states, their diplomatic and consular missions, intergovernmental organisations and for their respective officials. These issues will be addressed in more detail below, particularly in Chapter 7, Section 7.

2. States and statehood

States are the typical subjects and constituent pillars of international law. In line with the basic indications emerging from Chapter 1 on the sovereign equality of states as a constitutional and constituent principle of international law, the international legal order, observed as a matter of social fact, shows that states are social aggregates capable of independently exercising their threefold **internal sovereignty**: namely, their *jurisdiction to prescribe, to adjudicate and to enforce*. The condition of independence applies also to the exercise of its **external sovereignty**, in the sense that a state should be independent in making its foreign policy choices.

The exercise of these elements of a state's sovereignty, both internal and international, may well be constrained by both international customary and treaty law. In fact, as indicated in Chapter 1, the international law process is characterised, since its inception, by the formation of rules that impinge upon the exercise of state sovereignty.

Such constraints may apply to the exercise of both internal and external sovereignty. As to constraints on domestic sovereignty, suffice to recall, by way of example, the duty to treat aliens in a way which is not discriminatory or arbitrary, or that to afford tax privileges and jurisdictional immunities to foreign states, intergovernmental organisations and their respective officials, or environmental law obligations, which largely impinge upon conduct by administrative authorities.

Having regard to international law constraints on the exercise of the external sovereignty of states, apart from the fundamental prohibition to use force against the territorial integrity of other states, one may think of the international duties of **cooperation** as specified in MEAs or in treaties of judicial cooperation, including on extradition.

It is important to stress that the idea of international legal constraints on nation-states does not contradict the principle of independence as a corollary to state sovereignty. That is so insofar as such constraints are freely undertaken by states, precisely through the free exercise of their internal and external sovereignty. [1] That is, by freely entering into international agreements, or by producing customary law through the consistent conduct of domestic state organs, either belonging to the legislative, executive or judicial branch. As noted by the PCIJ, the predecessor of the ICJ, in 1927 in its landmark *Lotus* judgment:

> 'International law governs relations between independent States. The rules of law binding upon States therefore emanate from their own free will as expressed in conventions or by usages generally accepted as expressing principles of law and established in order to regulate the relations between these co-existing independent communities or with a view to the achievement of common aims.' [2]

Therefore, any given Government may feel politically, economically interested in entering into a given treaty, or to conduct itself in a certain manner that may be conducive to the creation of a given custom. But that pertains to the **cost-benefit analysis** inherent in any policy decision, which is an integral part of the exercise of state sovereignty.

As already alluded, the fact that states are endowed with international legal personality means that, by having the capacity to produce international law, at the same time, they are considered to have the capacity to become the bearers of the rights and duties which flow from it. Such legal capacity is subject to capacity as a matter of fact under the **principle of effectiveness**. In fact and in law, the three legal requirements for acquiring international legal personality coincide with the conditions for effective **independent statehood**: *a*) an independent and stable **Government**; *b*) a **territory** with settled borders within which the Government in question

---

[1] See above, Chapter 1, Section 2.

[2] *The Case of the S.S. "Lotus"* (France v Turkey) (Judgment) [1927] PCIJ Series A/No 10, para 18.

exercises its jurisdiction; and *c*) a permanent **population** settled in that territory and ruled by the Government in question.

In international law there is no central authority granting international legal personality, or an international registry recording incorporation and certifying its validity for all. The fulfilment of the above three legal requirements, being based on factual effectiveness, suggests an element of objectivity: namely, one might expect that once an entity effectively meets the requirements in question it would acquire the status of a state as a legal person objectively for all, until it does not lose such characteristics. However, as we shall see below, practice shows that, oftentimes, pre-existing states engage in acts of **recognition** of newly formed states, which might give a sense of arbitrary selection. This also suggests an element of relativism, but as we shall see, only in a political dimension.[3]

One may note that, nowadays and for a long time in the past, a new state is not created from nothing, but its formation is actually the result of a process of transformation stemming from a pre-existing state, or states. This is the case, for example, with the formation of the new states which have emerged from the process of **decolonisation**, or from the collapse of the Soviet Union, or the Former Yugoslavia. In descriptive legal terms this phenomenon of transformation may take different forms, namely, **dismemberment**, **secession** and **annexation**.

In fact, **annexation** seldom leads to the creation of a new state. It usually results in the mere expansion of the territory of the annexing state. Besides, when annexation is the result of occupation by unlawful military force, in principle, under international law states are under an obligation not to recognise its validity.[4] This gives rise to tensions between non-recognition and effectivity.

---

[3] For an in-depth analysis of the conditions of statehood see J Crawford, *The Creation of States in International Law* (2nd edn, OUP 2007), 96ff. See also K Knop, 'Statehood: Territory, People, Government' in J Crawford and M Koskenniemi (eds), *The Cambridge Companion to International Law* (CUP 2012), 95ff.

[4] Article 41(2) of the ASR specifies that: 'No State shall recognize as lawful

This historical background indicates how fraught with political sensitivity the issue of statehood is. The point will be illustrated further in relation to the elements of uncertainty which derive from the tension between the objective fulfilment of the requirements for the acquisition of statehood and the relativity of unilateral acts of recognition, or non-recognition, of new entities as states by pre-existing states.

2.1. *Recognition*

Some have considered as a further requirement for the acquisition of international legal personality the fact of being **recognised** as a state by pre-existing states. This approach reflects the so-called *constitutive recognition doctrine*. However, practice shows that under international customary law the above three requirements are sufficient for the acquisition of international personality by states. Therefore, we have to discard the validity of such doctrine.

Already in 1929, the Arbitration Tribunal in *Deutsche Continental Gas-Gesellschaft v Polish State* observed that:

> 'According to the opinion rightly admitted by the great majority of writers of international law, the recognition of a State is not constitutive but merely declaratory. The State exists by itself and the recognition is nothing else than a declaration of this existence, recognised by the State from which it emanates.' [5]

It is now established practice in international relations that the uni-

---

a situation created by a serious breach [by a State of an obligation arising under a peremptory norm of general international law], nor render aid or assistance in maintaining that situation.' See also F Salerno 'L'obbligo di non riconoscimento di situazioni territoriali illegittime dopo il parere della Corte internazionale di giustizia sulle Isole Chagos' (2019) 102 Rivista di diritto internazionale 729.

[5] *Deutsche Continental Gas-Gesellschaft v Polish State*, collected in (1936) 5 Annual Digest of Public International Law Cases 11, 15.

lateral act of recognition is considered to be merely declaratory of the recognising state's **political acceptance** or, rather, **endorsement** of a new social aggregate as a new state (*declaratory recognition doctrine*).

Suffice to recall that the US recognised the PRC only in 1979, whilst the latter had met the three requirements in question since 1949, conducted international relations with the large part of the international community, was admitted as a Member of the UN in 1971, and the following year received the visit by the then US President Richard Nixon. It could not possibly be said that the 1979 recognition by the US was in any way constitutive of the PRC's international legal personality. Similarly, this had not been the case with the PRC admission to the UN in 1971, since it had existed as a state and acted as such, including entering into international treaties, under the three requirements in question for the previous twenty years.

The **admission to the UN as a Member state** can undeniably be taken as a strong indicator of statehood. However, this should not be confused with a formal recognition of statehood from the UN institution as such. Such a **process of admission** would be relevant, on a case-by-case basis, only for the purposes of assessing the recognition by the individual UN Members that have voted in favour of the request for admission in any given case, which is not necessarily unanimous.

The conditions for membership of the UN go beyond those required for statehood. Namely, under Article 4 of the *UN Charter*, the applicant should prove to be a 'peace-loving country' – *i.e.* one which undertakes to comply with the ban on the use of force under Article 2(4) of the *UN Charter*, and to be 'able and willing' to carry out the obligations deriving from the *UN Charter* itself. By clear implication, this provision indicates that membership is not a requirement for statehood. That is, that a state may not accept the fundamental obligations stemming from the *UN Charter* and, therefore, not become a Member of the UN, without this depriving the state in question of its statehood. Furthermore, as stressed by the ICJ in its 1948 advisory opinion on the *Conditions of Admission of a State to Membership in the United Nations,*[6] each Member state, when casting its vote on a given application for membership, expresses its individual assessment simply on whether the applicant meets the conditions for admission, *i.e.*, not on its statehood.

By way of example, one may, again, refer to the case of the PRC, which is now one of the five permanent Members of the Security Council. Its admission took place in 1971 through the adoption of a General Assembly resolution by a roll-call vote of 76 to 35, with 17 abstentions.[7] However, as already indicated, the PRC had already been conducting itself, domestically and internationally, as a fully independent state and, no less importantly, had been treated as such by the large majority of states for a long time.

It would be impossible for an international customary rule to establish a precise threshold of the number of recognitions required, beyond which the international legal personality of a state would become valid for all. There is neither practice, nor *opinio juris*, to that effect, and it is difficult to imagine that a customary rule of the kind in question might evolve in the international society.

As a matter of fact, the occurrence of a significant number of recognitions of a given entity as a new state may bring along the political and economic support which is empirically necessary for a social aggregate to consolidate its legal personality in the form of a state. That is to say, that a newly formed state is likely to lose the capacity to effectively meet the three requirements in question – *i.e.* an effective Government over a population within a defined territory – without a sufficiently widespread political recognition by other states. That is particularly so in an ever increasingly interdependent world.

---

[6] *Conditions of Admission of a State to Membership in the United Nations (Article 4 of the Charter)* (Advisory Opinion) [1948] ICJ Rep 57, 63.

[7] UN General Assembly, Res 2758(XXVI) of 25 October 1971.

The above qualifications and distinctions are not merely of a theoretical or academic relevance. Indeed, the declaratory character of recognition realistically gives the benefit of the doubt to the effective completion of the process of formation of a new state and allows pre-existing states to fully rely on their political interest and discretion in their **political communication** without legally binding themselves to their political choices. Even more practically, the declaratory, instead of constitutive, connotation of recognition allows for the public authorities and domestic courts of a state that has not recognised another state to give effect to the latter's **public acts** and laws, such as certificates of birth, marriage, or divorce.

Elements of state practice after the end of the Cold War concerning the dismemberment of the Former Yugoslavia and the Soviet Union may prompt the question whether conditions additional to the above three requirements for statehood have been introduced in customary international law. One may recall the 1991 Declaration by the Ministers for Foreign Affairs of the then EC (now EU) on the *Guidelines on Recognition of New States in Eastern Europe and the Soviet Union.*[8] It announced the readiness of the EC Member states to recognize new states upon condition that, next to complying with 'international practice,' they are not the result of aggression, they comply *inter alia* with the prohibition of the use of force and the principles of territorial integrity, human rights, the protection of national minorities, and that they 'have constituted themselves on a democratic basis.'

It would be wrong to consider this Declaration as an element of practice and *opinio juris* purporting to introduce a new customary requirement for the acquisition of the legal personality of states, as much as it might be desirable. In fact, the Badinter Commission, named after the French lawyer who presided over it and which was established by the EC for the purpose of advising on applications

---

[8] Collected in (1992) 31 ILM 1486.

for recognition to be submitted to it, clearly stated from the outset of its advisory activity that, in any case, it considered recognition to be of a 'purely declaratory' nature.[9] Therefore, the Declaration in question should be considered as nothing more than what it is meant to be, *i.e.* a set of political guidelines for the then EC Member states, with a view to enhancing political coordination in the matter of recognition of the newly formed states.

2.1.1. *Two difficult cases, among others: Kosovo and Crimea*

A. Kosovo

After a series of dramatic ethnic conflicts which resulted in the formation of newly independent states ensuing from the dissolution of the Former Socialist Federal Republic of Yugoslavia in 1992, in 1998 a harsh civil strife broke out between the Former Yugoslav Government of Serbia and the Kosovo Liberation Army (KLA). In June 1999, within the UN Security Council agreement could finally be reached among its permanent Members on the text of a binding resolution (Resolution 1244(1999)) addressing the complex matter in point.[10] Given the beginning of tensions between the US and Russia, the former in favour of Kosovo achieving independence, the latter against a detachment from Serbia, the resolution in question could only be one of compromise. Namely, it demanded that both parties would end any form of violence, establishing a peace-keeping force also in charge with civil, administrative and police functions in the region in support of the local autonomous authorities. However, the resolution in question fell short of expressly ad-

---

[9] Opinion No 1 of the Arbitration Committee, reported in the Appendix to A Pellet 'The Opinions of the Badinter Arbitration Committee: A Second Breath for the Self-Determination of People' (1992) 3 European Journal of International Law 178, 182. On the Badinter Commission see also M Fitzmaurice, 'Badinter Commission (for the Former Yugoslavia)' in A Peters (ed), *Max Planck Encyclopaedia of Public International Law* (online edn, OUP 2019).

[10] UN Security Council, Res 1244(1999) of 10 June 1999.

dressing the issue of the sovereign independence of Kosovo, and simply demanded a political settlement of the situation.

Right after the self-declaration of independence by Kosovo in 2008, [11] Serbia promoted the adoption of a UN General Assembly resolution requesting the ICJ an advisory opinion as to whether such declaration was in accordance with international law. [12] The Court did not come down in so many words to a finding as to whether Kosovo had, or not, acquired the legal personality of a sovereign state, which was the true issue in question, but one fraught with political sensitivity. It strictly confined itself to the wording of the request, simply opining that the self-declaration in question was **in accordance with international law**, as there is no general prohibition on declarations of independence under international law. [13] It also found that the declaration was not contrary to Security Council Resolution 1244(1999), since not even the latter addressed the issue of independence. [14]

Be that as it may, at the time the present book is going to press, 97 states have recognised Kosovo as an independent sovereign state, from the EU, NATO and the OIC. Serbia, Russia and most Slavic countries have not, as well as other states experiencing secessionist drives, such as Spain, and have branded the 2008 self-declaration of independence as illegal. [15]

Most importantly for our purposes, despite the above and the increasing tensions between Kosovo and Serbia, the two are regular

---

[11] See C Warbrick, 'Kosovo: The Declaration of Independence' (2008) 57 International and Comparative Law Quarterly 675, esp at 679.

[12] UN General Assembly, Res 63/3 of 8 October 2008.

[13] *Accordance with International Law of the Unilateral Declaration of Independence in Respect of Kosovo* (Advisory Opinion) [2010] ICJ Rep 403, para 84.

[14] *Ibidem*, para 119.

[15] On the issue of Kosovo and statehood, see E Milano, *Formazione dello Stato e processi di State-building nel diritto internazionale. Kosovo 1999-2013* (Editoriale Scientifica 2013).

trading partners and in 2013 they concluded the First Agreement of Principles Governing the Normalization of Relations ('Brussels Agreement') which provides for the *de facto* recognition of Kosovo by Serbia in exchange for guarantees on the treatment of Serbian ethnic minorities in the northern provinces of Kosovo. As a matter of fact and law, the political relations between the two may improve or precipitate as between two sovereign states. And indeed, the Serbian President Alexander Vučić has recently made the headlines for declaring that the Brussels Agreement 'no longer exists,' citing alleged repeated violations by the Kosovar authorities, including the purges of ethnic Serbs from civil and administrative local institutions.[16] The EU is acting as mediator between the parties but no new agreement has been brokered so far.

B. Crimea

The history of the legal status of Crimea and of its people are exemplary of the tidal ebb and flow between international law and politics. After having been an autonomous entity under the sovereignty of the former Soviet Union, in 1992, the Crimean authorities adopted a declaration of independence, subject to confirmation by referendum. The independent Republic of Crimea was short-lived, however. Its sovereign independence was persistently opposed by Ukraine and no referendum ever endorsed the new Constitution, which was eventually abolished by the Ukrainian parliament in 1995.

The fate of Crimea followed that of the Russia-Ukraine relations. Based on the Russian-Ukrainian Friendship Treaty of 1997, the following year Crimea was formally made an 'Autonomous Republic' – *i.e.*, not an independent one – under the sovereignty of Ukraine. Since 2008 the tensions between Russia and Ukraine have been soaring, together with those within Crimea between pro-Russian and pro-Western militants, political parties and statesmen.

---

[16] 'Serbian President: "Brussels Agreement No Longer Exists"' (24 March 2022), available at: <www.serbiandaily.com>.

It so happened that, in February 2014, after the ousting of a pro-Russian President in Ukraine, out of concerns to lose its grip on the peninsula, its energy and logistical hubs on the Black Sea, pro-Russian armed militants, wearing uniforms without insignias, took effective military control over Crimea. Shortly after, in March of the same year, such military control was complemented by the support from the Crimean Russian-backed political authorities who, with very short notice, organised a referendum which resulted in favour of independence from Ukraine and the transferring of sovereignty over from Ukraine to Russia. Despite strong objections to the validity of the referendum having been raised by international electoral observers,[17] it was immediately endorsed by the pro-Russian local Crimean political authorities. This formula allowed Russia to advance the legal argument, as a matter of **political communication policy**, that it had not forcibly annexed Crimea, but that the latter, after gaining independence from Ukraine, would exercise its sovereignty so as to freely decide to merge with Russia.

Be that as it may and as a matter of fact, the sovereign control over the territory and people of Crimea is now being exercised by the Russian Federation. That is so, despite the **lack of recognition** of this state of affairs as a matter of international law, and even the adoption of sanctions against Russia, who is being regarded as the illegally annexing state, by a number of Western countries, namely Canada, the EU Members states, Japan and the US.

The events occurred in Crimea in 2014 recall aspects of those underway in Ukraine at the time the present volume is going to press, also referred to above in Chapter 1, Section 4. Under both circumstances legal arguments have been advanced by Russia to

---

[17] See A Peters, 'Sense and Nonsense of Territorial Referendums in Ukraine, and Why the 16 March Referendum in Crimea Does Not Justify Crimea's Alteration of Territorial Status under International Law' in *EJILTalk!* (16 April 2014). For a more elaborate analysis on the lawfulness of the referendum under international law, see J Vidmar, 'The Annexation of Crimea and the Boundaries of the Will of People' (2015) 16 German Law Journal 365.

justify its conduct while such conduct and arguments have been objected to by a significant number of states in different forms, including the adoption of sanctions, and in different forums, including the UN General Assembly, the ECtHR, the ICC and the ICJ. [18] While the annexation of Crimea remains a matter of fact, despite objections to its legality by multiple countries, dramatic hostilities are ongoing in Ukraine.

3. Intergovernmental organisations

Until the 20th century, states were the only legal subjects of international law, until they felt the need to enhance their cooperation on the international level through permanent intergovernmental organisations. Such organisations have been endowed by their constituent treaties with organs whose functions were primarily inward oriented, *i.e.* addressed to its Member states. That is still so nowadays. Taking the UN as the most representative example of intergovernmental organisations, suffice to consider the importance of the UN General Assembly and Security Council, which provide political negotiating *fora* for its Member states, within the regulatory framework of its founding treaty, *i.e.* the *UN Charter*.

At the same time, in the pursuit of their statutory aims, intergovernmental organisations through their organs often undertake activities in which they appear to act on behalf of a legal subject separate from their Member states. One may think, for instance, of the conclusion of treaties, such as those on the treatment of peace-keeping personnel with the state in which such missions take place. They are so-called **Status of Forces Agreements** (SOFAs).

Generally, the constituent treaties of international organisations, including the *UN Charter*, do not contain express provisions concerning the legal personality and capacity of the organisation in

[18] See Chapter 1.

question. Equally, until the middle of the 20th century, international customary law on legal personality had developed only in relation to states. It is therefore no surprise that, back in 1948, when a UN official was killed in the course of the first peace-keeping operation in Palestine, there was uncertainty regarding the state of the law as to whether the UN itself, or the state of nationality (Sweden) of the victim, were entitled to hold Israel internationally responsible and lodge a claim for reparation for the killing in question. Accordingly, the General Assembly requested an advisory opinion from the ICJ, which became a landmark judicial statement on the point at issue. [19]

The Court started from the premise that '[t]he subjects of law in any legal system are not necessarily identical in their nature or in the extent of their rights, and their nature depends upon the needs of the community.' [20] It then continued, following a ***functional approach***, as follows:

> '[T]he Organization was intended to exercise and enjoy, and is in fact exercising and enjoying, functions and rights which can only be explained on the basis of the possession of a large measure of international personality and the capacity to operate upon an international plane.
> [I]t must be acknowledged that its Members, by entrusting certain functions to it, with the attendant duties and responsibilities, have clothed it with the competence required to enable those functions to be effectively discharged. Accordingly, the Court has come to the conclusion that the Organization is an international person. That is not the same thing as saying that it is a State, which it certainly is not, or that its legal personality and rights and duties are the same as those of a State. (…)
> Under international law, the Organization must be deemed to have these powers which, though not expressly provided in the Charter,

---

[19] *Reparation for Injuries Suffered in the Service of the United Nations* (Advisory Opinion) [1949] ICJ Rep 174.

[20] *Ibidem*, 178.

> are conferred upon it by necessary implication as being essential to the performance of its duties. (…)
> Having regard to its purposes and functions already referred to, the Organization may find it necessary, and it has found it necessary, to entrust its agents with important missions to be performed in disturbed parts of the world. (…)
> The obligations entered into by States to enable the agents of the Organization to perform their duties are undertaken not in the interest of the agents, but in that of the Organization. When it claims redress for a breach of these obligations, the organization is invoking its own right, the right that the obligations due to it should be respected.' [21]

The functional approach followed by the ICJ led it to the acknowledgment of a legal personality and capacity of the UN on the basis of the **implied powers doctrine**. Namely, the Court found such legal personality and capacity to have been implicitly afforded to the UN by its Members as a necessary corollary of the functions expressly entrusted to it and in order for the Organisation to properly fulfil them. In so doing, the Court also introduced a gradual concept of legal personality, acknowledging for the UN one of a kind that falls short of the 'fully fledged' personality attached to statehood, but which is merely proportional to the functions in question. [22]

In sum, one can conclude from the above that intergovernmental organisations – irrespective of explicit provisions in their constituent treaties on the matter in hand – are generally to be considered as subjects of international law, while their legal capacity is confined to the rights and duties strictly related to their statutory functions on a case-specific basis. As a bare minimum, such capacity envisages that of concluding international agreements, to become the recipients of the

[21] *Ibidem*, 179, 184.

[22] 'Whereas a State possesses the totality of international rights and duties recognized by international law, the rights and duties of an entity such as the Organization must depend upon its purposes and functions as specified or implied in its constituent documents and developed in practice,' *ibidem*, 180.

rights and duties stemming from the agreements they are parties to, and to hold and be held internationally responsible for their breaches of such agreements by themselves or other parties, respectively.[23]

4. Non-state entities

4.1. *Individuals*

Initially and until the mid-1900s, individuals were relevant in international law only insofar as they were nationals of a given state when in a foreign country, thus, protected under the international customary rules, possibly complemented by bilateral treaties, on the **treatment of aliens**.

Prior to the introduction of international human rights law since the mid-1900s, the way individuals were treated by the authorities of their state of nationality, or even residence, would fall outside the scope of application of international law (*domaine réservé*). The absolute freedom of states regarding the treatment of their nationals and residents within their borders was originally considered as a corollary to the principle of sovereign equality and independence of states. Accordingly, such freedom would flow from the principle of non-interference in the internal affairs of other states, which would translate into the so-called concept of *domestic jurisdiction*. The latter is generally considered to be no longer legally effective since the coming into being of the international body of human rights law, whereby states are supposed to be internationally accountable, in principle, for the treatment of any individuals irrespective of their nationality.[24]

---

[23] For more on this topic, see D Sarooshi, 'Legal Capacity and Powers' in JK Cogan, I Hurd and I Johnstone (eds), *The Oxford Handbook of International Organizations* (OUP 2017), 985ff.

[24] On the human rights branch of international law, see Chapter 7, Section 4.

Aside from and parallel to international human rights law, when individuals abroad receive treatment by the host country which is considered to be in breach of international minimum standards, such individuals should resort to local remedies, where available and effective. But, after having exhausted the internal remedies of the foreign state in question to no avail (**the rule of the previous exhaustion of local remedies**), could in the past look for remedy only by asking their state of nationality to exercise **diplomatic protection** in their favour.

Diplomatic protection consists of the state of nationality bringing up, or *espousing*, the claim for the alleged unjust, arbitrary, or discriminatory treatment at diplomatic level *vis-à-vis* the state where the facts complained of have occurred. That is, through diplomatic protests accompanied by claims of restitution or compensation.[25] If both states have consented to international adjudication or arbitration relevant to the facts in question, the claimant state may submit the dispute for settlement to the ICJ, the ITLOS, or an arbitration tribunal.[26]

The problem is that states exercise diplomatic protection at their absolute discretion based on **utilitarian considerations** of appropriateness according to their foreign policy, or domestic, considerations. This is strictly connected to the fact that, even in the present day, the recipients of the rights deriving from the international rules on the treatment of aliens are not private individuals and companies, who are the **material beneficiaries** of such rules, but the states of which they have the nationality. This conforms to the traditional state-centred model of international law epitomised by the statement made in 1928 by the PCIJ in its advisory opinion on the *Jurisdiction of the Courts of Danzig* whereby 'an international

[25] On this topic see CF Amerasinghe, *Diplomatic Protection* (OUP 2008) and the ILC Draft Articles on Diplomatic Protection with commentaries (2006) II(2) Yearbook of the International Law Commission 23. On the law of state responsibility see Chapter 5.

[26] On the adjudicative aspects of dispute settlement, see Chapter 6, Section 4.

agreement, cannot, as such, create direct rights and obligations for private individuals.'[27]

However, as indicated, the formation of **human rights law** over the last seventy years has *pierced the veil* of domestic jurisdiction, significantly reducing the shield of national sovereignty against international scrutiny. It is to be stressed, again, that this is not in contradiction with the principle of sovereign equality and independence of states, insofar as such constraints have been produced by states themselves, precisely through the free exercise of their sovereignty by joining international human rights treaties or by expressing their *opinio iuris* and following conforming practice, including the adoption of domestic legislation and case-law.[28]

On the other hand, having regard to the body of law on the treatment of aliens with specific regard to the **protection of foreign direct investment**, through a net of bilateral and multilateral treaties, an arbitration system of dispute settlement has been developed, since the end of the 1960s, that does away with diplomatic protection for this particular but important area within the field of the law concerning the treatment of aliens.[29] In fact, under such treaties, with minor procedural differences between one another, foreign investors, usually corporations, having the nationality of one of the treaty parties in question, may directly sue before an international arbitral tribunal the state, also party to the same treaty, where the investment was made.[30]

As to international human rights law, it is to be noted that its rules explicitly benefit individuals, irrespective of their nationality,

---

[27] *Jurisdiction of the Courts of Danzig* (Advisory Opinion) [1928] PCIJ Series B/No 15, 17. The point ties in with the thorny issue of self-executing, or no self-executing international rules at the domestic law level, which is addressed in Chapter 4, Section 4.

[28] See the remarks in Chapter 1, Section 5.

[29] International investment law is addressed in Chapter 7, Section 2.1.

[30] This peculiar mechanism will be further explored in *ibidem*.

and that the material rights stemming therefrom are often complemented by procedural rights directly addressed to individuals. Such rights include the right to sue a state before a supranational adjudicative forum, such as the IACtHR, or the ECtHR.

The same applies to foreign investors in relation to their substantive rights and their right to sue states before international arbitration tribunals.

Those developments, while contradicting the above PCIJ opinion whereby international agreements do not accrue international rights and obligations for individuals, have raised the question whether this does not entail also affording individuals with international legal personality. The same question is raised by developments concerning the evolution of **international criminal law**. This is particularly the case with the establishment of the ICC, under which individuals may be found responsible for international crimes of war or against humanity.[31]

The question whether individuals are vested with international legal personality, or not, does not seem to the present author to bear significant practical legal consequences. Answering this question in the affirmative, or in the negative, would not add to, nor detract from, the actual rights and duties created for them by states, primarily by treaty law. However, a consideration militating in favour of an answer in the negative is that, even when afforded the procedural right to sue states before international adjudicative bodies, individuals are deprived, as a matter of fact, of an effective power to enforce their rights. Such a power lies only in states and intergovernmental organisations.

The above pragmatic consideration may find substantiation in legally formal terms. Namely, when creating substantive rights for individuals through treaties and customs, states undertake the obligation to respect such human rights towards all the other states par-

---

[31] See further, for both questions, A Kjeldgaard-Pedersen, *The International Legal Personality of the Individual* (OUP 2018).

ties to a given treaty (*erga omnes partes* obligations), and/or the other members of the international community as a whole (just *erga omnes* obligations). When individuals resort to an international adjudicative forum or to a compliance review body under a human right treaty, after the exhaustion of the municipal remedies, such adjudicative or treaty bodies can be said to act as common organs of the states parties to the treaty in question, asserting their common and indivisible right that human rights obligations be respected by each and all of the other parties. The same may formally be considered to apply when a foreign investor sues the host state before an arbitral tribunal established under a bilateral, or multilateral investment treaty, to which the state of the investor and the state hosting the investment are parties.

The above considerations conform to the way international law operates generally. As emphasised by James Crawford, '[m]any of the things international law tries to do have to be done at the national level.' [32] This is all the more the case with human rights, particularly with respect to which states have the tridimensional duty to **respect, protect and fulfil**.

Parallel considerations apply with regard to the operation of international criminal law. States have assumed the right and duty to domestically prosecute certain conducts that, under the international rules which they have created and implemented, amount to international crimes. When domestically prosecuting individuals accused of such crimes, a state would be at the same time exercising an international right and complying with an international obligation owed to the international community as a whole to suppress such crimes. Where a state having criminal jurisdiction over an individual accused of any of the crimes in question were unable, or unwilling, to prosecute, the ICC, by exercising its complementary criminal jurisdiction, would be acting as the adjudicative body

---

[32] J Crawford, 'Chance, Order, Change: The Course of International Law' (2013) 365 Collected Courses of the Hague Academy of International Law 13, 214.

common to the states parties to the *Rome Statute* – or the *UN Charter* when triggered by the Security Council. [33]

4.2. *NGOs*

In traditional liberal democracies, civil society, organised through NGOs, participates in the process for the pursuit of the public good on the domestic political and administrative levels under domestic constitutional guarantees. Against this background, one would assume that relevant input from civil society on the international level would be filtered through the governmental foreign policy. In fact, international bilateral and multilateral diplomatic negotiations are, still to the present day, carried out by state representatives.

Over the last few decades, the increasing international relevance of domestic ethical, social, scientific, economic, environmental and health factors, amongst others, has promoted the development of NGOs which are engaged in cross-border activities, and have highly specialised expertise in each specific area in which they operate.

To mention only few amongst so very many international NGOs, one may recall *Amnesty International*, *Human Rights Watch* or the *Fédération Internationale des Droits de l'Homme* in the field of human rights; *Greenpeace International* or the *World Wildlife Fund* on environmental protection and the *World Development Movement* in the economic sector.

Being registered under the municipal law of a state, NGOs have legal personality under that domestic law, but not under international law. They are not the addressees of international rights and obligations; hence, they cannot hold a state internationally responsible, nor incur international responsibility themselves and, therefore, cannot be parties before international courts and tribunals.

However, given the usually considerable **expertise** to be found in such organisations, in combination with their engagement on

[33] Under Article 13(b) of the *Rome Statute*.

public interest concerns of international relevance, they are increasingly being formally admitted in the international negotiations instrumental in international law-making, where they may contribute substantively in the discussions, as observers, but cannot vote.

One may also note a timid trend in international adjudication to admit NGOs in proceedings as non-parties. To that end, the common law procedural institution called ***amici curiae*** is increasingly being referred to by international adjudicative bodies according to which specialised NGOs may submit briefs on aspects of the dispute which are deemed to affect the interest of the public, next to that of the disputing parties.

The founders of the UN foresaw the possibility of interaction between NGOs and one of its principal bodies, most concerned with economic and social issues, *i.e.* the ECOSOC. To that end, Article 71 of the *UN Charter* reads as follows:

> 'The Economic and Social Council may make suitable arrangements for consultation with non-governmental organizations which are concerned with matters within its competence. Such arrangements may be made with international organizations and, where appropriate, with national organizations after consultation with the Member of the United Nations concerned.'

Throughout the years, the ECOSOC has adopted a number of resolutions to that effect. In particular, in 1996 a resolution has also introduced regulation governing the participation of NGOs in UN bodies beyond the ECOSOC itself.[34] By and large, the most qualified NGOs in the economic, social and cultural fields whose application to participate in any given UN diplomatic exercise is accepted, are given access to the preparatory documents. Equally, they may even propose additional items in the agenda and may participate in the workings in question with rights inherent with observer status. This includes the power to make both **oral and written**

[34] UN ECOSOC, Res 1996/31 of 25 July 1996.

statements. Such statements may influence the outcome of debate, including drafting formulas in the text under negotiation, irrespective of the fact that NGOs are not afforded the right to vote. It is to be noted that the state where the NGO in question has been incorporated, or another Member state, may object to the application of a particular NGO for admission in any given negotiations. Under such circumstance, the NGO in question is afforded the **right to reply** to the arguments advanced against its admission, and the UN Secretariat in charge of the workings in question may approve the application nonetheless, if persuaded by the arguments contained in the reply.

One may recall the key role of the NGO *No Peace Without Justice* in the negotiations of the 1998 UN Conference for the preparation of the *Rome Statute*. Next to taking an active part in the negotiations, it trained a number of legal experts on the specific international criminal law issues that would be tackled at the conference. Those experts would then be made available to, and employed by, a number of governmental delegations that took part in said Conference.[35] In the 1992 UN Rio Conference on Environment and Development the accredited NGOs were 1,378, whilst a parallel non-governmental conference was attended by 17,000 of them. The *Climate Action Network* alone ensured the participation at the 2015 Paris CoP to the *UN Climate Change Convention* of more than 1,100 NGOs, coming from over 120 countries.

While the governmental staff in charge of specific negotiations – from health to environmental protection, or judicial cooperation – that take part in diplomatic exercises geared towards the adoption of international conventional, and non-conventional, instruments, often find it difficult to keep up to date with a considerable number of dossiers over a wide spectrum of subjects and negotiations, the staff of NGOs are usually focused on a narrower spectrum of topics on which they are specialised. This accounts for the fact that,

---

[35] See F Benedetti and JL Washburn, 'Drafting the International Criminal Court Treaty: Two Years to Rome and an Afterword on the Rome Diplomatic Conference' (1999) 5 Global Governance 1.

thanks to the high degree of **preparation of their representatives**, NGOs often bear a significant impact on the final drafting formulas of international instruments, irrespective of the fact that their prerogatives fall short of the right to vote.

NGOs may exert significant pressure on domestic and international political bodies engaged in the international law-making process. Many NGOs have constructively exercised pressure over state delegations from the perspective of the pursuit of global public good, beyond purely **domestic short-term** governmental interests. However, an issue of transparency and accountability may arise. Namely, whilst governmental activities are subject to the political constitutional checks and balances, as well as to domestic social and judicial control, the monitoring of NGOs' international activities is difficult and their funding is not always **transparent**.

Similar considerations apply to the role of NGOs as *amici curiae* in international judicial or arbitral proceedings, mentioned above. While a number of NGOs have constructively participated in international proceedings, particularly in the field of human rights and investment law, concerns have been raised with regard to their impartiality, requiring increased 'transparency standards' concerning their identity, affiliation and financial resources. [36]

4.3. *Corporations*

In addressing NGOs, we have so far considered those of a non-profit nature, namely, those concerned exclusively with the promo-

---

[36] See, for instance, the newly adopted (July 2022) ICSID Arbitration Rules 67(2)(c), 67(2)(d) and 67(2)(e) dedicated to the conflict of interests, affiliation and funding of 'Non-Disputing Parties' filing submissions in the proceedings, respectively. See also C Baltag, 'The Role of *Amici Curiae* in Light of Recent Developments in Investment Treaty Arbitration: Legitimizing the System?' (2020) 35 ICSID Review 279 and GM Farnelli, 'Amicus Curiae' in D Mantucci (ed), *L'arbitrato negli investimenti internazionali. Trattato di Diritto dell'arbitrato* (vol XIII, Editoriale Scientifica 2021), 577.

tion of the public interest. They are called, in jargon, PINGOs. One can also signal the trend featuring corporations and the business community, the already mentioned BINGOs,[37] in the international law discourse on the protection of human rights, the environment and health.

To that end, in the year 2000 the then UN Secretary General, supported by Member states, introduced the *Global Compact* initiative. It aimed to promote the **voluntary adherence** to universal principles on human rights, labour, environment and anti-corruption by corporations in their business conduct, especially with respect to the business organisation, production process, infrastructure building or public utilities supply. The expression capturing the goal of this initiative – and of the many more of this kind both at the intergovernmental and corporate level – is ***corporate social responsibility*** (CSR). Whilst the adjective *social*, as opposed to *legal*, emphasises the voluntary basis of compliance with the standards in question, the consistency and increase in number of such international documents – intergovernmental and not – is promoting the application of international human rights, environmental and health legal standards to corporations as well.

One is to recall, amongst others, the 1976 *OECD Guidelines on Multinational Enterprises*, revised in 2011; the 1977 *ILO Tripartite Declaration on Multinational Enterprises*, revised in 2017; the 1999 *OECD Principles of Corporate Governance*; the 2007 *OECD Principles for Private Sector Participation in Infrastructure*; and the 2011 *Report of the Special Representative of the Secretary-General on the Issue of Human Rights and Transnational Corporations and Other Enterprises*.

In line with the reasoning followed above on the issue of the international legal personality of individuals, acknowledging, or not, **international legal personality** for corporations would not add or detract to the legal accountability of corporations for breaches of

---

[37] See Chapter 1, Section 1.

international legal standards. As to the judicial application of such legal standards, irrespective of the unlikely establishment of an international permanent court with specific jurisdiction over corporate conduct, the general principle remains that it would be for domestic courts and tribunals to apply the international legal standards in question to corporations and their managers. This is all the more the case in the area of human rights where states are under the obligation to *respect, protect and fulfil.* That is to say that states, not only have a duty not to infringe human rights directly through conduct of their authorities, but also **the obligation to protect** their residents under their laws from breaches of human rights carried out by private individuals and companies.

Further reading

Chiussi Curzi L, *General Principles for Business and Human Rights and International Law* (Brill 2021);

Dupuy PM and Vierucci L (eds), *NGOs in International Law: Efficiency in Flexibility?* (Edward Elgar Publishing 2008);

Gaeta P, Viñuales JE and Zappalà S (eds), *Cassese's International Law* (3rd edn, OUP 2020);

Klabbers J, *An Introduction to International Organisations Law* (4th edn, CUP 2022);

Peters A, *Beyond Human Rights: The Legal Status of the Individual in International Law* (CUP 2016);

Reinisch A, 'The Changing of International Legal Framework for Dealing with Non-State Actors' in P Alston (ed), *Non-State Actors and Human Rights* (OUP 2005), 37ff;

Tanzi A, *Introduzione al diritto internazionale contemporaneo* (7th edn, CEDAM 2022);

Wiik A, *Amicus Curiae before International Courts and Tribunals* (Hart 2018), 41-174.

Chapter 3

Making and changing international rules

1. Sources of law and sources of international law

For legal rules to make up a particular legal order which governs the interactions within a given society, there must be some sources generally recognised in that society as capable to bring about such legal rules. It is this type of general recognition by the members of the society in question which makes certain facts, statements or documents become authoritative pieces of law. The sources of the law in force in any given legal order are, **themselves**, legal rules. They are rules about 'who' and 'how' produces the rules of conduct which are addressed to the subjects of a given legal order. The rules which identify the sources of law are of a **constitutional nature** and, as such, they are peculiar to each one legal order and define it. As indicated in Chapters 1 and 2, the social and political process which produces international law is, still nowadays, characterised by the relations between states and between states and intergovernmental organisations.

Given the **constituent principle of sovereign equality and independence of states**, as further illustrated in Section 1.1., the ways and means by which international legal rules are produced have been envisaged in terms different from those we are used to into domestic jurisdictions. As already alluded, the main feature of the sources of international legal rules lies in their **participatory nature**. Namely, they are basically produced by the will of states, or by their actual conduct, when widespread and associated with the conviction that such an attitude conforms to the law (*opinio juris*) or to what ought to be law (*opinio necessitatis*). Such participatory feature is epitomized by **agreements** and **custom**, which are the primary sources of international law.

In municipal legal systems there are two main approaches to the sources of law, depending on whether they belong to a **common law** or **civil law system**. In **common law jurisdictions**, authoritative evidence of the law is looked for in jurisprudential precedents of the same or higher courts. Here, the *doctrine of precedent* applies whereby lower courts are **bound** to follow decisions of higher courts in similar cases. This is the so-called *stare decisis* principle. Increasingly, also in common law jurisdictions, the law is to be found in statutes enacted by legislative bodies; academic legal writings may also be considered as authoritative, as well as considerations of conventional wisdom, in order to decide a case.

In **continental civil law jurisdictions**, law is primarily to be found in civil and penal codes and statutes. True, continental lawyers and courts also often rely on previous case-law. However, differently from common law systems, prior decisions are not binding following the *doctrine of precedent* under the *stare decisis* principle, but bear persuasive authority according to the so-called *jurisprudence constante* doctrine. This proceeds from the **legal positivist approach** followed in civil law legal systems according to which only the legislature makes law. Therefore, as opposed to the natural law/equitable approach whereby common law judicial decisions represent authoritative evidence of the law on a par with statutory law, judgments in civil law countries are supposed to merely interpret and apply legislation (as the Baron of Montesquieu famously stated, judges are, or should be, *la bouche de la loi*).[1]

Even though legislation in municipal jurisdictions is of relatively recent origin, it is now the main source of law in most legal orders around the world. International law, being the product of the law-making interactions between countries of common law and civil law, reflects the increased diffusion of the legal positivist approach since the 20th century.

Statutory law-making by a legislative body has been introduced

---

[1] C de Secondat de Montesquieu, *De l'esprit des lois* (re-edited, Éditions Gallimard 1995), 116.

constitutionally in most countries with a view to pursuing the degree of **clarity and precision** which could not be found in unwritten customary law. Most importantly, it was envisaged as being able to **change** the law more expeditiously in order to meet the needs for social change.

As emphasised by a great American lawyer of the 20th century, Roscoe Pound:

> 'Law must be stable and yet it cannot stand still. Hence all the thinking about law has struggled to reconcile the conflicting demands of the need of stability and of the need of change.' [2]

Another reason for the increased statutory means of law-making in domestic legal systems has to do with the fact that national societies are evolving in ever more diversified, often fragmented, fashions within themselves. Until a few decades ago, the common values and conventional wisdom in any given national society were relatively easy for domestic judges to infer from the social process, and to interpret and apply on a case-by-case basis. Such judicial law-making function, at least in common law systems, was met with the general acknowledgment of its authoritative nature to an extent that is difficult to be found in fragmented, polarised or in any way highly conflictual societies. Such basic difficulties in the national social and legal processes inevitably impact on the international social and legal processes, reminding us of the realistic observation by Friedrich Martens quoted above [3] about the imprecisions and pitfalls of international law being the inevitable reflection of the imperfections and lack of stability of the domestic legal systems in force at any given point in time.

Reverting to the national level by way of comparison, such critical factors account for the fact that law-making in domestic juris-

---

[2] R Pound, *Interpretations of Legal History* (re-edited, CUP 2013), 1.

[3] See Chapter 1, Section 7.

dictions has proved slow and difficult also through legislation. Politically sensitive social issues calling for new legislation give rise to impassioned parliamentary debates between opposing factions, some militating for change, others against. Amongst the progressive factions, different forms of new legislation are usually proposed. Against this background, the **legislative process** is frequently long. Long negotiations often produce statutes which represent a compromise between multiple different views. Therefore, their drafting is hardly ever clear enough to avoid a cumbersome, potentially subjective **interpretation**.[4] Oftentimes, such interpretation produced new complementary legislation, which may not, in turn, provide sufficient clarity, while introducing new problems of interpretation concerning compatibility and priority with respect to previous legislation. Eventually, the interpretation and application of any legislative setting in any given field ends up with the judiciary. Paradoxically, under such circumstances the expansion of statutory law causes an expanded role for the judiciary. When confronted with unclear, sometimes contradictory, legislation, we are witnessing, even in civil law countries, inevitable trends towards *creative jurisprudence*, which is aimed at mending the vagueness, inconsistency or pitfalls of legislation.

In international law, due to the absence of compulsory adjudication, legal interpretation is often left to self-interpretation by states. That explains the importance of the linguistic dimension of international law as a means of communication for the peaceful settlement of differences. On that score, it is worth remembering that disputes are generally settled by agreement which, as we shall see in the following Sections, is at the same time a source of international law. Suffice to recall the 1905 *Rio Grande Agreement*, illustrated

---

[4] On the unpredictability of the application of the law, be it written or unwritten, domestic or international, see Chapter 1, Section 7.1. See also the interesting remarks by Ph Allott, 'Interpretation – An Exact Art' in A Bianchi, D Peat and M Windsor (eds), *Interpretation in International Law* (OUP 2015), 373ff.

above,[5] which settled an age-old dispute between Mexico and the US, setting out the **equitable and reasonable utilisation rule**. That is to say that agreements, especially bilateral ones, while **producing new rules**, at the same time, mark the **settlement of a dispute**. Also, a new clear legal setting mutually agreed between states provides ground for **dispute avoidance, or management**, in the future.

As a final introductory note to law making in the international society, one is to recall that, nowadays, most areas of international relations are expressly governed by some specific rule or general principle of international law. A type of conduct or situation which is not expressly governed by international law will fall within the scope of application of some general rule, or principle, implicitly allowing or forbidding it. Therefore, one should not lose sight of the fact that **making new law** inevitably amounts to **changing the law**. This accounts for the importance of the rules governing the relationship in time between the sources of international law addressed below in Section 5.

1.1. *The absence of legislation in international law*

As it appears from the previous introductory pages, international law shares many of the features and problems about law making with other legal orders, including national jurisdiction. But there is one **crucial difference** between international law and municipal legal systems concerning sources of law and their functioning: namely, the **absence of an institutional legislator in international law**. That is to say that, as already anticipated in Chapter 1, the international constitution does not provide for a legislative body comparable to a national parliament, or congress, that produces statutory law binding on all the legal subjects of that legal system, nor a system of courts endowed with compulsory jurisdiction and the power to render judgments having a legislative binding force for all.

[5] See Chapter 1, Section 4.1.

This feature flows from the still largely decentralised and scarcely institutionalised nature of the international society of states, which derives from the original constitutional principle of **sovereign equality** and independence of states discussed above in Chapter 1, Sections 5 and 6.

The UN General Assembly is a permanent organ composed of basically all the states of the international community, nearly 200, who are also UN Member states. It is the universal forum in which states express their views on all sorts of areas that cover virtually the whole spectrum of the subject-matters governed by international law, from outer-space to terrorism, environment, health, trade and development, *inter alia*. Debates over those subjects between governmental delegations often result in the adoption of carefully crafted resolutions, after long and painstaking negotiations among governmental delegations.

However, **General Assembly resolutions** cannot be equated to anything close to parliamentary legislation. According to Article 10 of the *UN Charter*, General Assembly resolutions have merely hortatory effect:

> 'The General Assembly may discuss any questions or any matters within the scope of the present Charter (…) and (…) may make recommendations to the Members of the United Nations or to the Security Council or to both on any such questions or matters.'

Accordingly, General Assembly resolutions cannot be considered as sources of law in any statutory way. However, in combination with their *travaux préparatoires* – which involve official statements by governmental representatives and their votes – General Assembly resolutions may bear significant persuasive relevance in the identification of customary international law. It is no accident that General Assembly resolutions are oftentimes relied upon as authoritative instruments in diplomatic exchanges in order to substantiate, or reject a claim, as well as in international, or national, judicial decisions.

Considering that **custom and agreements** are the two main sources of international law, as we shall see, it is to be stressed that General Assembly resolutions **do not coincide** with either of them, even though they may be considerably relevant to the formation of custom and the diplomatic background work paving the way to the negotiation of agreements.

The argument – posited by some scholars and endorsed by developing countries in the 1960s[6] – that the adoption of a General Assembly resolution may produce some kind of *instant custom*, as an expression of a widespread *opinio juris* by states, irrespective of repeated uniform and extensive practice, never found much support.

On the other, neither state practice nor international courts and tribunals, or legal literature have substantiated the view that a General Assembly resolution would amount to the conclusion of a *treaty in simplified form – i.e.* a treaty that would enter into force without parliamentary ratification – which would be binding on the Member states that have voted in favour of its adoption. While it is true that state consent is the constituent element of international agreements, the governmental delegates who vote in favour of a resolution have been authorised to express their Government's consent only to the adoption of an instrument which, under the *UN Charter*, has a merely hortatory effect, and not one comparable to that of a binding agreement. The international practice and case-law show that when General Assembly resolutions are invoked as authoritative instruments, this is never based on their putative treaty relevance.

However, and most importantly, General Assembly resolutions – as well as **similar diplomatic instruments**, such as the final declaration of a diplomatic conference on a specific matter – may be instrumental in the formation of a new custom as evidence of the

---

[6] Among others, B Cheng, 'United Nations Resolutions on Outer Space: "Instant" International Customary Law?' (1965) 5 Indian Journal of International Law 23.

opinio juris of the states voting in favour. This point will be illustrated further below.[7]

As already alluded, General Assembly resolutions may have a significant role in treaty law-making, on a case-by-case basis.

Oftentimes, UN Conventions are preceded by a General Assembly resolution on the same subject-matter. Most importantly, the drafting is usually very similar. In this case, one may say that the previous negotiations of the resolution in question have provided a diplomatic test of the political will of states to undertake **engagements** on a given subject **in a non-legally binding form**. Once such engagements have been undertaken, it becomes politically difficult to later reject them in the course of negotiations aimed at the adoption of a conventional instrument. This has been the general attitude of states for decades. Over the last few years, the general perception of the need for good faith consistency in one's own conduct and over the reliance of third parties has regrettably been diminishing in international diplomacy, just like in the interpersonal relations.

Moreover, under Article 13(1)(a) of the *UN Charter*, the General Assembly is vested with the aim of 'encouraging the progressive development of international law and its codification.' This aim has been pursued through the establishment, in 1947,[8] of the ILC, a body of thirty-four 'persons of recognized competence in international law'[9] elected by the General Assembly as **independent experts**. They are tasked with elaborating studies – which may take the form of draft-articles or draft-principles – on topics selected by the General Assembly with a view to consolidating existing international law or promoting its progressive development through codification in different forms.

---

[7] See Section 4.

[8] UN General Assembly, Res 174(II) of 21 November 1947.

[9] *Statute of the International Law Commission* (annexed to *ibidem*), Article 2(1).

The ILC is one of the most influential bodies involved in the international law-making process.[10] Its reports on the topics assigned to it by the General Assembly – usually, upon proposal from the ILC itself – may serve as the basis for governmental negotiations of a codification convention. This was the case with the 1961 *Vienna Convention on Diplomatic Relations*, the 1963 *Vienna Convention on Consular Relations* or the VCLT, to mention the first amongst many others **codification conventions**, and which will be illustrated in due course.

The outcome of the ILC work may take formats other than that of a convention. They consist of a wide spectrum of **soft-law instruments**, ranging from simple draft articles to model rules, guidelines, principles, or simply studies. Such instruments are usually regarded as authoritative and are, thus, recurrently relied upon in diplomatic notes, or before international courts and tribunals, as evidentiary of the law which substantiates a claim.

The authoritative character of such instruments flows from the thorough research of state and international practice in the preparatory works of the ILC and from the recognised legal expertise of its members, who represent the different legal systems and cultures.[11] Consideration should be given also to the fact that the end product of the work of the ILC is always the outcome of repeated exchanges with the state representatives sitting in the **Sixth Committee of the General Assembly**. That accounts for the fact that reference to the ILC work is frequently found in international judgments and

[10] See, in general, L Boisson de Chazournes, 'The International Law Commission in a Mirror – Forms, Impact and Authority' in The United Nations (ed), *Seventy Years of the International Law Commission: Drawing a Balance for the Future* (Brill 2020), 133ff.

[11] See *Statute of the International Law Commission*, Article 8: '[T]he persons to be elected to the Commission should individually possess the qualifications required and that in the Commission as a whole representation of the main forms of civilization and of the principal legal systems of the world should be assured.'

awards to corroborate the reasoning of international adjudicative decisions, with special regard to the identification of customary law.

Over time, apart from the three codification Conventions just recalled, the ILC has significantly contributed in different forms to the codification a large number of sensitive issues of international law. One may recall the ILC's studies on the most-favoured nation clause (1967-1991; 2008-2015), the law of the non-navigational uses of international watercourses (1976-1994), jurisdictional immunities of states (1977-2004), diplomatic protection (1995-2016), the prevention of transboundary damage from hazardous activities (1997-2001), fragmentation of international law (2002-2006), international liability in case of loss from transboundary harm arising out of hazardous activities (2002-2006), the law of transboundary aquifers (2003-2008), jurisdictional immunities of state officials (2006-ongoing), and identification of customary law (2011-2016).

Recently, the scope of the areas of international law addressed by the ILC has sensibly widened, as its most recent works and long-term programme of works demonstrate. While the ILC still retains its primary interest in topics pertaining to general theory of law, such as *jus cogens* (2015-ongoing) and general principles of law (2018-ongoing), it has increasingly focused on sectorial areas, such as environmental law – *e.g.*, the protection of the environment in relation to armed conflicts (2013-ongoing) and the protection of the atmosphere (2013-2021) – and procedural law, with special regard to the production of evidence before international courts and tribunals.

In sum, as much important the role the General Assembly plays in boosting the international law-making process, such a role is nowhere close to legislation of the kind we are used to in domestic jurisdictions. First, the General Assembly is not mandated by the *UN Charter* to pass statutory law. Second, the function that the General Assembly fulfils under the *UN Charter* in promoting the international law-making process is one of **facilitating customary law and treaty law-making**, both of which are firmly in the hands of states.

2. Article 38 of the Statute of the International Court of Justice

The sources of international law are generally recognised to be those listed in Article 38 of the *ICJ Statute*, which is an integral part of the *UN Charter*, both adopted in 1945. It spells out the sources of law the Court would apply in deciding disputes between states.

It reads as follows:

> '1) The Court, whose function is to decide in accordance with international law such disputes as are submitted to it, shall apply:
> *a*) international conventions, whether general or particular, establishing rules expressly recognized by the contesting States;
> *b*) international custom, as evidence of a general practice accepted as law;
> *c*) the general principles of law recognized by civilised nations;
> *d*) (…) judicial decisions and the teachings of the most highly qualified publicists of the various nations, as subsidiary means for the determination of rules of law.
> 2) This provision shall not prejudice the power of the Court to decide a case *ex aequo et bono*, if the parties agree thereto.'

This provision echoes the parallel one enshrined in the 1920 Statute of the PCIJ, the predecessor to the ICJ. It reflects the **legal positivistic**, or strictly consent based, approach alluded to above, in Section 1, that prevailed at that time over the previous somewhat natural law approach. This is evidenced by treaty law being listed before the other sources of international law, as well as by the fact that such consensual approach is not only emphasized in relation to treaty law through the expression 'expressly recognised,' as appropriate, but also to custom and general principles which, in order to properly qualify as sources of international law are to be, respectively, 'accepted' and 'recognised' by states.

However, as it will be shown below, the consensual attitude required as a constituent element of international agreements under the expression 'expressly recognised' under Article 38(1)(a), is different from the concept of 'acceptance' of general practice as evidence of international custom, as well as from the 'recognition' of the general principles of law, Articles 38(1)(b) and (c), respectively.

One is inclined to believe that the provision under consideration can be said to enunciate the sources of international law in a rather simplified way, but also in terms sufficiently general as to allow international courts and tribunals to interpret it in order to capture the dynamics that produce authoritative manifestations of international law. Ever since its adoption, international practice and case-law have developed in a much more precise way the contents of the rules about making agreements, as well as on the formation and identification of customary law and general principles.

3. International agreements. Introductory qualifications

Before addressing the matter of international agreements, one should stress, once more, that **issues** such as those on their coming into being and validity, existence, scope and effects of reservations, interpretation or extinction, are **of key relevance also for domestic attorneys and operators**. Suffice to recall international agreements on trade, investment, taxation, copyright, judicial cooperation and, of course, human rights. Indeed, sight should not be lost of the fact that the domestic laws implementing international agreements will be interpreted and applied at the domestic level – including by domestic courts and tribunals – according to the assessment of the above issues under the international law on the law of treaties.

Under the international constitutional customary law principle *pacta sunt servanda*, international agreements produce international rights and obligations for the legal subjects that are parties to them. The principle in point is articulated through a complex set of rules making up the international body of **treaty law** codified in the VCLT. The latter governs *inter alia* the conclusion, validity, or nullity, duration, scope of application and interpretation of international **written agreements**, which form the largest majority of international agreements. [12]

Terminology and form in this area are flexible. An **international agreement** may be labelled as, or take the form of, a **convention**, **treaty**, **protocol**, **statute**, **charter**, **exchange of notes**, or otherwise. The terminological designation of an agreement, or whether it consists of a single document or more documents, does not bear normative consequences. The VCLT defines a treaty as an international agreement, but does not define what an international agreement is. Basically, an international agreement can be said to consist of the **expression of consent** by two or more international legal subjects – basically, states and intergovernmental organisations – over the regulation of the subject-matter which constitutes the substantive scope of the agreement in question. [13]

In the not-too-distant past, international case-law followed a 'liberal approach' to the definition of an instrument, or combination of diplomatic exchanges, that make up an international agreement, irrespective of its form and label. One may refer to the *Qatar v Bah-*

---

[12] Article 3(a) of the VCLT specifies that: 'The fact that the present Convention does not apply to international agreements concluded between States and other subjects of international law or between such other subjects of international law, or to international agreements not in written form, shall not affect the legal force of such agreements.' Although very rare, treaties may also be concluded orally or tacitly, that is through the interaction of their behaviours clearly signalling their common will to regulate a given matter in a given way, for instance in the field of delimitation agreements.

[13] Although the VCLT only applies to treaties concluded between states, Article 3(c) specifies that Article 3(a) of the VCLT specifies that: 'The fact that the present Convention does not apply to international agreements concluded between States and other subjects of international law or between such other subjects of international law, or to international agreements not in written form, shall not affect the application of the Convention to the relations of States as between themselves under international agreements to which other subjects of international law are also parties.'

rain 1994 ICJ judgment.[14] Contrary to Bahrein's objection to the Court's jurisdiction based on the argument that the signatories of the minutes of a meeting never intended to conclude an international agreement, but only a political understanding, the ICJ found that:

> '[T]he Minutes are not a simple record of a meeting (…) [t]hey enumerate[d] the commitments to which the Parties have consented (…) thus create[ing] rights and obligations in international law for the Parties.'[15]

Interestingly, the Court did not draw any inference to the contrary from the fact that the agreement in question had not been submitted to parliamentary ratification, as required under the constitutional law of the disputing countries.

In the 2018 judgment in the case between Bolivia and Chile on the *Obligation to Negotiate Access to the Pacific Ocean*, the ICJ applied the same reasoning and the same test quoted above in order to assess the existence, or not, of a binding agreement invoked by Bolivia according to which Chile was under the obligation to enter into negotiations over Bolivia's access to the Pacific Ocean.[16] Under the circumstances of the case, the Court found in the negative.[17] Having regard to one of the disputed documents, the Court observed that:

> '[It] does not enumerate any commitments and does not even summarize points of agreement and disagreement. Moreover, the penultimate clause of these minutes records that the Foreign Minister of Bolivia stated that "the present declarations do not contain provi-

---

[14] *Maritime Delimitation and Territorial Questions between Qatar and Bahrein* (Qatar v Bahrain) (Preliminary Objections) (Judgment) [1994] ICJ Rep 112.

[15] *Ibidem*, 121.

[16] *Obligation to Negotiate Access to the Pacific Ocean* (Bolivia v Chile) (Judgment) [2018] ICJ Rep 507.

[17] *Ibidem*, 543.

sions that create rights, or obligations for the States whose representatives make them". The Chilean Minister Plenipotentiary did not contest this point. Thus, even if a statement concerning an obligation to resort to negotiations had been made by Chile, this would not have been part of an agreement between the Parties.' [18]

Referring to another document claimed by Bolivia to make up the alleged international agreement in question, the ICJ further found that:

> '[It] could be considered a politically significant step. However, it was not addressed to Bolivia and did not contain any wording that could show the acceptance on the part of Chile of an obligation to negotiate or the confirmation of a previously existing obligation to do so.' [19]

The Court's statement prompts consideration of the controversial distinction between **international agreements** and **unilateral declarations** as sources of international rights and obligations, and the role of the good faith principle in the sources discourse. [20] While the ICJ requires good faith promises to be met with acceptance, or consent, by their addressees for such promises to create rights and obligations between the actors involved in an international agreement context, unilateral promises containing engagements with regard to future conduct by the state making the promise have been considered by the same ICJ as a source of obligations for the state making unilateral statements publicly announcing unilateral commitments.

---

[18] *Ibidem.*

[19] *Ibidem.*

[20] See the seminal R Kolb, *Good Faith in International Law* (Hart Publishing 2017), 41ff. On unilateral declarations see the ILC work, 'Guiding Principles Applicable to Unilateral Declarations of States Capable of Creating Legal Obligations' (2006) II(2) Yearbook of the International Law Commission 159.

Obviously, the **good faith principle**, in combination with the principle of estoppel, or *forclusion*, based on the legitimate expectation of consistency with one's public statement, may provide for the unilateral creation of obligations for oneself – for some kind of interest – but not for others, at will.

In the *Nuclear Tests* cases, between Australia and New Zealand, respectively, against France, the ICJ discontinued the proceedings considering the case moot – *i.e.*, considering the dispute terminated – based on the public announcement of the then President of France before the press that France would hold no further nuclear tests in the South Pacific.[21] Basically, the ICJ found that, in so doing, France had undertaken the obligation to that effect and that, therefore, the applicants' claim no longer had any object. The Court stated as follows:

> 'It is well recognized that declarations made by way of unilateral acts, concerning legal or factual situations, may have the effect of creating legal obligations. [A]n undertaking of this kind, if given publicly, and with an intent to be bound, even though not made within the context of international negotiation, is binding.'[22]

The consensual factor of international agreements brings us to the limitation of their **subjective scope**. Namely, an international agreement is binding, as such, only on its parties, under the so-called principle *pacta tertiis neque nocent neque iuvant.* This principle is codified under Article 34 of the VCLT, which provides that '[a] treaty does not create either obligations or rights for a third State without its consent.'[23] Such consent is to be expressed in the form

[21] *Nuclear Tests* (Australia v France) (Preliminary Objections) (Judgment) [1974] ICJ Rep 253 and *Nuclear Tests* (New Zealand v France) (Preliminary Objections) (Judgment) [1974] ICJ Rep 457.

[22] *Australia v France* (n 21) 267, *New Zealand v France* (n 21) 472.

[23] See also Article 26 of the VCLT: 'Every treaty in force is binding upon the parties to it (…).'

of acceptance in the unlikely case in which a provision of a treaty purports to establish obligations for states which are not parties to the treaty in point (Article 35 of the VCLT). Conversely, the consent is considered as presumed when a treaty purports to afford rights to third states (Article 36 of the VCLT). Obviously, under the principle of good faith, such rights may be exercised in compliance with the conditions provided for in the treaty in question.

This rule whereby a treaty is binding on its parties only will be further qualified in connection with the situation in which a specific provision in a treaty coincides with the content of an international custom which, by definition, is general in its scope of application. We shall revert to this point below when addressing precisely the relationship between treaties and customs in Section 6.

Until the beginning of the 20th century, custom was the prevailing source of international law. In fact, until then, international law was made up of few customary rules, generally based on the principle of freedom and competition. Treaty law was a secondary source of international law, mainly consisting of **bilateral treaties**, which would usually supplement customary law by confirming, specifying, or adding to, customary rights and obligations on a **reciprocal** basis.

A significant degree of decline of customary law has occurred together with the waning of the social homogeneity in the international society around the time the First World War was over. The latter accelerated the gradual downfall of the Great European Powers of the 19th century, marked the birth of the Soviet Union in 1917, paved the way to populist dictatorial Governments in Europe and, eventually, to the Second World War, which definitely introduced deep ideological and political divisions in the international society. Namely, the East-West confrontation between Socialist countries and liberal democracies characterising the Cold War, on the one hand, and the North-South violent decolonisation process, on the other. This latter was followed by the strong tensions in the post-decolonisation period, through the 1970s and the 1980s, between newly formed developing countries and industrialised ones, with special regard to the rules governing economic relations.

Such divisions and erosion of liberal common values customarily protected throughout centuries on the interstate level initially caused an unquestionable decline of custom and a tentative replacement of this source with treaty law, especially with a view to renegotiating old customs by taking into account new values and interests from Soviet and decolonised developing countries.

After the Second World War, the net of bilateral agreements protecting individual state interests on a reciprocity basis began to be complemented by new kinds of **multilateral treaties** which addressed newly perceived global or regional societal interests, despite the mentioned divisions. First of all, one should mention the **constituent treaties** of intergovernmental organisations at the global or regional level, such as those establishing the very UN, or the WB, IMF, ICAO, WTO, Mercosur, OAS, OAU, and EU. The mentioned East-West and North-South divides prompted a series of thorough diplomatic exercises of renegotiation of the key bodies of international law which led to the adoption of major **codification conventions**. Apart from VCLT itself, complemented by the 1986 *Vienna Convention on the Law of Treaties between States and International Organizations or between International Organizations*, one could recall the already mentioned 1961 *Vienna Convention on Diplomatic Relations* and 1963 *Vienna Convention on Consular Relations*, and also, among others, the four 1949 *Geneva Conventions and Their Additional Protocols* (also known as the 'Laws of Warfare'), the 1982 UNCLOS, the 1997 *Convention on the Law of Non-Navigational Uses of International Watercourses* and the 2004 *Convention on Jurisdictional Immunities of States and their Property*.

One also may add consideration of those multilateral conventions giving special protection to **collective interests**. This is particularly the case with **human right treaties**, the two 1966 *International Covenants on Human Rights*, respectively, *on Civil and Political Rights* and on *Economic, Social and Cultural Rights*, or the multiple MEAs, such as the 2015 *Paris Agreement*, supplementary to the 1992 *United Nations Framework Convention on Climate Change*. Having special regard to human rights treaties, reference has already been made above to the *erga omnes partes* nature of their obligations in relation to the legal structure of the rights and obligations that may be vindicated by individuals, respectively, in Chapter 1, Sections 2 and 5, and Chapter 2, Section 4.1. Further illustration of such treaties and their functioning will be provided in Chapter 7, Section 4.

MEAs often contain rules which provide for a two-tier kind of obligations. Namely, obligations that operate at the traditional bilateral level with regard to transboundary issues, on the one hand, and obligations that protect indivisible collective interests, on the other. This is particularly, but not exclusively, the case with regard to the protection of areas beyond national jurisdictions. One may take fisheries protection agreements – such as the 1995 *Fish Stock Agreement* – as an example.

On the basis of an assessment of the sustainable amount of total yearly fishing in order to preserve fish stocks in a given maritime area concerning the states parties, such agreements provide mechanisms that set quotas on a periodical basis. Each state party is under the obligation not to issue licences that would lead to fishing beyond the fixed threshold. To that end, states have to adopt the necessary controls over fishing methods by vessels under their jurisdiction, as well as over the documentation from fish processing factories concerning the provenance of the incoming fish. Infringements by one state of its quota would alter the capacity to avoid the depletion of fishing stock in the maritime area, affecting the right of all the states parties to the agreement. In that sense, the obligation breached is one of an ***erga omnes partes* character**, namely, one owed to all the states parties to the agreement. Further illustration of such MEAs and their functioning will be provided below in Chapter 7, Section 5.

The extraordinary increase of multilateral treaty practice has not supplanted bilateral treaties in contemporary international affairs.

Suffice to recall the diffused bilateral treaty practice, *inter alia*, in the fields of investment promotion and protection (BITs), the avoidance of double taxation, extradition or other forms of judicial cooperation. Bilateral treaty-making may take place even in areas covered by the scope of application of multilateral treaties, as the latter may even require their parties to subsequently enter into further bilateral treaties in order to implement, on the bilateral level, the general standards agreed upon in the multilateral context. This is particularly the case with regard to certain MEAs which are characterised by a so-called 'framework' nature, precisely because they lay down a general legal framework which requires further specification on the bilateral or a restricted multilateral level, according to the circumstances. Article 9 of the 1992 *UNECE Convention* is illustrative of the point at issue:

> '1) The Riparian Parties shall on the basis of equality and reciprocity enter into bilateral or multilateral agreements or other arrangements, where these do not yet exist, or adapt existing ones, where necessary to eliminate the contradictions with the basic principles of this Convention, in order to define their mutual relations and conduct regarding the prevention, control and reduction of transboundary impact. The Riparian Parties shall specify the catchment area, or part(s) thereof, subject to cooperation. These agreements or arrangements shall embrace relevant issues covered by this Convention, as well as any other issues on which the Riparian Parties may deem it necessary to cooperate.
> 2) The agreements or arrangements mentioned in paragraph 1 of this article shall provide for the establishment of joint bodies (…).'

3.1. *Treaty law*

3.1.1. *Negotiations, adoption, manifestation of consent and entry into force*

Treaties are written agreements and are governed by the VCLT, which is now unanimously regarded in international state practice and case-law to reflect the international customary law in this field.

Treaties are the end-product of **negotiations** conducted by governmental delegations. The latter are usually composed of state officials from the Ministries which are competent in the subject-matter of the negotiations in question, such as environment, health, military or judicial cooperation. Officials from the Ministry for Foreign Affairs often, but not necessary always, head state delegations with a view to coordinating members of theirs from other Ministries. Scientific or legal experts and advisors may also become members of governmental delegations.

Multilateral negotiations are obviously more complex than those aimed at the conclusion of a bilateral treaty. They may take place between relatively few states and in an *ad hoc* – regional or sub-regional – context or in the wider format of a diplomatic conference under the auspices of a global international organisation. Their secretariats are in charge of the organisation of the workings, while the elected officials – *i.e.* the bureau, composed of the president, one or more vice-presidents – conduct the negotiation, starting from the proposal for adoption of the agenda and the rules.

The **final stage of the negotiations** of multilateral agreements may be particularly complex. Article 9(1) of the VCLT requires in principle the unanimity of the negotiating states for **the adoption** of the text. Here, the envisaged situation is one in which the negotiating states are in a relatively little number and in an *ad hoc* negotiating context. Article 9(2) refers to the adoption of the text of a treaty in the context of an **international conference**, requiring the vote of the two thirds of the negotiating states. But it also provides that, by the same two third majority, the negotiating states may decide the adoption by a different rule. Nowadays, in international conferences the practice goes in the direction of deciding the adoption by the so-called ***consensus***. In diplomatic jargon, this expression refers to the rule whereby the president of the conference proposes the adoption without a vote, *i.e.* without objections. If only one delegation asks for the vote, then the two third majority vote rule applies.

The attention to rules governing the process of **conclusion of the negotiations** of multilateral agreements should not lead one to conflate them with those governing the means and conditions for the negotiated text to become legally binding, and for whom. In fact, a treaty is a treaty as a source of international rights and obligations only upon its **entry into force** and only for the states for which it has entered into force and until it remains in force for them. Before it has entered into force, a treaty may be a persuasive or even authoritative instrument, like General Assembly resolutions, based on the support received by state representatives during the negotiations, possibly in combination with other elements of practice in the same direction. As already anticipated, the **adoption** of the text of a multilateral treaty should not be conflated with its **entry into force**. For the consent to the adoption, or authentication, of the negotiated text only purports to **close the negotiations** so that the text may no longer be changed, and such final version be submitted to the competent authorities for consideration as to whether to consent to be bound by it.

As a matter of principle, a treaty enters into force for the states that have expressed their **consent** to be bound by it. The VCLT leaves states free to choose by agreement the means by which they express their consent to be bound by a treaty. Article 11 enunciates that:

> 'The consent of a State to be bound by a treaty may be expressed by signature, exchange of instruments constituting a treaty, ratification, acceptance, approval or accession, or by any other means *if so agreed* [italics added].'

Each such means of expressing consent to be bound by a treaty – from signature to approval or accession – is in turn illustrated, from Articles 12 to 15 of the VCLT, only by indicating that each particular formula constitutes a **valid means** to express consent to be bound by a treaty *if the parties have so agreed.*

One would wonder which would be the residually prescribed form under the VCLT when no agreement in the matter can be inferred from the negotiated text or otherwise. The VCLT offers none. The fact that VCLT has taken a **descriptive approach** to the point in hand, rather than a prescriptive one, was certainly not a negligent oversight by the negotiators in Vienna. On the contrary, it was the purported result of a carefully crafted compromise. The then newly formed States which had emerged from decolonisation resisted the idea of an international law prescription on the subject fearing that it could provide legal ground to so-called 'unequal treaties,' *i.e.*, treaties imposed over weak countries by powerful ones having more leverage over negotiations. The corollary argument was that the former countries would be weary, as a matter of principle, of an international rule impinging upon the domestic constitutional regulatory freedom over the way in which a state would freely express its consent to be bound by an international treaty.

The above explains the **non-prescriptive** nature of the VCLT provisions (Articles 11-15) to the effect that it allows for the total freedom of States to regulate the forms of expression of their own consent to be bound by an international agreement by means of their own choice, usually by constitutional law.

This negotiating victory for developing countries was compensated by the fairly stringent rules on the possibility to invoke the invalidity, termination and suspension of the operation of a treaty, in Part V of the VCLT, which will be addressed below.

Apart from the rationale of the negotiating history, precisely based on the diffused constitutional practice of states, **ratification** upon parliamentary authorisation is by far the preferred means for states to express their consent to become parties to treaties. That reflects the generally felt constitutional need for **parliamentary control** over the foreign policy conducted by the Government.

Bilateral treaties usually **enter into force** when both negotiating states have expressed their consent, while normally multilateral treaties provide for a minimum number of states consenting to it, as alluded, usually by ratification. In principle, a multilateral treaty would enter into force for the first two states having expressed their consent to be bound by the treaty. However, the decision to subject the entry into force of the would-be treaty precisely to a **minimum**

number of expressions of consent to it corresponds to the purpose pursued by the negotiating states of producing a homogeneous body of law governing a certain area for a sufficiently wide group of states in a sub-regional, regional or global context.

By way of example, Article 84(1) of the VCLT provides that '[t]he present Convention shall enter into force on the thirtieth day following the date of deposit of the **thirty-fifth** instrument of ratification or accession.' The VCLT was adopted in 1969 and entered into force in 1980, and has now 116 states parties. However, most of the states which have not ratified it regularly invoke most of its provisions in diplomatic exchanges or in international litigation as **reflecting customary law**, their recalcitrance to ratify being explained by their opposition to certain specific provisions in the Convention.

Prior to its entry into force, a treaty may bear a special legal relevance for the signatory states, even where the expression of consent to be bound by the treaty in question is subject to ratification. Under the **principle of good faith**, as codified by Article 18(a) of the VCLT,[24] those states are precluded from adopting conduct in contrast with the object and purpose of the treaty, until they declare that they do not intend to ratify the treaty. The signing of a treaty by a state is taken to amount to **an indication of intent** by the signatory state to engage in the necessary internal constitutional procedures aimed at expressing its consent to become a party. And this would generate the **legitimate expectation** that the state in question would not act contrary to the object and purpose of the treaty in question, at least until it renders manifest that the domestic procedure of ratification will not be completed. That usually occurs for political reasons linked to a change of Government.

---

[24] Which states that: 'A State is obliged to refrain from acts which would defeat the object and purpose of a treaty when it has signed the treaty or has exchanged instruments constituting the treaty subject to ratification, acceptance or approval, until it shall have made its intention clear not to become a party to the treaty.'

One may recall that, whilst one of the last acts of the Clinton Presidency was the signing of the *Rome Statute* establishing the ICC, the following Bush Jr Administration started in 2001 a systematic diplomatic policy aimed at concluding bilateral treaties which, *inter alia*, would provide for the commitment by partner countries not to ratify the *Rome Statute* and, in any case, never to surrender US nationals to the ICC. Soon after the beginning of this policy, in line with Article 18(a) VCLT, the US Government, officially announced the intention not ratify the *Rome Statute*.[25] Russia, which had signed the *Rome Statute* in 2000, did the same in 2016.[26]

3.1.2. *Invalidity, termination and suspension of treaties*

As anticipated above, the loose descriptive character of the VCLT approach to the means for states to express their consent to be bound by a treaty – in compliance with their freedom to determine the matter by the constitutional means of their own choice – has been compensated by a restrictive approach to the **causes of invalidity**. The manifest violation of the internal constitutional rules on the conclusion of treaties by a contracting state represents, indeed, one of the **causes of invalidity** of a treaty – together with **error** (Article 48 of the VCLT), **fraud** (Article 49 of the VCLT), **corruption** of a state representative (Article 50 of the VCLT), or **coercion** against a state representative (Article 51 of the VCLT), or of a state itself (Article 52 of the VCLT).[27] As already alluded, the area of

[25] 'U.S. Announces Intent Not To Ratify International Criminal Court Treaty' in *ASIL Insights* (11 May 2002).

[26] 'Russia Withdraws Signature From International Criminal Court Statute' in *The Guardian* (16 November 2016).

[27] Article 52 establishes that 'A treaty is void if its conclusion has been procured by the threat or use of force in violation of the principles of international law embodied in the Charter of the United Nations.' The applicability of this ground of invalidity has proved to be particularly problematic in relation to peace treaties bringing an end to armed conflict and settling related issues such as the delimitation of borders and payment of damages. In this case, the agree-

treaty law governing the causes of invalidity, termination or suspension of the operation of treaties under Part V of the VCLT takes a restrictive approach with a view to enhancing the **stability of treaties** and the predictability of the legal relations falling within the scope of application of such treaties.

Article 46 of the VCLT entitled to the provisions of internal law regarding competence to conclude treaties provides as follows:

> '1) A State may not invoke the fact that its consent to be bound by a treaty has been expressed in violation of a provision of its internal law regarding competence to conclude treaties as invalidating its consent unless that violation was manifest and concerned a rule of its internal law of fundamental importance.
> 2) A violation is manifest if it would be objectively evident to any State conducting itself in the matter in accordance with normal practice and in good faith.'

The negative drafting formulation of this key provision would in principle suggest that only exceptionally could the cause of invalidity in question be successfully invoked by a contracting state. In this respect this provision reflects the *pacta sunt servanda* good faith principle codified in more general terms in Article 27 of the VCLT according to which 'a party may not invoke the provisions of its internal law as justification for its failure to perform a treaty.'

However, this general provision makes express 'without prejudice' reference to Article 46, under which a manifest violation of a domestic rule of 'fundamental importance' regarding the conclusion of treaties may be invoked as a ground invalidating a treaty so concluded. And it is a matter of fact that internal rules on treaty-making are laid down in the **Constitution**, which almost by defini-

---

ment is usually considered valid, but it is clear that, at least when the losing party is forced to accept an unfavourable solution, its conclusion will appear to be at odds with Article 52. On this point, see S Forlati, 'Coercion as a Ground Affecting the Validity of Peace Treaties' in E Cannizzaro (ed), *The Law of Treaties Beyond the Vienna Convention* (OUP 2011), 320ff.

tion renders them 'of fundamental importance' and their violation objectively manifest. This might appear to introduce an element of uncertainty, as states having concluded a treaty in contrast with their constitutional rules on treaty-making could at will one day – when required to comply with the treaty – decide to invoke its invalidity. In order to avoid abuses of this provision and retain its restrictive rationale, its contextual interpretation in the light of the overall VCLT and the principle of good faith, requires, firstly, that the state's manifestation of consent was *actually* in violation of its constitutional order.

For instance, in the *Case concerning the delimitation of maritime boundary*, Guinea-Bissau disputed the validity of a 1960 agreement delimiting its maritime boundary with Senegal concluded by the then colonial powers – respectively, Portugal and France.[28] Its argument went that said agreement was null and void because it had been concluded by Portugal in violation of Article 91(1) of its own 1933 Constitution, which provided that all treaties entailing a change to the national borders had to be ratified with parliamentary authorisation.[29] However, in 1960 the Portuguese Constitution, although formally in force, had long since been suspended by dictator Oliveira de Salazar. In this regard, the arbitral tribunal established by the parties to settle the dispute noted that:

> 'Pour examiner si un traité a été conclu conformément au droit interne d'un État, il faut tenir compte du droit en vigueur dans le pays, c'est-à-dire du droit tel qu'il est réellement interprété et appliqué par les organes de l'État, y compris par ses organes judiciaires et administratifs,'[30]

concluding that Portuguese institutional and constitutional practice

---

[28] *Case concerning the delimitation of maritime boundary between Guinea-Bissau and Senegal* (Award) [1989] UNRIAA vol XX 119.

[29] *Ibidem*, 139.

[30] *Ibidem*, 141.

'at that time' had been respected and that 'le Gouvernement français a eu des raisons de croire, en toute bonne foi, que le traité signé était valable.' [31]

Secondly, it is worth stressing that a good-faith-oriented application of Article 46 entails that a state should invoke the cause of invalidity as soon as possible after becoming aware of its occurrence. In fact, for the avoidance of doubt, this aspect of **good faith** – which permeates the whole body of treaty law and gives effect to the general principle *pacta sunt servanda* – has been codified in Article 45 of the VCLT concerning the invocation of any cause of invalidity, termination or suspension of the operation of a treaty, as follows:

> 'A State may no longer invoke a ground for invalidating, terminating, withdrawing from or suspending the operation of a treaty (…) if, after becoming aware of the facts:
> *a*) it shall have expressly agreed that the treaty is valid or remains in force or continues in operation, as the case may be; or
> *b*) it must by reason of its conduct be considered as having acquiesced in the validity of the treaty or in its maintenance in force or in operation, as the case may be.'

A cause of invalidity of great significance, which was introduced by the VCLT – one which was innovative at the time of its adoption in 1969, insofar as it introduced a new category of international rule for the protection of collective interests – is that of a treaty which is, or becomes, in conflict with a **peremptory rule** – so-called of ***jus cogens*** – protecting the international community as a whole. Article 53 provides that:

> 'A treaty is void if, at the time of its conclusion, it conflicts with a peremptory norm of general international law. For the purposes of the present Convention, a peremptory norm of general international

[31] *Ibidem*, 142.

> law is a norm accepted and recognized by the international community of States as a whole as a norm from which no derogation is permitted and which can be modified only by a subsequent norm of general international law having the same character.'

The circular drafting of this provision provides no concrete guidance as to the identification of the substantive international rules having peremptory character. The international case-law and practice following the adoption of the VCLT indicate that examples of *jus cogens* rules can be found in the ban on genocide, on aggression, slavery or on torture.[32] At first, an agreement of this kind may seem difficult to imagine; however, one could think of a treaty providing for an offensive alliance, or one on judicial cooperation with a country whose new Government practices systematic torture on suspected dissidents.

Article 66 of the VCLT tries to adjust the international law of adjudicative dispute settlement, traditionally based on consensual jurisdiction, with the introduction of an element of **compulsory jurisdiction** precisely with regard to disputes over claims of invalidity of a treaty due to an alleged contrast with a peremptory rule of international law, as follows:

> '[A]ny one of the parties to a dispute concerning the application or the interpretation of article 53 or 64 may, by a written application, submit it to the International Court of Justice for a decision unless the parties by common consent agree to submit the dispute to arbitration.'

The apparent limitation that emerges from this provision lies in the fact that the claimant in such a case can only be 'one of the parties,'

[32] On *jus cogens* see, among others, A Orakhelashvili, *Peremptory Norms of International Law* (OUP 2006), E Cannizzaro (ed), *The Present and Future of Jus Cogens* (Sapienza Università Editrice 2015), D Shelton, *Jus Cogens* (OUP 2021) and D Tladi (ed), *Peremptory Norms of General International Law (Jus Cogens)* (Brill 2022).

and not – as would be more logical from a systemic perspective – any state member of the international community, as a whole, in the pursuit of a superior and indivisible community interest. It is difficult to imagine a state which, one day, concludes such a treaty and, the other day, files a claim before the ICJ to have it invalidated. Since such treaties represent a form of extreme foreign policy choices, a similar case could be brough after a radical change of Government. However, under such circumstances, the new Government could be well entitled to withdraw unilaterally from the treaty in question under Article 65 of the VCLT, that is precisely invoking the violation of *jus cogens* as a ground for impeaching the validity of the treaty. And it would seem little defensible for the other states parties to challenge such a unilateral withdrawal, further to exposing the issue internationally.

As to the **duration of treaties**, they may be subject to grounds for termination (or suspension) that are *internal* or *external* to them. By internal grounds of termination, one refers to the situation when the very text of the treaty indicates the lapse of time during which it will remain in force, and the means by which a party may unilaterally invoke the expiry date within the prescribed frame of time preceding such date. That is to say that treaties often provide for unilateral termination by denunciation or withdrawal, setting a period of notice for the communication of the intention to denounce or withdraw from the treaty (usually twelve months), a prominent example being Article 50 of the TEU.

Obviously, the contracting states may at any time decide the termination of a treaty by mutual agreement, even implicitly (Article 54 of the VCLT). Both cases are not problematic, apart from when the terminating agreement is of a tacit character deriving from a successive treaty which does not explicitly indicate the intention of the parties to derogate from the earlier treaty, in part or in its entirety, also conflating with the case of the tacit conclusion of subsequent agreement amending (but not terminating) a former one under Article 39 of the VCLT.

Treaty provisions setting means and dates for termination by denunciation or withdrawal commonly also stipulate a period of time during which the treaty **continues to remain in force** after having been terminated by denunciation or withdrawal. Such provisions are called ***sunset clauses***. For instance, they are frequently provided in BITs, so as to afford predictability of international legal protection to those that have invested in a foreign country relying on a BIT. Such clauses usually afford **a ten-year extension after termination**, during which the investors from the two states parties remain entitled to rely on the protections found in the treaty. Such protections include the right to sue the foreign country hosting the investment before an investment arbitration tribunal. For example, even if Indonesia has unilaterally terminated its BIT with the Netherlands as of 1 July 2015, Dutch investors in Indonesia, and *vice-versa*, will continue to benefit from the protections of the BIT for the following fifteen years based on the sunset clause to that effect.

On the multilateral level, a recent illustrative example is given by the *Comprehensive Economic and Trade Agreement* (CETA) adopted in 2014 by the EU and Canada after six years of painstaking negotiations. The CETA is currently applied on a provisional basis with ratification process still ongoing at the EU Member states level, whilst Canada has completed its ratification process. Article 30(9) reads as follows:

> '1) A Party may denounce this Agreement by giving written notice of termination to the General Secretariat of the Council of the European Union and the Department of Foreign Affairs, Trade and Development of Canada, or their respective successors. This Agreement shall be terminated 180 days after the date of that notice. The Party giving a notice of termination shall also provide the CETA Joint Committee with a copy of the notice.
> 2) Notwithstanding paragraph 1, in the event that this Agreement is terminated, the provisions of Chapter Eight (Investment) shall continue to be effective for a period of 20 years after the date of termination of this Agreement in respect of investments made before that date.'

Among the external grounds for termination (or suspension) of a treaty, one is to recall the **material breach of the treaty** by one of its parties, which would ground some form of reciprocal conduct by the other states parties. Such reactions to a breach of treaty may be complemented by other forms of response based on the law of state responsibility regarding the consequences of an internationally wrongful act, such as countermeasures and claims of reparation. In this regard, Article 60 of the VCLT reads as follows:

> '1) A material breach of a bilateral treaty by one of the parties entitles the other to invoke the breach as a ground for terminating the treaty or suspending its operation in whole or in part.
> 2) A material breach of a multilateral treaty by one of the parties entitles:
> *a*) the other parties by unanimous agreement to suspend the operation of the treaty in whole or in part or to terminate it either: *i*) in the relations between themselves and the defaulting State; or *ii*) as between all the parties;
> *b*) a party specially affected by the breach to invoke it as a ground for suspending the operation of the treaty in whole or in part in the relations between itself and the defaulting State;
> *c*) any party other than the defaulting State to invoke the breach as a ground for suspending the operation of the treaty in whole or in part with respect to itself if the treaty is of such a character that a material breach of its provisions by one party radically changes the position of every party with respect to the further performance of its obligations under the treaty.
> 3) A material breach of a treaty, for the purposes of this article, consists in:
> *a*) a repudiation of the treaty not sanctioned by the present Convention; or
> *b*) the violation of a provision essential to the accomplishment of the object or purpose of the treaty.
> 4) The foregoing paragraphs are without prejudice to any provision in the treaty applicable in the event of a breach.
> 5) Paragraphs 1 to 3 do not apply to provisions relating to the protection of the human person contained in treaties of a humanitarian

> character, in particular to provisions prohibiting any form of reprisals against persons protected by such treaties.'

There is a cause for treaty termination which goes to the heart of the international constitutional principle of treaty law – *pacta sunt servanda rebus sic stantibus*. Namely, a **fundamental change of circumstances** with respect to those existing at the time the agreement was concluded. During the negotiations in Vienna, the line promoted by the Western delegations eventually prevailed which safeguards the principle of stability of treaties. While those delegations originally even resisted the idea of providing for such a cause of termination, altogether, the final wording of the provision in point, that is Article 62 of the VCLT, proves restrictive enough to contain, if not avoid, its abuses. It reads as follows:

> '1) A fundamental change of circumstances which has occurred with regard to those existing at the time of the conclusion of a treaty, and which was not foreseen by the parties, may not be invoked as a ground for terminating or withdrawing from the treaty unless:
> *a*) the existence of those circumstances constituted an essential basis of the consent of the parties to be bound by the treaty; and
> *b*) the effect of the change is radically to transform the extent of obligations still to be performed under the treaty.
> 2) A fundamental change of circumstances may not be invoked as a ground for terminating or withdrawing from a treaty:
> *a*) if the treaty establishes a boundary; or
> *b*) if the fundamental change is the result of a breach by the party invoking it either of an obligation under the treaty or of any other international obligation owed to any other party to the treaty.
> 3) If, under the foregoing paragraphs, a party may invoke a fundamental change of circumstances as a ground for terminating or withdrawing from a treaty it may also invoke the change as a ground for suspending the operation of the treaty.'

In sum, there are four basic conditions to be *cumulatively* met for the cause of termination in point to be validly invoked to justify a diplomatic action of unilateral termination of a treaty. Firstly, the change is to be assessed with respect to the circumstances existing at the time of the conclusion of the treaty. The change in question must be of a fundamental character. Secondly, objective political changes may be relevant, but the principle of good faith prevents governmental changes or mere policy changes in a given state to be validly invoked by that state as a fundamental change. This condition conforms to the general principle of good faith, whereby a ground for termination may not be validly invoked if it is the result of conduct by the state invoking it. Thirdly, the change should have not been foreseeable by the parties at the time when the treaty was concluded. Fourthly, the circumstances subject to the change invoked must have constituted an essential basis of the consent of the parties to be bound by the treaty.

The restrictive rationale of the provision in point has been well emphasized by the ICJ in the 1997 *Gabčíkovo-Nagymaros Project* judgment, between Hungary and Slovakia, as follows:

> 'The negative and conditional wording of Article 62 of the Vienna Convention on the Law of Treaties is a clear indication (…) that the stability of treaty relations requires that the plea of fundamental change of circumstances be applied only in exceptional cases.' [33]

Another ground for termination of a treaty restrictively codified by the VCLT (Article 61) consists of the **supervening impossibility of performance**. It may be validly invoked on the basis of objective grounds, such as 'the permanent disappearance or destruction of an object indispensable for the execution of the treaty,' for example, a river or a lake. On the basis of the general principle of good faith, this ground may not be validly invoked if the circumstances in question are the result of conduct by the state invoking it. If the im-

[33] *Gabčíkovo-Nagymaros Project* (Hungary/Slovakia) (Judgment) [1997] ICJ Rep 7, 65.

possibility is temporary, such situation will operate only as a ground of suspension of the operation of the treaty.

3.1.3. *Reservations and treaty interpretation*

The consent to be bound by an agreement may be affected by **reservations** when a state wishes to become a party to a treaty except for certain provisions, or except for a certain interpretation of them, or of the whole treaty. According to Article 2(1)(d) of the VCLT, a reservation is a 'unilateral statement (...) made by a State when signing, ratifying, accepting approving or acceding to a treaty, whereby it purports to exclude or to modify the legal effect of certain provisions of the treaty in their application to that State.'

Issues about reservations may apply only to multilateral treaties. Formulating a reservation when expressing consent to a bilateral treaty amounts to a rejection of the negotiated text and a proposal to reopen the negotiations.

In the absence of express provision on the admissibility of reservations, a reservation is not admissible when in contrast with the object and purpose of the treaty in question. Absent a centralised body deciding, once and for all, on the admissibility of a given reservation, it falls to each state party to the treaty to assess the admissibility of a reservation and whether, on the basis of its assessment, to consider the reserving state as a party to the treaty in relation to itself.

Under the VCLT (Articles 19-23), depending on the reaction of the states parties to a reservation, the latter may produce different effects giving rise to a web of **different legal relations** stemming from the same treaty. Obviously, the treaty applies in its entirety between the reserving states and the other states that have accepted the reservation. The treaty will apply, except for the provisions to which the reservation relates, between the reserving state and the states which have objected to the reservation, but not to the entry into force of the treaty between them and the reserving state. The treaty will not enter into force between the reserving state and the states objecting to the reservation as incompatible with the object and purpose of the treaty.

The problem of the lack of a centralized system of assessment on the admissibility of a given reservation is especially problematic in relation to human rights treaties where the negotiating states have avoided to expressly rule on the admissibility of reservations with a view to encouraging as many ratifications, or accessions, as possible. It was in this context, in the 1951 advisory opinion on *Reservations to the Convention on the Prevention and Punishment of the Crime of Genocide*, that the ICJ addressed the problem of the admissibility of reservations, as follows:

> '[A] State which has made (…) a reservation which has been objected to by one or more of the parties to the Convention but not by others, can be regarded as a party to the Convention if the reservation is compatible with the object and purpose of the Convention.' [34]

The negotiating states of human rights treaties have generally been prepared to pay the price of such relativity and inhomogeneity in the subjective scope of application of the provisions of the treaty in order to promote the number of ratifications.

Since treaties, like statutes, often represent a compromise resulting from difficult negotiations, their text is seldom clear enough not to require **interpretation**. Treaty interpretation is governed by customary treaty law as evidenced in Articles 31-33 of the VCLT, as recognised by international case-law and even by states that are not parties to VCLT. The commanding interpretive criteria are listed under Article 31 and follow a combination of the *literal* or *textual* approach (which comes first and follows the ordinary every day meaning of the language in question), the *intentions of the parties* approach and the *purposive* or *teleological* approach (which follows the object and purpose of the treaty leading to more liberal results than the literal interpretation).

---

[34] *Reservations to the Convention on the Prevention and Punishment of the Crime of Genocide* (Advisory Opinion) [1951] ICJ Rep 15, 29.

The balance between the three criteria in hand is to be found in the contextual approach, whereby a treaty provision is also to be interpreted in the light of the treaty as a whole – including its preamble and annexes. In wider terms, the interpretive context also comprises subsequent agreements between the parties and subsequent practice relevant to the interpretation and application of the treaty in question, as well as any other relevant rule binding on the parties, either of a treaty or customary source.

The *travaux préparatoires*, *i.e.* the negotiating history of a treaty, are referred to under Article 32 of the VCLT as a 'supplementary means' of interpretation, despite in international case-law and practice they are regularly relied upon in order to corroborate the proposed interpretation. In fact, their supplementary character lies precisely in the fact that reference to the *travaux* may be relied upon, either when the textual, contextual and teleological means of interpretation lead to ambiguous results, or simply in order to buttress and further articulate an interpretation based on the textual, contextual and teleological means of interpretation, rather than to depart from it.

In sum, as observed by the ICJ in its 1991 judgment on the *Arbitral Award of 31 July 1989*, stemming from the previously mentioned award *Concerning the delimitation of maritime boundary* between Guinea-Bissau and Senegal:

> '[T]he first duty of a tribunal which is called upon to interpret and apply the provisions of a treaty, is to endeavour to give effect to them in their natural and ordinary meaning in the context in which they occur. If the relevant words in their natural and ordinary meaning make sense in their context, that is an end of the matter. If, on the other hand, their natural and ordinary meaning are ambiguous or lead to an unreasonable result, then and then only, must the Court, by resort to other methods of interpretation (including the investigation of the *travaux préparatoires*) seek to ascertain what the parties really did mean when they used these words.' [35]

---

[35] *Arbitral Award of 31 July 1989* (Guinea-Bissau v Senegal) (Judgment) [1991] ICJ Rep 53, 69.

Finally, it is worth remembering that, based on the relevance of international law at the municipal law level, issues of treaty interpretation, or the assessment as to whether a treaty is validly in force, concern **domestic civil servants**, lawyers of municipal law and judges as much as international law ones.[36]

4. International custom

International custom has been the primary source of modern international law for nearly three centuries since its inception in the 17th century, coinciding with the birth of nation-states. They were the so-called Great Powers, mostly European nations-states, which accounts for the consideration that international customary rules proceed from the habitual conduct of states in their relations. Such habits acquired an increasing degree of legality evolving into authoritative sources of law through the equally increasing expectations by states that such habitual conduct, perceived to be *natural*, would be reciprocally continued, respected, and eventually complied with. This accounts for the two constituent elements of custom: *a*) widespread **practice** consistently repeated over time (in Latin ***diuturnitas***) and *b*) the consciousness by state organs that such practice conforms to a legally binding rule or to what ought to be a legal rule (***opinio juris sive necessitatis***).

It is on the basis of consistent expectations of reciprocity that sovereign states have, for example, started respecting the immunity of foreign state representatives, treating aliens according to certain minimum standards and to mutually respect freedom of navigation and trade.

Such a natural law approach to international law-making was the

[36] On this latter issue see HP Aust, A Rodiles and P Staubach, 'Unity or Uniformity? Domestic Courts and Treaty Interpretation' (2014) 27 Leiden Journal of International Law 75.

preferred one, so long as the international community of states was characterised by a high degree of social and cultural homogeneity among their élites, or ruling class. The Great Powers of Europe for centuries spoke the same language, being inspired mostly by the same principles revolving around free political, economic and military competition within and outside Europe. Largely complemented and supplemented by the written source of treaty law, customary international law is still invoked nowadays to ground claims and to decide disputes.

A distinguishing feature of customary law – as a remnant of the natural law approach from which it stemmed – consists of its general scope of application with respect to its subjects, as opposed to treaty law. This accounts for the fact that in international law the expression '**general law**' is synonymous with customary law.[37]

State practice, as a constituent and evidentiary element of customary law, may consist of diplomatic practice (both bilateral and multilateral, such as public statements by state officials, notes verbales of protest, or the voting attitude of states concerning certain UN General Assembly resolutions) as well as legislative, administrative and judicial practice. It may also consist of operational conduct, such as conduct taken by the police, custom officers, or the coast guard. The conclusion of international agreements on certain matters (the so-called conventional practice) may, in suitable circumstances, provide significant elements of practice for the purposes of the identification of custom. Consistent conventional practice on certain matters, on the part of a significant number of states, may suggest their recognition and consolidation of customary law on such matters. Generally, the more uniformly widespread the practice of states on a certain matter, the shorter the duration required.

Even if each of the two constituent elements of custom is to be ascertained separately, as stressed by the ILC in its ongoing work

---

[37] See R Higgins, *Problems and Process: International Law and How We Use It* (Clarendon Press 1994), 26.

on the identification of customary international law,[38] the ***opinio juris*** of a state may be derived from much the same pieces of state practice just referred to. For instance, the parliamentary debates over the adoption of a given statute, or even its text, may indicate that it has been adopted to conform to, or to promote, a certain international custom. The same applies to a domestic judicial or administrative decision, or a ministerial circular note.

International judicial decisions, international agreements, resolutions of intergovernmental organisations and academic writings may provide authoritative elements for the identification of the existence and the contents of customs, with different degrees of authority. As already alluded, acts of international organisations stem from the multilateral diplomatic practice of Member states. Therefore, they may be taken as a form of expression of collective *opinio juris*, whose authoritative value may change, on a case-by-case basis, according to the voting record and the kind of language adopted in the international act in question.

One may also notice that, with some exceptions – state practice consisting of operational conduct, inaction, or silence, as indicative of acceptance, hence, of *opinio juris*, in relation to other states' conduct – most elements of *opinio juris* and other evidentiary materials, like international judicial decisions, are of a written character. This does not contradict the unwritten nature of customary law, in so far as no individual written piece of practice or *opinio juris* stands, on its own, as evidence of a certain custom and its contents.

4.1. *The role of precedents*

Special consideration should also be given to the role of **international case-law** in the international customary-making process, par-

---

[38] ILC, 'Draft Conclusion on Identification of Customary International Law, with Commentaries' (2018) II(2) Yearbook of the International Law Commission 122, 124.

ticularly in view of the fact that international judicial decisions, first, do not seem to emanate from the attitude of states and, second, are legally binding for the disputing parties only.[39] This means that the *stare decisis* principle, or rule of precedent, does not apply in international law. However, as a matter of fact, as the ILC Special Rapporteur on identification of customary law, Sir Michael Wood, singled out with regard to the attitude of the ICJ, '[the Court] seems very reluctant to depart from its previous Decisions.'[40] Indeed, starting from *Cameroon v Nigeria*, the ICJ has repeatedly noted that:

> 'It is true that, in accordance with Article 59, the Court's judgments bind only the parties to and in respect of a particular case. There can be no question of holding Nigeria to decisions reached by the Court in previous cases. The real question is whether, in this case, there is cause not to follow the reasoning and conclusions of earlier cases.'[41]

As put it by Dame Rosalyn Higgins when President of the ICJ:

> 'States which have no dispute before the Court follow the judgments of the Court with the greatest interest, because they know that every judgment is at once an authoritative pronouncement on the law, and also that, should they become involved in a dispute in which the same legal issues arise, the Court, which will always seek to act consistently and build on its own jurisprudence, will reach the same conclusions.'[42]

---

[39] With respect to the ICJ, see Article 94(1) of the *UN Charter* and 59 of the *ICJ Statute*.

[40] ILC, 'Third Report on Identification of Customary International Law by Michael Wood, Special Rapporteur' UN Doc A/CN.4/682 (27 March 2015), 121.

[41] *Land and Maritime Boundary between Cameroon and Nigeria* (Cameroon v Nigeria) (Preliminary Objections) (Judgment) [1998] ICJ Rep 275, 292.

[42] Higgins (n 37) 202-203.

Eventually, in its commentary to Draft-Conclusion 13 on identification of customary international law, the ILC observed as follows:

> 'Decisions of courts and tribunals on questions of international law, in particular those decisions in which the existence of rules of customary international law is considered and such rules are identified and applied, may offer valuable guidance for determining the existence or otherwise of rules of customary international law. The value of such decisions varies greatly, however, depending both on the quality of the reasoning (…) and on the reception of the decision, in particular by States and in subsequent case-law. Other considerations might, depending on the circumstances, include the nature of the court or tribunal; the size of the majority by which the decision was adopted; and the rules and the procedures applied by the court or tribunal. It needs to be borne in mind, moreover, that judicial pronouncements on customary international law do not freeze the law; rules of customary international law may have evolved since the date of a particular decision.' [43]

Interestingly, having regard to the development of customary international criminal law, the point just made with regard to the ICJ is corroborated in relation to the ICC by Article 21(2) of the *Rome Statute*, which provides that '[t]he Court may apply principles and rules of law as interpreted in its previous decisions.'

5. General principles of law

General principles of law are the third source of international law under Article 38(1)(c). [44] In the words of Sir Hersch Lauterpacht, they are:

---

[43] ILC (n 41) 149.

[44] Among the vast bibliography on the subject of general principles of international law, see B Cheng, *General Principles of Law as Applied by Inter-*

> '[T]hose principles of law, private and public, which contemplation of the legal experience of civilized nations leads one to regard as obvious maxims of jurisprudence of a general and fundamental character (…) a comparison, generalization and synthesis of rules of law in its various branches – private and public, constitutional, administrative, and procedural – common to various systems of national law.' [45]

From the summary records of the *travaux* that produced Article 38(c) of the *PCIJ Statute*, adopted in 1920, and then reproduced unchanged under Article 38(1)(c) of the *ICJ Statute*, it appears that one of the reasons for singling out 'general principles of law recognized by civilized nations' as a separate source of the law was the need to address the concern that the Court could find itself in the position of not being able to settle a dispute due the lack of any pertinent rule discernible from any applicable international treaty or custom. In legal language, this situation is defined after the Latin expression ***non liquet***. [46]

As stressed by the mixed Italian-Venezuelan arbitral commission in the old landmark *Gentini* case, where Italy acted in diplomatic protection for the imprisonment and mistreatment of an Italian businessman, whilst 'rules' are aimed to prescribe specific conducts,

---

national Courts and Tribunals (re-edited, CUP 2006), M Andenas, M Fitzmaurice, A Tanzi and J Wouters (eds), *General Principles and the Coherence of International Law* (Brill 2019), and A Gattini, A Tanzi and F Fontanelli (eds), *General Principles of Law and International Investment Arbitration* (Brill-Nijhoff 2018).

[45] Quoted in E Lauterpacht (ed), *International Law Being the Collected Papers of Hersch Lauterpacht* (vol I, CUP 1970), 74.

[46] On the issue of *non liquet* see A Tanzi, 'On Judicial Autonomy and the Autonomy of the Parties in International Adjudication, with Special Regard to Investment Arbitration and ICSID Annulment Proceedings' (2020) 33 Leiden Journal of International Law 57, 62-63. For a minority view on the possibility of *non liquet* see N Lanzoni, 'Il *non-liquet* e i limiti della funzione giudiziaria nell'ordinamento internazionale' (2018) 73 La Comunità internazionale 619.

principles are of a more general nature and provide the direction for state conduct.[47] Absent specific rules expressly regulating a given conduct, when such conduct runs contrary to the direction set by a general principle, the conduct in question can well be said to be unlawful. It is in that sense that general principles fulfil a **gap-filling** (almost law-making) **function** in the legal system.

This role of general principles of law as a supplemental source to conventional or customary sources of law, and potentially as a means through which new specific rules may develop, is widely used in international case-law.

By way of example, one can take the role of good faith with regard to the conduct of negotiations, which is not regulated, despite negotiation being the primary means of peaceful settlement of disputes under Article 33(1) of the *UN Charter*. In the *Lac Lanoux Affaire* arbitration between France and Spain over the use of the lake and the allocation of its waters, the tribunal, lacking explicit procedural provisions regulating the positive conduct due in negotiations, resorted to the general principle of good faith. It did so in order to determine by implication the kind of state conduct which would amount to a breach of the general obligation to negotiate – which, obviously, does not involve the obligation to reach an agreement – as follows:

> '[U]njustified breaking off of conversations, unusual delays, disregard of established procedures, systematic refusal to give consideration to proposals or adverse interests, and more generally (…) the case of infringement of the rules of good faith.'[48]

In its 1969 judgment on the delimitation of the *North Sea Continental Shelf* between Denmark and the Netherlands, on the one hand,

---

[47] *Gentini case (of a general nature)* (Award) [1903] UNRIAA vol X 551, 556.

[48] *Affaire de Lac Lanoux (Espagne, France)* (Award) [1957] UNRIAA vol XII 281, 306-307 (our translation).

and Germany, on the other, the ICJ has followed the same line of reasoning in order to assess that the parties to the dispute:

> 'Are under an obligation so to conduct themselves that the negotiations are meaningful, which will not be the case when either of them insists upon its own position without contemplating any modification of it.' [49]

The same applies to the 1974 judgment over disputed fisheries between the UK and Iceland in which the ICJ required the disputing parties 'to conduct their negotiations on the basis that each must in good faith pay reasonable regard to the legal rights of the other.' [50]

Reference has been made in legal literature to the **'interpretative' and the 'corrective' functions** of general principles. As to the former function, reference is obviously made to Article 31 of the VCLT according to which a treaty should be interpreted in good faith. As to the so-called 'corrective' function of general principles, it has been observed that:

> 'Some principles of general international law are or ought to be so compelling that they might be recognized by the international community for the purpose of invalidating or forcing revision in ordinary norms of treaty or custom in conflict with them.' [51]

It is apparent that in this case general principles coincide with the basic structural principles making up the constitutional basis of international law, such as the principles of sovereign equality, or *pacta sunt servanda*. One could add substantive core rules and princi-

---

[49] *North Sea Continental Shelf* (Federal Republic of Germany/Denmark) (Federal Republic of Germany/Netherlands) (Judgment) [1969] ICJ Rep 3, 47.

[50] *Fisheries Jurisdiction* (United Kingdom of Great Britain and Northern Ireland v Iceland) (Judgment) [1974] ICJ Rep 3, 33.

[51] GA Christenson, 'Jus Cogens: Guarding Interests Fundamental to International Society' (1988) 28 Virginia Journal of International Law 585, 586.

ples of *jus cogens*, such as the ban on the use of force, the principle of self-determination, the prohibition of torture and slavery,[52] and, as the ICJ put it in its *Corfu Channel* judgment in order to *legally* support the existence of an international obligation to notify the existence of minefields in territorial waters to foreign warships and ships in general not only in periods of war, but also in peacetime, all 'elementary considerations of humanity.'[53]

Against the above background, resorting to 'general principles of law recognized by civilized nations' would be tantamount to looking into municipal legal systems for a source of law that could not otherwise be found in international law. For example, in the *Barcelona Traction* case in which Spain was sued by Belgium acting in diplomatic protection for Belgian shareholders of a Canadian registered company which was hit by the Spanish nationalisation of the electricity sector, the ICJ stated that:

> 'In [the field of corporate law,] international law is called upon to recognize institutions of municipal law that have an important and extensive role in the international field. This does not necessarily imply drawing any analogy between its own institutions and those of municipal law, nor does it amount to making rules of international law dependent upon categories of municipal law. All it means is that (...) whenever legal issues arise concerning the rights of States with regard to the treatment of companies and shareholders, as to which rights international law has not established its own rules, it has to refer to the relevant rules of municipal law.'[54]

Not all **municipal general principles of law** necessarily apply in international law just because they are generally recognised in do-

---

[52] See Chapter 1, Section 5; above, Sections 3.1.2; and Chapter 5, Section 2.1.2.

[53] *Corfu Channel Case* (United Kingdom of Great Britain and Northern Ireland v Albania) (Judgment) [1949] ICJ Rep 3, 22.

[54] *Barcelona Traction, Light and Power Company, Limited* (Belgium v Spain) (New Application: 1962) (Judgment) [1970] ICJ Rep 3, 33.

mestic legal systems; only those **suitable for application to inter-state relations** and disputes apply in international law. Furthermore, once extensively and consistently applied at the international level, 'general principles of law recognized by civilized nations' inevitably transmigrate into international law under the label '**general principles of international law**.'[55]

At that point, the expression 'general principles of international law' would therefore not be indicative of the municipal provenance of the principles in question, but of their **content**: namely, such expression would indicate a set of international customary rules having a content widely shared among states and, as such, one that would be instrumental in forging the systemic consistency of the international legal order. In that sense, like in any legal system, those are the building blocks and pillars of the **rule of law** in international law.

To that end, such general principles (and rules) are both of a structural and a substantive legal character. They range from *pacta sunt servanda* to good faith – from its substantive and procedural law articulations, such as **unjust enrichment** or **estoppel** – to *res judicata*, or the principle that wrongful conduct is to be redressed and unlawful damage is to be compensated. Given their general and unwritten character, over the years those principles have inspired the transcription in writing of their articulations and specifications. Having regard to *pacta sunt servanda*, one may refer to most provisions of the VCLT, with special regard to those concerning the grounds for invalidity, termination and suspension.[56]

Rather than academic speculation, reference to general principles of international law is increasingly to be found in the international practice and case-law. The fact remains that, in their unwritten form, the general principles of international law would still largely per-

---

[55] On the relationship between national and international general principles see H Lauterpacht, *Private Law Sources and Analogies of International Law: With Special Reference to International Arbitration* (re-edited, The Lawbook Exchange 2012).

[56] See also Section 4.

form their gap-filling function with regard to the gaps left by the more specific treaty or customary rules. After all, as already noted, that was their main function as envisaged under Article 38 of the Statutes of the PCIJ and ICJ.

The topic of the general principles of law is currently underway by the ILC, which is expected to produce useful results about their identification and function.[57]

6. Relationship between the sources of international law

International legal rules stemming from different sources may supplement or complement each other. Other times, new international rules are brought about with a view to develop new law. As already anticipated, international law, lacking statutory legislation or the *res judicata* principle of the kind existing in domestic jurisdictions, also lacks a hierarchy between sources, with the exception of the peremptory rules or so-called *jus cogens*. That is to say that, in principle, an international treaty may derogate, only as between its parties, from an international customary rule, as much as a new custom may derogate from a previous treaty.

Against the above background, determining the scope of application in time and with regard to their addressees of international rules on the same subject-matter stemming from different sources, with special regard to which rules have priority, becomes particularly critical.[58]

---

[57] The last report by the ILC on 'General Principles of Law' is 'Report of the International Law Commission in Its Seventy-second Session' (26 April – 4 June and 5 July – 6 August 2021) GAOR 66th Session, Supplement No 10 (A/76/10), 150ff.

[58] See, in general, Report of the Study Group of the ILC, finalized by Mr Martti Koskenniemi, 'Fragmentation of International Law: Difficulties Arising from the Diversification and Expansion of International Law,' UN Doc A/CN.4/L.682 and Add.1 (13 April 2006).

6.1. *Relationship of compatibility*

In the 2006 concluding report on its study of the issue of the *Fragmentation of International Law*, the ILC asserted that:

> 'It is a generally accepted principle that when several norms bear on a single issue they should, to the extent possible, be interpreted so as to give rise to a single set of compatible obligations.' [59]

The possibility of such **compatibility** is to be tested looking at the contents of the rules in question on a case-by-case basis. When the test is positive 'one norm assists in the interpretation of another (...) for example as an application, clarification, updating, or modification of the latter. In such a situation, both norms are applied in conjunction.' [60] This conforms with the contextual approach to treaty interpretation considered above. [61]

There is a special kind of relationship of compatibility between international rules that deserves to be emphasised. That is the relationship between **codification conventions** and **customary law**. We are concerned primarily with codification conventions (purported to be the case), such as those prepared by the ILC, but also to treaties in general (according to their specific features on a case-by-case basis) with special regard to those of a multilateral character that address an entire body of law, such as the already mentioned *Geneva Conventions and Their Additional Protocols* and UNCLOS.

The point has been addressed most clearly by the ICJ in the also

---

[59] ILC, 'Conclusions of the Work of the Study Group on the Fragmentation of International Law: Difficulties Arising from the Diversification and Expansion of International Law' (2006) II(2) Yearbook of the International Law Commission 177, 178.

[60] *Ibidem*.

[61] See Section 3.1.3.

already mentioned *North Sea Continental Shelf* case. [62] The dispute, as the name suggests, was about the delimitation of the continental shelf between Germany, on the one hand, and Denmark and the Netherlands, on the other and, consequently, over the allocation of the respective economic rights of exploitation deriving from it.

The legal arguments involved revolved around the applicability to Germany of the equidistance principle of delimitation spelt out under Article 6 of the 1958 *Geneva Convention on the Continental Shelf*, despite Germany having not been a party thereto. The respondents contended that the rule in question was nonetheless applicable to Germany, since it coincided with a custom having the same contents. [63] The ICJ rejected this contention under the circumstances of the case and applied the principle that a treaty applies to its parties only. However, it upheld the legal reasoning which formed the basis of the defendants' argument and elaborated upon it.

In particular, the ICJ envisaged three circumstances in which a treaty rule may be binding even on a **non-state party**, insofar as it reflects an international custom: *a*) when the rule in question was, at the time of the adoption of the treaty from which it stemmed, **declaratory** of a pre-existent international custom; *b*) when the rule in question, through the process of its elaboration and adoption of the treaty in point, catalysed the **crystallisation** of a custom whose process of formation had reached an advanced stage prior to the negotiation of the treaty in point; and *c*) when the rule in question, since the adoption, or even entry into force, of the treaty to which it belongs, has promoted sufficiently extensive practice and *opinio juris* conforming to it so as to **generate** a new custom. [64]

---

[62] *North Sea Continental Shelf* (n 49).

[63] *Ibidem*, 20ff.

[64] *Ibidem*, 39.

6.2. *Relationship of conflict*

According to the ILC report on *Fragmentation of International Law* referred to above, 'where two norms that are both valid and applicable point to incompatible decisions (...) a choice must be made between them.' [65]

In municipal legal systems, similar conflicts are easily settled through some form of hierarchy of sources usually provided for by the Constitution. When conflict occurs between rules stemming from sources of the same level, the *lex specialis derogat generali* (**special law supersedes general law**) and *lex posterior derogat priori* (**later law supersedes earlier law**) principles govern the matter usually looking at the intention of the legislator, while 'hard cases' tend to be settled by the supreme, or constitutional, court of that country.

As repeatedly anticipated, conflict between rules is a more complex issue to settle when it comes to international law, where **treaties may derogate from customs and *vice-versa***, save for the limited core of peremptory norms (*jus cogens*) from which derogation is not permitted.

Second, the ***lex specialis* and *lex posterior* principles** also operate in international law, but there is no supreme court applying them in a way that is binding on all international legal subjects. The application of the relevant principles is relatively easy with regard to rules having the same number of recipients. However, one is to note that regarding conflicts between treaties, the VCLT appears to give priority to *lex posterior*, [66] while the ICJ (and other international court and tribunals') case-law tends to favour *lex specialis*. [67]

---

[65] ILC (n 59) 178.

[66] Article 30(3) establishes that: 'When all the parties to the earlier treaty are parties also to the later treaty but the earlier treaty is not terminated or suspended in operation under article 59, the earlier treaty applies only to the extent that its provisions are compatible with those of the later treaty.'

[67] See, for instance, *Legality of the Threat or Use of Nuclear Weapons* (Advisory Opinion) [1996] ICJ Rep 226, 240.

In this regard, it should be noted that, first, the *lex specials* principles may work as a rule of conflict when matters of a highly specialised branch (such as international investment law or international humanitarian law) are at play against the backdrop of 'general international law.' However, when two rules of a *generalis* or, as it is often the case, *specialis* nature are in conflict, objectively assessing which one should prevail over the other becomes problematic. Secondly, both the *lex posterior* and *specialis* principles do not entail that the conflicting rule is automatically or can be declared invalid or 'ineffective.' Therefore, the existence of two conflicting treaties with the same parties does not mean that the first should be considered invalid. Rather, it only means that the parties should not invoke the need to comply with the first treaty to justify the non-fulfilment of the second. In line with the 'horizontal' nature of the international legal system, it is therefore a matter of international responsibility, more than of hierarchy of sources. [68]

The matter is even more complex when the recipients of the rules stemming from the two different sources in conflict with each other are **not identical**. This occurs when a treaty falling short of general participation departs from general custom, or when the conflict is between different treaties on the same subject, but **without the same participants in each**. Under such circumstances, a state that is a party to both treaties is to choose between performance or breach, of either treaty *vis-à-vis* the parties to the earlier treaty that are not parties to the later one, or *vice-versa*.

Often, multilateral treaties contain **compatibility clauses** with the effect of providing for the **subordination**, or **priority**, of the provisions of the treaty in question with respect to pre-existing, or future agreements. An example of a subordination clause is to be found in Article 351 of the TFEU, which reads in part as follows:

---

[68] See also J Klabbers, 'Beyond the Vienna Convention: Conflicting Treaty Provisions' in E Cannizzaro (ed), *The Law of Treaties Beyond the Vienna Convention* (OUP 2011), 192ff.

> 'The rights and obligations arising from agreements concluded before 1 January 1958 or, for acceding States, before the date of their accession, between one or more Member States on the one hand, and one or more third countries on the other, shall not be affected by the provisions of the Treaties.
> To the extent that such agreements are not compatible with the Treaties, the Member State or States concerned shall take all appropriate steps to eliminate the incompatibilities established. Member States shall, where necessary, assist each other to this end and shall, where appropriate, adopt a common attitude.'

The most prominent example of a priority clause is Article 103 of the *UN Charter*:

> 'In the event of a conflict between the obligations of the Members of the United Nations under the present Charter and their obligations under any other international agreement, their obligations under the present Charter shall prevail.'

The near-universal participation in the *UN Charter* and the prominence generally accorded thereto have triggered much debate in the international scholarship as to whether Article 103, along *jus cogens* rules, should not merely be intended as a priority clause, but as the provision elevating the *UN Charter* into a full-fledged Constitution of the international community.[69]

[69] See K Zemanek, 'The Metamorphosis of Jus Cogens: From an Institution of Treaty Law to the Bedrock of the International Legal Order?' in E Cannizzaro (ed), *The Law of Treaties Beyond the Vienna Convention* (OUP 2011), 398ff and J Vidmar, 'Norm Conflict and Hierarchy in International Law: Towards a Vertical International Legal System?' in E de Wet and J Vidmar (eds), *Hierarchy in International Law: The Place of Human Rights* (OUP 2012), 18ff.

7. So-called 'soft-law instruments'

In the debate about the sources of international law, reference is often made to so-called '**soft-law**.' This expression looks like a contradiction in terms, as the binary proposition that law *is* law or *is not* law applies. There is no denying that, when looking for elements which form evidence of the sources of law on a given subject, one can resort to more or less authoritative or persuasive instruments to that effect. The latter instruments can be constituted by codes of conduct adopted by intergovernmental bodies or non-governmental bodies, such as the ILA, reports and draft-articles by the ILC, General Assembly resolutions, final declarations of international diplomatic conferences, or adopted multilateral treaties prior to their entry into force. However, the end result of a process of ascertainment of the law worthy of any argumentative **legal relevance** will be to the effect of either the existence or non-existence of a given rule.

Accordingly, whilst one can refer to so-called 'soft-law' instruments and to their legal relevance, it would indeed be contradictory to speak of 'soft-law' *per se*. This is not contradicted by the category of international rules producing **due diligence obligations**. Such provisions – usually to be found in environmental agreements, or in human rights conventions concerning economic, social or cultural rights – are drafted in terms whereby the parties are to 'take all appropriate measures' aimed to pursue a given result. [70] Those are fully fledged legal obligations that, as such, are to be complied with or may be infringed upon. To enhance their clarity, such obligations are usually supplemented by standards, criteria and parameters, or reporting obligations aimed to evidence compliance.

In summary, the fact that the obligation of harm prevention is

---

[70] See, in general, R Pisillo Mazzeschi, *Due diligence e responsabilità internazionale degli Stati* (Giuffrè 1989), J Kulesza, *Due Diligence in International Law* (Brill 2015) and A Ollino, *Due Diligence Obligations in International Law* (OUP 2022).

couched in due diligence terms, as opposed to an absolute obligation, is intended to avoid the finding of automatic international responsibility for the occurrence of transboundary harm resulting from activities under a state's jurisdiction, despite all best efforts having been made to prevent such occurrence.

The same applies to the field of human rights with respect to those provisions that allow for their progressive realisation. The 1966 *Covenant on Economic, Social and Cultural Rights* is exemplary of such rules. Under its Article 2(1), each state party is 'to take steps to the maximum of its available resource with a view to achieving progressively the full realization of the rights recognized in the (...) Covenant by all appropriate means.'

As authoritatively stated by the Committee of experts established by the same Covenant, despite the 'progressive' nature of the normative contents of its provisions, the latter 'imposes various obligations that are of immediate effect.' [71] Among those, the Committee singled out the undertaking in Article 2(1), 'to take steps' in order to stress that 'while the full realization of the relevant rights may be achieved progressively, steps towards that goal must be taken within a reasonably short time after the Covenant's entry into force.' [72] Most importantly, the Committee underlined that 'the fact that realization over time, or in other words progressively, is foreseen under the Covenant should not be misinterpreted as depriving the obligation of meaningful content.' [73]

Aversion to the idea of 'soft-law' as a category of law, does not mean rejecting the legal relevance of international instruments that, as such, fall short of constituting a source of law, but that, **cumulatively with other factors**, may produce customary law. For instance,

---

[71] See Committee on Economic, Social and Cultural Rights, 'General Comment No 3: the Nature of States Parties' Obligations (Art 2, Para 1, of the Covenant)' UN Doc E/1991/23 (14 December 1990), para 1.

[72] *Ibidem*, para 2.

[73] *Ibidem*, para 9.

General Assembly resolutions – as well as similar diplomatic instruments, such as the final declaration of a diplomatic conference on a specific matter – may be instrumental in the formation of a new custom as evidence of the *opinio juris* of the states voting in favour. [74] Such resolution would not be constitutive of any soft-law, but only evidence of customary law.

Until the full formation of a custom, in line with the contents of the instruments in question, said instruments would still provide the basis for the application of the principles of **good faith**, **reliance** and **estoppel**, in the sense that they could still be invoked against those states that, despite having participated in their adoption, have later adopted conduct contrary to them.

As put by the late American international lawyer Oscar Schachter:

> 'When States enter into a non-legal commitment, they generally assume a political (or moral) obligation to carry it out in good faith. Other States concerned have reason to expect such compliance and to rely on it. What we must deduce from this is that the non-binding declarations that express political or moral commitments are governed by the general principle of good faith. Inasmuch as good faith is an accepted general principle of international law, it is appropriate to apply it to such commitments. There is no reason for distinguishing the legal meaning of 'good faith' from a supposed political meaning of that concept. Whether called legal or political, its meaning is essentially the same. A significant legal consequence of the 'good faith' principle is that a party which committed itself in good faith to a course of conduct or to recognition of a legal situation would be stopped from acting inconsistently with its commitment or position.' [75]

---

[74] See also above, Section 4.

[75] O Schachter, 'Non-Conventional Concerted Acts' in M Bedjaoui (ed), *International Law: Achievements and Prospects* (Martinus Nijhoff Publishers 1991), 267.

Further reading

Akehurst M, 'Custom as a Source of International Law' (1976) 44 British Yearbook of International Law 1;

Baxter RR, 'Treaties and Custom' (1970) 129 Collected Courses of the Hague Academy of International Law 36;

Cannizzaro E (ed), *The Law of Treaties Beyond the Vienna Convention* (OUP 2011);

Chinkin CM, 'The Challenge of Soft Law: Development and Change in International Law' (1989) 38 International and Comparative Law Quarterly 850;

Fitzmaurice M, 'The Practical Working of the Law of Treaties' in M Evans (ed), *International Law* (5th edn, OUP 2018), 138ff;

Gaja G, 'General Principles of Law' in A Peters (ed) *Max Planck Encyclopaedia of Public International Law* (online edn, OUP 2013);

Kolb R, *Peremptory International Law: Jus Cogens* (Bloomsbury 2015);

Mendelson M, 'The Formation of Customary International Law' (1998) 272 Collected Courses of the Hague Academy of International Law 197;

Pellet A and Müller D, 'Article 38' in A Zimmermann et al (eds), *The Statute of the International Court of Justice: A Commentary* (3rd edn, OUP 2019), 819ff;

Tanzi A, *Introduzione al diritto internazionale contemporaneo* (7th edn, CEDAM 2022);

Titi C, *The Function of Equity in International Law* (OUP 2021);

Thirlway H, *The Sources of International Law* (OUP 2014).

Chapter 4

International law and domestic jurisdictions

1. Background

We have seen how domestic jurisdictions can be instrumental in transforming the **general principles** existing in their legal systems into a source of international law. We have also seen how state conduct, including legislation, adjudication and enforcement, provides elements of state practice and *opinio juris* instrumental in the formation of international **custom**.

Also, international courts and tribunals can find themselves considering domestic statutes, administrative regulations or court decisions which are invoked, or complained of, by the parties before them. Suffice to think of domestic courts incurring denial of justice or entertaining jurisdiction over a foreign state or diplomat, of local entities adopting discriminatory measures against a foreign company, or of police carrying out torture or deprivation of liberty which amounts to arbitrary detention.

The relationship between international law and municipal law works both ways. Namely, it also needs to be considered with regard to the relevance, implementation or application of international law into domestic jurisdictions. As put it by the late Judge Crawford in the words recalled above in Chapter 2, '[m]any of the things international law tries to do have to be done at the national level.' [1]

As we have seen in Chapter 1, many, if not most, international rules have a bearing on the exercise of the internal sovereignty of states – from the treatment of foreigners, foreign goods, or foreign officials, to the control of activities carried out within their jurisdiction that may have a transboundary environmental impact. The fact

---

[1] J Crawford, 'Chance, Order, Change: The Course of International Law' (2013) 365 Collected Courses of the Hague Academy of International Law 13, 214.

that states implement international rules and obligations within their own legal orders (either by **recognising**, **incorporating or transforming such law**) is essential for the operation and effectiveness of international law.

The knowledge of how states recognise, incorporate or transform international rules and obligations within their own legal orders is key to those officials (*i.e.*, civil servants in the central or local public administration, police, custom officers and ultimately courts and tribunals) who are required to apply international rules and principles, either directly or indirectly through the domestic legislation transforming international law into domestic law.

The present Chapter, first, introduces very briefly the two principal competing approaches to the relationship between international law and domestic law, namely, **monism** and **dualism**. Second, Section 3 will briefly show the relevance of domestic law from the standpoint of international law and its adjudicative bodies. Sections 4, 5 and 6 will present the different domestic constitutional attitudes towards the implementation and application of international law based on the main division between **common law** and **civil law jurisdictions**. Irrespective of how international rules are 'received' into each given domestic jurisdiction, the **crux of the matter** will be shown to consist in the criteria that apply in any given jurisdiction in order to determine which rule has **priority in case of conflict** with earlier or later domestic legislation or a judicial decision intended to 'receive' international obligations. Section 7 is devoted to this matter. This Chapter is drawn to a close with reflections, in Section 8, on the recently increasing trends towards legal nationalism.

2. The monism v dualism controversy and balancing

The **monist approach**, propounded by the Austrian legal philosopher Hans Kelsen (1881-1973), and followed prominently, amongst others, by the British scholar and Judge at the ICJ, Sir Hersch Lauterpacht (1897-1960), views law as a unitary global phenomenon governed by international law envisaged as hierarchically superior to domestic legal systems. According to this approach, domestic jurisdictions would be grounded in international law, with special regard to the basic international rule regarding the sovereign equality of states. Consequently, conflict between a domestic rule and international law would result in the prevalence of international law. Cases in which this does not occur, would only represent instances of the shortcomings of international law. [2]

As a corollary of this unitary view, international rules would have direct effect in domestic jurisdictions as if the latter were mere components of the international legal system. That is to say that international rules would produce rights and obligations **directly** addressed to states and individuals alike. As Sir Hersch Lauterpacht once noted:

> 'It is true that international law is made for states, and not states for international law, but it is true only in the sense that the state is made of human beings and not human beings for the state.' [3]

On the other hand, according to the **dualist approach**, the relationship between international law and the municipal legal systems would be one of separation, each one governing respectively different legal relationships. Namely, international law would govern relationships between states – or between states and intergovernmental organisations – whilst municipal legal systems would regulate relations between individuals, or private companies, *inter se* (with

---

[2] See H Kelsen, *Principles of International Law* (re-edited, 2nd edn, The Lawbook Exchange 2003). This theory was first developed in the 1920s, see H Kelsen, *Il problema della sovranità e la teoria del diritto internazionale* (Giuffrè 1989) and H Kelsen, 'Les rapports de système entre le droit interne et le droit international public' (1926) 14 Collected Courses of the Hague Academy of International Law 227. As for H Lauterpacht, see *The Function of Law in the International Community* (re-printed, OUP 2011), esp 428ff.

[3] Lauterpacht (n 2) 439.

each other), or between them and the national public administration of the country where they reside.[4]

The dualist approach appears to reflect, in a more realistic manner, the present state of affairs in domestic and international practice. Nonetheless, from a descriptive perspective, one can see merit in both doctrines, insofar as each of them (prevailingly the dualist approach) reflects some aspects of the various national constitutional attitudes towards international law. That is to say that some jurisdictions appear partly less dualist, or a little more monist, than others. The fact remains that under international law each state enjoys its **sovereign freedom** to choose the means by which to incorporate, transform or recognise, international law.

In line with the dualist approach, each kind of legal order has, from its own perspective, **supremacy** over the other, with the qualifications that we will see below.

At the same time, there is a key fact that is all too often overlooked by domestic lawyers. Namely, that **international agreements and customs are the end-product of the combination of the exercise of states' external sovereignty with the distillation of the exercise of their domestic sovereignty in matters relevant to international law**.

In light of the above, the old-fashioned expression '**law of nations**' – a synonym with 'international law' – most aptly conveys the sense of collective ownership of international law by its very recipients, *i.e.*, states and intergovernmental organisations. This is a point that will be recurrently singled out in the present treatise as key to understand the basic sense of international law as it has been produced and conceived up to the present day.

---

[4] On the monism/dualism debate see further, among others, JG Starke, 'Monism and Dualism in the Theory of International Law' in SL Paulson (ed), *Normativity and Norms: Critical Perspectives on Kelsenian Themes* (OUP 1999), 537ff. and GRB Galindo, 'Revisiting Monism's Ethical Dimension' in J Crawford and S Nouwen (eds), *Select Proceedings of the European Society of International Law* (vol III, Hart Publishing 2012), 141ff.

3. Municipal law in international law and before international courts and tribunals

The most apparent manifestations of the international law process corroborate the view of the **separation** between international law and domestic jurisdictions. This separation provides the **premise for the customary law on *the responsibility of states for internationally wrongful acts***, which will be illustrated in Chapter 5. For the present purposes, suffice to recall that this body of international law has been codified by the ILC in a set of 'draft articles' which have been endorsed by the UN General Assembly in 2001 [5] and are widely referred to by international courts and tribunals as an authoritative restatement of custom.

Article 3 of the ASR, entitled to the characterization of an act of a state as internationally wrongful, is particularly relevant to our discussion on the relationship between international law and domestic jurisdiction. It reads as follows:

> 'The characterization of an act of a State as internationally wrongful is governed by international law. Such characterization is not affected by the characterization of the same act as lawful by internal law.'

This provision is paralleled by Article 27 of the VCLT which provides that '[a] party may not invoke the provisions of its internal law as justification for its failure to perform a treaty.'

In line with the above, international courts and tribunals, treating international law and municipal law as separate from one another, refer to domestic legislations, administrative measures and case-law, as **mere facts** and not as law. This is so precisely because international adjudicative bodies do not consider the municipal sources of law as part of the sources of international law. A

---

[5] UN General Assembly Res 56/83 of 28 January 2002.

parallel of this may be found in the way domestic courts and tribunals regard foreign statutes, administrative measures or judicial decisions. Domestic judges also usually consider foreign law as a fact and, as such, evidence about it is usually produced through expert witnesses and, in common law countries, also through the expertise of ***amici curiae***.

From the perspective of international law, **separation** does **not** mean **irrelevance**. As already alluded to, not only may a piece of domestic legislation or a judicial decision be a relevant element of state practice, or *opinio juris*, instrumental in the formation of an international custom (hence, relevant for the purpose of its identification), but they may also constitute an act of **compliance with**, or a **breach of**, **international law**.

Accordingly, Article 12 of the ASR, on the existence of a breach of an international obligation, provides that:

> 'There is a breach of an international obligation by a State when an act of that State is not in conformity with what is required of it by that obligation, regardless of its origin or character.'

As a consequence of the separation between international law and domestic law, domestic statutes, administrative measures or judicial decisions that are found by an international court or tribunal in breach of international law **cannot be repealed**, **quashed** or **declared invalid** by the international court or tribunal in question. The latter would rather enjoin the wrongdoing state to do so under its own legal system by means of its choosing.

The decisions of international courts and tribunals are legally binding pursuant to those agreements by means of which the disputing parties have conferred jurisdictional competence to such courts and tribunals with regard to the dispute in question. For instance, Article 94(1) of the *UN Charter* provides that '[e]ach Member of the United Nations undertakes to comply with the decision of the International Court of Justice in any case to which it is a party.' Accordingly, a state who does not comply with an international judgment or arbitration award would commit an internationally wrongful act additional to the one found to have been committed by the international adjudicative body.

3.1. *Jurisdictional immunities case between Germany and Italy*

All of the above notions have been recently considered in relation to the *Jurisdictional Immunities of the State* case **between Germany and Italy**, decided by the ICJ in 2012.[6] The case was about whether the exercise of jurisdiction by Italian national courts over civil claims filed against Germany demanding compensation for the crimes committed by Nazi officials during the Second World War was in breach of the international custom on the sovereign immunity of states.

The ICJ rejected the arguments advanced by Italy, which argued that the international custom in hand had not been breached as it had evolved over time to the extent of excluding states' immunity in relation to civil suits for compensation of damages caused by international crimes. Therefore, the Court concluded that:

> '1) [T]he Italian Republic has violated its obligation to respect the immunity which the Federal Republic of Germany enjoys under international law by allowing civil claims to be brought against it based on violations of international humanitarian law committed by the German Reich between 1943 and 1945; (...)
> 2) [t]he Italian Republic has violated its obligation to respect the immunity which the Federal Republic of Germany enjoys under international law by taking measures of constraint against Villa Vigoni; (...)
> 3) [t]he Italian Republic has violated its obligation to respect the immunity which the Federal Republic of Germany enjoys under international law by declaring enforceable in Italy decisions of Greek

[6] *Jurisdictional Immunities of the State* (Germany v Italy: Greece intervening) (Judgment) [2012] ICJ Rep 99.

> courts based on violations of international humanitarian law committed in Greece by the German Reich.' [7]

Accordingly, it enjoined Italy to act as follows:

> '[B]y enacting appropriate legislation, or by resorting to other methods of its choosing, ensure that the decisions of its courts and those of other judicial authorities infringing the immunity which the Federal Republic of Germany enjoys under international law cease to have effect.' [8]

In 2013, Italy passed a specific law with a view to complying with this ICJ judgment, which was of a **declaratory nature** whilst, at the same time, requiring the cessation of, and reparation for, the assessed breach of international law. [9]

However, the constitutional legitimacy of this law – along with the 1957 law ratifying the *UN Charter* and, therefore, 'receiving' in the Italian legal order the above-mentioned Article 94(1) on the compulsory compliance with ICJ decisions [10] – was challenged by a domestic judge before the Italian Constitutional Court which ultimately did find it to be unconstitutional due to the fact that it was in conflict with fundamental constitutional rights, such as the right of judicial defence. [11]

This judgment of the Italian Constitutional Court (No 238/2014) was clearly in contrast with the 2012 judgment of the ICJ and would provide the precondition for the Italian judiciary to (re-)entertain its jurisdiction, including of an **executive nature**, over Germany and its property in Italy. Were this to occur, it would amount, at the in-

---

[7] *Ibidem*, 154.

[8] *Ibidem*, 155.

[9] Law No 5 of 14 January 2013.

[10] Law No 848 of 17 August 1957.

[11] Italian Constitutional Court, Judgment No 238 of 22 October 2014. More specifically, with Articles 2 and 24 of the Italian Constitution.

ternational law level, to a breach of the international obligations stemming from international customary law on sovereign immunities and the 2012 ICJ judgement.

The Italian Constitutional Court judgment has indeed been followed by multiple judgments by Italian courts against Germany – in disregard of its sovereign immunity – awarding compensation to the victims or the victims' families for the crimes committed by the Third Reich. Most importantly, some of those judgments had given rise to the beginning of enforcement proceedings geared towards the seizure of German state-owned immovable property in Italy, such as the buildings hosting the German Archaeological Institute, the German Cultural Institute, the German Historical Institute and the German School in Rome.

These developments eventually led Germany to bring once more Italy before the ICJ, on 29 April 2022. Germany's application to the ICJ did not incur a violation of the *ne bis in idem* principle, for it argued that the Italian Constitutional Court's judgment No 238/2014 has been 'adopted in conscious violation of international law and of Italy's duty to comply with a judgment of the principal judicial organ of the United Nations' and that the practical consequence of this judgment was that Italy was infringing Germany's sovereign immunity 'in a widespread and systematic manner.' [12] Germany also claimed 'full reparation for any injury' deriving from the exercise by the Italian courts of their jurisdiction, even though none had been caused by the time of the filing of the application. [13]

Interestingly, Germany's application also contained an urgent request to the ICJ for provisional measures. [14] This procedural move reveals the trigger-event behind Germany's decision to bring again

[12] *Questions of Jurisdictional Immunities of the State and Measures of Constraint against State-owned Property* (Germany v Italy) [2022] (Application instituting proceedings and request for the indication of provisional measures of 29 April 2022), 4.

[13] *Ibidem*, 20.

[14] *Ibidem*, 23ff.

Italy before the ICJ. Namely, the fact that, 'in clear disregard of Germany's right to sovereign immunity,' [15] the Court of Appeal of Rome had authorised the sale of above-mentioned German immovable property at a public auction to be held on 25 May 2022. [16]

Remarkably, on 30 April 2022 Italy passed a Decree-Law (No 36/2022) that, for the relevant part, establishes a mechanism to which the victims of the crimes in question and their relatives can resort to for compensation, as a remedy alternative to judiciary proceedings. [17] This solution would combine abidance by the right to access to justice of the victims with respect for Germany's right to immunity from execution. The passing of this Decree-Law, which was later converted into law, [18] prompted Germany's withdrawal of its request for provisional measures before the ICJ. At the time the present text is going to press, Germany's application remains pending, possibly until the compensation mechanism is actually put in place and the pending cases against Germany before Italian courts are dropped or extinguished.

4. International law in municipal law and before domestic courts and tribunals

As already alluded, the age-old doctrinal controversy between monism and dualism can be settled by the observation that, as a matter of social fact, the absolute majority of national legal systems regard themselves and operate as **separate** from international law.

There is still some merit in the monist theory though, insofar as it conceptually helps to qualify the **degree of dualism** adopted in any given national jurisdiction. For instance, one can detect in cer-

---

[15] *Ibidem*, 23.

[16] Court of Appeal of Rome, Judgment No 5446 of 4 November 2020.

[17] Decree-Law No 36 of 30 April 2022, Article 43.

[18] Law No 79 of 29 June 2022.

tain jurisdictions aspects of monistic features, *e.g.*, with regard to the incorporation of international custom in common law systems, as we will see in the following Section. However, one is to note that, even in those national jurisdictions where the Constitution, originally inclined towards monism, provides that 'international law is part of the law of the land,' [19] its interpretation and application falls ultimately to the hands of their constitutional or supreme courts. [20] In recent times, more than ever before, the latter are inclined to rely primarily on their own domestic constitutional legal values over the international legal ones.

Indeed, the main issue concerning the matter in hand boils down to the question of **which rules prevail** in national jurisdictions in case of conflict between international customary or treaty rules and domestic statutes and judicial decisions.

National law on this point varies from state to state. The next Section will give a brief overview of the constitutional attitudes in different legal systems with respect to the matter in hand.

The domestic constitutional rules on the matter are often general and imprecise, hence, lending themselves to different constructions according to the circumstances of the case, or the of the **legal policy climate** at the time of their application. Giving prevalence to a domestic statute or judicial decision in conflict with an international rule – hence, infringing the latter and leading to the incurrence of international responsibility on the part of the state – may be the result of **inadvertence** or of a deliberate **political choice**, often, for instance, in cases of operational conduct decided by the Government. It may also be a matter of **legal culture**, particularly in cases of judicial decisions, given the diffused attitude of judiciaries to focus exclusively on their domestic legislation.

---

[19] See R O'Keefe, 'The Doctrine of Incorporation Revisited' (2008) 79 British Yearbook of International Law 7.

[20] See the interesting remarks in K Keith, ''International Law is Part of the Law of the Land': True or False?' (2013) 26 Leiden Journal of International Law 351.

That explains the importance of appropriate training in international law for civil servants, municipal law practitioners and judges. It often escapes domestic lawyers that international law does not stem from the will, or whims, of an international legislator which is by definition antagonistic to the domestic legal system, but that, on the contrary, it proceeds either from states' positive consent, or from their repeated conduct and views. Such states' consent, conduct and expression of views about the law represent the exercise of sovereignty. Therefore, domestic constitutional legislation and practice giving prevalence to international law – directly or as transformed into domestic law – would basically enhance the consistency of the domestic legal system, until and unless an overriding need for change would base a politically deliberate breach of international law geared towards its change.

5. The doctrine of *incorporation* of customs and *transformation* of treaties in common law jurisdictions

As repeatedly indicated and for the historical reasons that have been illustrated, until the beginning of the 20th century, custom has been the main source of international law.[21] Given its unwritten and natural law character, it was only consequential for the states that produced customary rules to consider them as 'part of the law of the land.' That is to say that international customs were incorporated into municipal law without the need for domestic law-making organs having to engage in any specific process of case-by-case statutory implementation. This reflected the (monistic) approach whereby international law and domestic law would be part and parcel of the same unitary legal order.

As to domestic law **adaptation to international customary law**,

---

[21] See Chapter 3, Section 4.

in line with the above, according to the **English common law**, an international custom would automatically apply as part of domestic law and should therefore be enforced as such. This practice – corresponding to the so-called **incorporation doctrine** – involves state officials, and ultimately domestic courts and tribunals, to engage in the difficult task of ascertaining the existence and contents of international customs.

As a corollary of the incorporation doctrine, any change in international customary law would automatically imply the same **change** in English law. In 1977, in *Trendtex v Central Bank of Nigeria,* Lord Denning, presiding over the Court of Appeal, referring to international customary law, held as follows:

> 'International law does change, and the courts have applied changes without the aid of any Act of parliament. Thus, when the rules of international law were changed (by the force of public opinion) so as to condemn slavery, the English courts were justified in applying the modern rules of international law.' [22]

The same applies under **Scots law**. Still in 1999, in two criminal cases (usually referred to as *John v Donnelly* and *Greenock*) in which the accused, charged with the sabotage of British nuclear weapons, invoked the illegality of holding such weapons under international customary law, the Court of Appeal maintained that 'a rule of customary international law is a rule of Scots law' without relying on any legislative, or constitutional transformation. [23]

Another corollary of the incorporation doctrine, whereby international (customary) law and domestic law are part of the same unitary legal order, is that international customs are **directly applicable** and **effective** at the national level. This means that an individual

---

[22] *Trendtex Trading Corporations Ltd v Central Bank of Nigeria* (1983) 64 ILR 111, 128.

[23] Quoted in SC Neff, 'International Law and Nuclear Weapons in Scottish Courts' (2002) 51 International and Comparative Law Quarterly 171, 172.

may invoke an international custom in his or her defence before a domestic court or tribunal.

In recent times, as a result of the increase of parliamentary legislation, the doctrine of automatic incorporation has been **sensibly tempered** in English and Scots law. Namely, international customary rules are automatically incorporated only insofar as they are not incompatible with domestic statutory legislation or a judicial precedent of final authority.

One is not to overlook the somewhat paradoxical fact that a given international custom, once directly incorporated into UK law by a judicial decision of final authority, becomes, as such, **transformed** into domestic law and binding under the principle of *stare decisis*. The incorporation doctrine does not prevent the Government and parliament from adopting an international custom and making it part of the law of England and Wales by legislation, *i.e.* by **transformation**. An example comes in the form of the UK *State Immunity Act* of 1978. State practice has shown so far that both judicial decisions and statutes, safe for rare cases of inadvertence, tend to interpret and apply international law in full conformity with the international rule in question. Exceptionally, one can also find cases of deliberate breaches of international law, possibly aimed to promote its change.

As for domestic law **adaptation to treaties**, in the UK and in Commonwealth countries in general, their conclusion and ratification are part of the prerogative of the Government. In England, since 1924, according to the so-called 'Ponsonby constitutional convention', and since 2010, under the *Constitutional Reform and Governance Act*, all treaties are submitted by the Government to parliamentary scrutiny.

In the UK, if implementation of a treaty requires further implementing legislation to be enacted, as is the case, for instance, when the treaty calls for **changes in the law**, this is taken care of before ratification. This is in stark contrast with the practice of many countries where, despite parliamentary approval of the ratification of the treaty in question, necessary implementing legislation is often enacted **long after**.

The ECHR was incorporated by the *Human Rights Act* of 1998. It provides the obligation for any public body to act in full conformity with the ECHR and ECtHR judgments and opinions, and to interpret likewise domestic legislation and authoritative judicial precedents. In cases of clear incompatibility by primary domestic legislation, domestic judges are to issue a 'declaration of incompatibility.' This does not invalidate the domestic incompatible legislation, but triggers a fast-track legislative procedure to amend the statutory provision in question.

The '**tempered incorporation**' doctrine referred to above and as it has developed over the years in English law, has characterised the **US legal system** from the outset. Namely, international law is automatically incorporated as part of federal law subject to the US Constitution.

As for the relationship with **international customs**, the US Supreme Court delivered a landmark judgment in 1900 in the *Paquete Habana* and *Lola* case, named after the two fishing vessels flying the Spanish flag, captured off the Cuban coast by the US Navy during the Spanish-American War.[24] There, the Supreme Court reversed a District Court decision, by ascertaining an ancient international custom protecting freedom of navigation, according to which fishing vessels were exempt from prize capture. It applied the **doctrine of incorporation** as follows:

> 'International law is part of our law and must be ascertained and administered by our courts of justice of appropriate jurisdiction as often as questions of right depending on it are duly presented for their determination. For this purpose, where there is no treaty or controlling executive or legislative act or judicial decision, resort must be had to the customs and usages of civilized nations.'[25]

---

[24] Supreme Court of the United States, *The Paquete Habana; The Lola* (1900) 175 USR 677.

[25] *Ibidem*, 700.

There is also a peculiar statutory means of incorporation of international custom into the US system through the judiciary. That is the ***Alien Tort Claims Act*** of 1789 (ATCA), also referred to as the *Alien Tort Statute* (ATS), providing that '[t]he district courts shall have original jurisdiction of any civil action by an alien for a tort only, committed in violation of the law of nations.' [26]

This old piece of US legislation was rediscovered in the 1980s by a young practitioner who assisted a Paraguayan national whose son had been tortured to death in Paraguay by a Paraguayan police officer, and whose case would become famous as the *Filártiga v Peña-Irala* case of 1980. [27] Since the case lacked the nationality and territoriality criteria for a US criminal court to entertain jurisdiction over it, based on the damages claim of the relatives of the victim, the federal court entertained its civil jurisdiction over the case instead, having ascertained that the claim was founded upon a breach of the international customary rule prohibiting torture and eventually ruling in favour of the claimant.

Whilst this precedent has inspired a long series of claims for damages before the US federal courts based on breaches of international human rights, the Supreme Court has adopted a rather restrictive attitude since its 2004 decision in *Sosa v Alvarez-Machain*. [28] Such a restrictive jurisprudential attitude was corroborated by its 2013 judgment in *Kiobel v Royal Dutch Petroleum Co*. [29] There, the Supreme Court unanimously rejected the argument that the statute in hand may ground the exercise of universal, or simply extraterritorial, jurisdiction by US federal courts, namely with regard to

---

[26] The ATCS/ATS is today codified at 38 US Code §1350.

[27] United States Court of Appeals for the Second Circuit, *Filártiga v Peña-Irala* (1980) 630 F.2d 876.

[28] Supreme Court of the United States, *Sosa v Alvarez-Machain* (2004) 542 USR 692.

[29] Supreme Court of the United States, *Kiobel v Royal Dutch Petroleum Co.* (2013) 569 USR 108.

claims that have **no territorial or subjective links with the US**.[30] While claims of universal jurisdiction pertain to the exercise of national criminal jurisdiction over the alleged commission of international crimes, the ATCA/ATS provides for the jurisdictional competence of US federal courts in relation to claims for damages.

As for **the adaptation to treaty law**, Article VI(2) of the 1787 US Constitution provides that:

> '[A]ll Treaties made, or which shall be made, under the authority of the United States, shall be the Supreme Law of the Land, and the Judges in every State shall be bound thereby, any Thing in the Constitution or Laws of any State to the Contrary.'

This provision is also known as the '**supremacy clause**,' as its last sentence places treaties regularly concluded by the US authorities **above** state constitutions and statutes. However, since the early 19th century, the Supreme Court has introduced a significant element of **judicial discretion** in the application of this constitutional provision.

In the 1829 *Foster and Elam v Neilson* case, it held that an international treaty validly concluded by the Government would not be given effect as law if *non-self-executing*.[31] A treaty provision is considered to be **self-executing** when its text is sufficiently precise to create rights and obligations that may be enforceable in the domestic courts.[32] A non-self-executing treaty could therefore not be invoked before domestic courts, until the necessary implementing legislation has been enacted. In such cases, however, the applicable law would be the implementing legislation *and not the treaty*.

---

[30] *Ibidem*, 121.

[31] Supreme Court of the United States, *Foster and Elam v Neilson* (1829) 27 USR 253, 254.

[32] See further, T Buergenthal, 'Self-Executing and Non-Self-Executing Treaties in National and International Law' (1992) 235 Collected Courses of the Hague Academy of International Law 305.

However, since the landmark *Murray v The Charming Betsey* case, decided as early as 1804,[33] in the US, like in the majority of jurisdictions, there has been for a long time a **presumption of compatibility** between an international treaty in force for it and its domestic legislation.

The problematic part of the principle whereby non-self-executing treaties do not have legal force before the domestic courts of the US, revolves around the judicial discretion in determining whether an international treaty is self-executing, or not. We will revert to this point below in Section 8 with reference to the *Breard v Green* (1998) and *Medellín v Texas* (2008) cases, amongst others making up the so-called US and the 1963 *Vienna Convention on Consular Relations* saga.

6. The 'receipt' of international law in civil law jurisdictions

In **Italy**, under Article 10(1) of the Constitution 'the Italian legal system conforms to the generally recognised rules of international law.' This is a case of constitutional *a priori* transformation of international customary law. This transformation at the **constitutional level** implies that an international custom would prevail over prior, or later, legislation incompatible with it.

However, the Constitutional Court may 'halt,' by way of interpretation, the transformation of an international custom when alleged to be in conflict with constitutional provisions. This was the case, for instance, in the judgment No 238/2014 referred to above in Section 3.1.

As for **treaties**, Article 80 provides that:

---

[33] Supreme Court of the United States, *Murray v The Charming Betsey* (1804) 6 USR 64.

> 'The Houses authorise by law the ratification of international treaties which are of a political nature, or which call for arbitration or legal settlements, or which entail changes to the national territory or financial burdens or changes to legislation.'

The parliamentary authorisation of the ratification of a treaty (the latter being the formal prerogative of the President of the Republic under Article 87(8)) is usually contained in the statute which provides for the receipt and **execution** of the treaty, once the latter has entered into force. That would be fully sufficient for the treaty in question to be implemented, provided its provisions are of a self-executing character. Otherwise, further implementing legislation will be required.

After the constitutional reform of 2001,[34] Article 117(1) provides that '[l]egislative powers shall be vested with the state and the regions in compliance with the constraints of EU legislation and international obligations.' It aims to ensure that international law, both customs and treaties, received in the Italian legal system, takes precedence over a conflicting statute, whether it is earlier or later in time.

The Preamble of the 1958 **French Constitution** fulfils the same function of Article 10(1) of the Italian Constitution in providing for the automatic transformation of international customary law. However, it does not expressly spell out whether international custom would be applicable in the domestic law even if inconsistent with the acts of parliament. Article 55 provides that treaties that have been duly ratified by virtue of a law take precedence over earlier or later legislation.

In Germany, Article 25 of the Basic Law (*Grundgesetz*), significantly entitled to the primacy of international law, not only spells out that '[t]he general rules of public international law shall be a part of federal law,' but also provides that '[t]hey shall take precedence over the laws and shall directly create rights and duties for

---

[34] Constitutional Law No 3 of 18 October 2001.

the inhabitants of the federal territory.' Moreover, German domestic courts have interpreted Article 59(2) on the authority to conclude treaties with the effect being that ratified treaties become part of German law.[35] When ratification has been subject to parliamentary authorisation, the treaty is recognised as ranking equal to domestic legislation and may be superseded by later legislation (*lex posterior derogat priori*).

German case-law recognises the **direct applicability** of treaties regularly transformed into domestic law. According to German courts, this implies that individuals and companies may base a judicial claim on a treaty provision provided it be a self-executing treaty provision.[36]

The **1993 Russian Constitution**, adopted after the dismemberment of the former Soviet Union, provides for the transformation of international customary law, as well as for treaties in force for Russia. Article 15(4) provides that '[u]niversally recognised principles and norms of international law and the international treaties of the Russian Federation shall constitute part of its legal system.' Given the constitutional ranking of the rules stemming from the two international sources of law in question, they should both be accorded precedence over national legislation, either earlier or later. The same provision addresses expressly the issue of hierarchy only in relation to treaties, as follows: '[i]f an international treaty of the Russian Federation establishes rules which differ from those stipulated by law, the rules of the international treaty shall apply.' This provision is supplemented by Article 17(1) providing that '[i]n the Russian Federation human and civil rights and freedoms shall be recognized and guaranteed according to the universally recognized principles and norms of international law and this Constitution.'

---

[35] German Constitutional Court (*Bundesverfassungsgericht*), Order of the Second Senate of 15 December 2015.

[36] See further D Lovric, 'A Constitution Friendly to International Law: Germany and its *Völkerrechtsfreundlichkeit*' (2006) 4 Australian Yearbook of International Law 75.

Throughout the 1990s, the Russian domestic judiciary, with special regard to the Constitutional Court, showed significant openness towards international law, recognising the direct applicability and direct effect of international law rules stemming from both sources, including in the delicate field of human rights. In 1998, for instance, seized to review the constitutional compatibility with Article 17 of administrative measures reintroducing certain residence permits by a number of local administrations (so-called '*propiska* system'), the Constitutional Court struck down such measures holding that they were invalid because they conflicted with the right to freedom of movement and free choice of the place of residence as recognised under the 1966 *Covenant on Civil and Political rights*, and by Protocol No 4 to the ECHR, as well as by human rights law.[37]

Since then, however, Russia has been involved in a 'regressive trend,' both political and judiciary, further addressed below in Section 8, and ideally culminated in the 2020 amendments to the Russian Constitution, whose new Article 79 provides that:

> 'The Russian Federation in conformity with relevant treaties may participate in international associations and delegate to them part of its powers, if this does not limit the rights and freedoms of the individual and the citizen or contradict the fundamentals of the constitutional system of the Russian Federation. Decisions of interstate bodies, adopted on the basis of provisions of international treaties of the Russian Federation, where construed in a manner contrary to the Constitution of the Russian Federation, shall not be subject to enforcement in the Russian Federation.'[38]

---

[37] Russian Constitutional Court, Judgment No 4-P of 2 February 1998.

[38] See further L Mälskoo, 'International Law and 2020 Amendments on the Russian Constitution' (2021) 115 American Journal of International Law 79, esp 86ff.

7. The crux of the matter: conflict and precedence

Against the background of the above cursory overview of the attitude of various national jurisdictions towards the matter at hand, it appears that they generally reflect a mixture of both monist and dualist features, with a prevalence of some form of 'mitigated dualism.'

Be that as it may, the heart of the matter concerns which rule has **priority** when an international rule so incorporated, transformed, or received is found to be in conflict with a domestic statute or judicial decision of final authority, whether earlier or later.

On balance, it appears that domestic case-law generally accords precedence to incorporated or transformed international rules over conflicting domestic rules, unless subsequent statutes are passed with the express aim of superseding prior treaty law. This is based either on express constitutional provisions or practice.

However, even in those cases where the domestic constitution provides for the automatic incorporation of international customs and both international customs and treaties, duly concluded and ratified, take precedence over conflicting domestic sources of law, a constitutional limitation (so-called '*controlimiti*') nearly always applies.

That is to say that, even where international law is afforded a constitutional place within the hierarchy of the municipal sources of law, the issue of the compatibility of international rules so received with other constitutional rules and principles may always arise. Accordingly, such issues fall on the constitutional or supreme court of the country in question to be decided, and its decision is binding on all state organs.

Given the inevitably strong political factors affecting such courts, together with the discretion that they usually enjoy and the fact that their decisions are inherently exempt from further appeals, they often reflect the domestic political trends prevailing at any point in time, despite the impartiality of their role in the *checks and balances* of the constitutional process.

A comparative analysis of the case-law of the constitutional and supreme courts – which may not be thoroughly dealt with here for the purposes of the present treatise[39] – can be highly indicative of the state of the matter in any given country at any point in time. For our purposes, it may be sufficient to note that, in the last decade, the trend has been shifting from an openness towards international legal values to a nationalist closure.

Until the turn of the century, the pendulum-like unfolding of the judicial and policy debate on the matter in hand – swinging between the promotion of the international rule of law at home and strenuous attachment to national sovereignty – has been fairly contained within the framework of a broad consensus which allowed for a limited degree of difference. Even when realistically dictated by cost-benefit considerations, such debate was carried out in legally educated terms. International law was being relied upon, even though from differing perspectives, as a common language with which to pursue individual advantages through worldwide competition, never losing sight of the sense of the global interdependence of all the factors producing or threatening domestic and international security, alike.

Until then, the tension between an openness towards international law and an adherence to domestic legal values seemed to be more a matter of legal technicalities and culture rather than one of a political nature.

As lucidly portrayed in the following passage by Dame Rosalyn Higgins, former President of the ICJ, this debate and the actual practice around it has been significantly marked by the international law background, or the lack of it, by domestic legal practitioners and judges (and one would add law-makers and administrative civil servants to the list):

> 'Related to this great jurisprudential debate [over monism and dualism] is a further reality not to be found in the textbooks, but which must be mentioned. This is the reality of legal culture. In some ju-

[39] See, for instance, 'Constitutional Courts and International Law: Revisiting the Transatlantic Divide' (2016) 129 Harvard Law Review 1362.

risdictions international law will be treated as a familiar topic, one that both the judge and the counsel before him will expect to deal with on a routine basis (…). Of course, this attitude is more to be expected in systems accepting the monist view. But I speak of very practical matters: the judge and lawyers in his court will have studied international law and will be familiar with it, as they are familiar with it, just as they are familiar with other everyday branches of the law. But there is another culture that exists, in which it is possible to become a practicing lawyer without having studied international law, and indeed to become a judge knowing no international law. Psychologically that disposes both counsel and judge to treat international law as some exotic branch of the law, to be avoided if at all possible, and to be looked upon as if it is unreal, of no practical application in the real world.' [40]

8. Jurisprudential nationalism

Contemporary state practice presents significant indications in the direction of increasing juridical nationalism resulting in extreme forms of domestic judicial unilateralism purporting to set international obligations and judicial decisions at naught. This is combined with political unilateralist attitudes by an increasing number of states inclined to cancel international cooperative engagements and the international rule of law. For the purposes of the present Chapter, it is notable that such attitudes are carried out through the assertion of the absolute supremacy of domestic constitutional law and justice over international law.

Particularly representative of a heavily regressive attitude towards the international rule of law and cooperation is the position of the US judiciary and Government – at times mutually supportive, at other times conflicting.

---

[40] R Higgins, *Problems and Process: International Law and How We Use It* (Clarendon Press 1994), 206.

The long string of US Supreme Court cases concerning the interpretation and application of the 1963 *Vienna Convention on Consular Relations* epitomises the nationalist trend under consideration. Legally, the bone of contention was whether Article 36 of this Convention, entitled to communication and contact with nationals of the sending state, is of a self-executing character. Namely, whether it has, *vel non*, direct effect in the US legal system, so as to afford foreign individuals charged with crimes in the US the right to enjoy consular assistance as a right that may be invoked by such individuals *directly* before US domestic courts. If in the affirmative, the outcome of a trial in which the right in point has not been complied with, may be validly appealed on procedural grounds. The treaty provision in question reads in part as follows:

> '1) With a view to facilitating the exercise of consular functions relating to nationals of the sending State:
> *a*) consular officers shall be free to communicate with nationals of the sending State and to have access to them. Nationals of the sending State shall have the same freedom with respect to communication with and access to consular officers of the sending State;
> *b*) if he so requests, the competent authorities of the receiving State shall, without delay, inform the consular post of the sending State if, within its consular district, a national of that State is arrested or committed to prison or to custody pending trial or is detained in any other manner. Any communication addressed to the consular post by the person arrested, in prison, custody or detention shall be forwarded by the said authorities without delay. The said authorities shall inform the person concerned without delay of his rights under this subparagraph;
> *c*) consular officers shall have the right to visit a national of the sending State who is in prison, custody or detention, to converse and correspond with him and to arrange for his legal representation. They shall also have the right to visit any national of the sending State who is in prison, custody or detention in their district in pursuance of a judgement. (…).
> 2) The rights referred to in paragraph 1 of this article shall be exer-

> cised in conformity with the laws and regulations of the receiving State, *subject to the proviso, however, that the said laws and regulations must enable full effect to be given to the purposes for which the rights accorded under this article are intended.*' [41]

The *Breard v Greene* case, decided by the US Supreme Court on 14 April 1998, [42] started a particularly harsh arm-twisting between the US judiciary and the ICJ, which eventually resulted in the US withdrawal from the *Optional Protocol to the Vienna Convention on Consular Relations concerning the Compulsory Settlement of Disputes* in 2005.

The case is the following: Mr Angel Francisco Breard, a Paraguayan national, before execution due in 1996 for conviction for attempted rape and capital murder, applied in federal courts for a stay of execution and a federal *habeas corpus* petitions, invoking a breach of his rights to consular assistance under the 1963 *Vienna Convention*. The applications were rejected on the so-called 'procedural default doctrine' – a legal principle which forbids the reviewing of *habeas corpus* petition when the petitioner failed to follow reasonable state-court procedures – and Mr Breard was scheduled to be executed on 14 April 1998 by the authorities of the Commonwealth (*i.e.*, state) of Virginia.

On 3 April 1998, Paraguay sued the US before the ICJ, also submitting an urgent request for provisional measures, namely, to indicate '[t]hat the Government of the US take the measures necessary to ensure that Mr Breard not be executed pending the disposition of this case.' [43] Five days later, on 8 April, the ICJ issued an order upholding the provisional measures requested by Paraguay. [44]

---

[41] Emphasis added.

[42] *Breard v Greene* (1998) 523 USR 371.

[43] *Vienna Convention on Consular Relations* (Paraguay v United States of America) (Order) [1998] ICJ Rep 248, 251.

[44] *Ibidem*, 258.

Breard and Paraguay then brought the ICJ decision to the attention of the US Supreme Court in two separate motions for relief, filed on April 10 and 13, basically arguing that the applicability of the 1963 *Vienna Convention* was to be intended as trumping the procedural default doctrine and the ICJ decision was binding domestic law that the Supreme Court was obliged to enforce. [45]

In the meanwhile, the case has brought national attention. On 13 April the then US Secretary of State under President Clinton, Madeleine Albright, wrote to the Governor of Virginia requesting a stay of the execution in compliance with the ICJ Order. She wrote in part as follows:

> 'The immediate execution of Mr Breard in the face of the Court's April 9 action could be seen as a denial by the United States of the significance of international law and the Court's processes in its international relations and thereby limit our ability to ensure that Americans are protected when living or travelling abroad.' [46]

On 14 April, just hours before the planned execution, in a *per curiam* opinion issued without oral argument, the US Supreme Court finally denied the application for the stay and other reliefs on a number of grounds, including the putatively non-self-executing character of Article 36 of the 1963 *Vienna Convention*. [47] Mr Breard was therefore executed that very same day.

It is notable how two years later, the then US Permanent Representative to the UN under the Presidency of George Bush Jr, Amb John R Bolton, wrote, in an article provocatively entitled 'Is There Really 'Law' in International Affairs?,' as follows:

---

[45] The background of the case is thoroughly described in CA Bradley, 'Breard, Our Dualist Constitution and the Internationalist Conception' (1999) 51 Stanford Law Review 529, 534ff.

[46] Quoted in JI Charney and WM Reisman, 'Agora: Breard' (1998) 92 American Journal of International Law 666, 672.

[47] *Breard v Greene* (n 42) 375.

> 'Albright's failure, and those who supported the intrusion of "international law" into the Breard case, was ignoring the legitimate, indeed overwhelming, national interest in honouring our own laws and our own Constitution.' [48]

Ten years later, in *Medellín v Texas*, [49] the US Supreme Court took an even firmer stand against compliance with judgments of the ICJ. The latter in 2004 found that a number of Mexican nationals, including Mr Medellín, were entitled to reconsideration of their conviction based, again, on the breach of their right to consular assistance. [50] The following year, President George Bush Jr sent the Attorney General a Memorandum ordering a review of convictions against foreign nationals who had not been advised of their rights to consular assistance under the 1963 *Vienna Convention*.

After a complex judicial process, consisting of appeals, rejections and counter-appeals, the case once again landed before the US Supreme Court. In its final judgment, delivered on 24 March 2008, the latter rejected the presidential authority as binding on state courts, and found, *inter alia*, that the international obligation for the US to comply with the ICJ decision under Article 94(1) of the *UN Charter* is of a non-self-executing character. Accordingly, Article 94(1) cannot afford rights directly to individuals and cannot, therefore, be directly applicable by domestic courts. [51] As a consequence, Mr Medellín was executed on 5 August 2008.

As for the UK, the idea of the repeal of the *Human Rights Act* of 1998 with a *British Bill of Rights* has recently been put on the political agenda of the British Government. One of the changes pro-

---

[48] JR Bolton, 'Is There Really 'Law' in International Affairs?' (2000) Transnational Law and Contemporary Problems 1, 34.

[49] *Medellín v Texas* (2008) 552 USR 491.

[50] *Avena and Other Mexican Nationals* (Mexico v United States of America) (Judgment) [2004] ICJ Rep 12.

[51] *Medellín v Texas* (n 49) 501ff.

posed would be to reverse the direct applicability of the ECHR and of the ECtHR's judicial decisions.[52] Another signal of the potential reduction of the relevance of international legal standards in the running of public administration emerges from the 2016 *Ministerial Code* amending the 2010 *Ministerial Code*. The *Ministerial Code* provides for the standards of conduct for Ministers. Whilst the 2010 edition provided for an 'overarching duty on Ministers to comply with the law including international law and treaty obligations and to uphold the administration of justice and to protect the integrity of public life,' the 2016 version has been shortened to say on the point in hand that there is an 'overarching duty on Ministers to comply with the law and to protect the integrity of public life.'[53] It is arguable that in substance little has changed as international law is part of the law of the land anyhow. On the other hand, one could consider the implication and interpretation of the deletion in the new *Ministerial Code* of the words 'international law and treaty obligations.'

As for Italy, similar results, even though through different reasoning, were reached by the Italian Constitutional Court in the already discussed judgment No 238/2014, rejecting the applicability of the 2012 ICJ judgment in the *Jurisdictional Immunities of the State* case.[54]

As for Russia, apart from the 2020 amendments mentioned above, note is to be taken of the 2015 amendments to the 1993 Russian Constitution enabling the Constitutional Court to declare an international judicial decision 'non-executable.'[55] On the basis of such amendments, the Russian Ministry of Justice resorted to the Constitutional Court pleading the 'possible inapplicability' of the 2013

---

[52] See 'No 10 To Set Out Sweeping Plans To Override Power Of Human Rights Court' in *The Guardian* (21 June 2022).

[53] Principle 1.3.

[54] See Section 3.1.

[55] Federal Constitutional Law No 7 of 14 December 2015.

ECtHR judgment in the *Anchugov and Gladkov v Russia* case.[56] The Constitutional Court decided the case starting from the very 'dualistic' premise that the Russian legal order is not subordinate to the ECHR system. The Constitutional Court then found that, given the Russian legislation in force on criminal sentences, the ECtHR decision in question could not be executed, unless the Russian criminal legislation were changed.[57]

In 2016, the Constitutional Court replied in the negative to the question submitted to it by the Russian Ministry of Justice whether Russia was to comply with the ECtHRs' *Yukos* judgement of 2014 ordering Russia to pay almost 2 billion euros to the shareholders of the company Yukos as compensation for the Governmental sanctions against them.[58] The Russian Constitutional Court argued that compliance with the judgement would not be constitutionally admissible because it infringed the principles of fairness and proportionality enshrined in the Russian Constitution. This reasoning has been criticised in the legal literature as a pretext by the Russian Government not to honour the pecuniary obligations stemming from the judgement.[59]

The Russian Federation has marked the apex of an increasingly diffused resistance by various states parties to the ECHR against the authority of the ECtHR.[60]

---

[56] ECtHR, *Case of Anchugov and Gladkov v Russia*, Apps Nos 1157/04 and 15162/05, Judgment (4 July 2013).

[57] Russian Constitution Court, Judgment No 12-П of 19 April 2016.

[58] ECtHR, *Case of OAO Neftyanaya Kompanya Yukos v Russia*, App No 14902/04, Judgment (31 July 2014).

[59] Russian Constitutional Court, Judgment No 1-П of 9 January 2017. See also K Dzehtsiarou and F Fontanelli, 'Unprincipled Disobedience to International Decisions: A Primer from the Russian Constitutional Court' (2018) European Yearbook of Human Rights 319.

[60] See, in general, F de Londras and K Dzehtsiarou, 'Mission Impossible Addressing Non-execution through Infringement Proceedings in the European Court of Human Rights' (2017) 66 International and Comparative Law Quarterly 467.

At the time of writing of the present volume and with respect to the foreseeable future, abidance by and confidence in the international rule of law and cooperation will be put to a serious test by various challenges. Amongst others, the fragmented reactions in Europe, and the US, to waves of humanitarian migration, mostly originating from poverty, underdevelopment and political persecution following the civil wars in Syria and Northern Africa; terrorism; climate change; the continuing economic crisis; the upsurge of extreme nationalism and competing hegemonism in the PRC, Russia and the US. The ongoing war in Ukraine and the tensions over Taiwan are but wearying signs of such trends.

Further reading

Bantekas I and Papastravidis E, 'The Relationship between International and Domestic Law' in Id (eds), *International Law Concentrate: Law Revision and Study Guide* (4th edn, OUP 2019), 45ff;

Cassese A, 'Modern Constitutions and International Law' (1985) 192 Collected Courses of the Hague Academy of International Law 368ff;

Ferrari Bravo L, 'International and Municipal Law: Complementarity of Legal Systems' in RS Macdonald and DM Johnston (eds), *The Structure and Process of International Law* (Martinus Nijhoff Publishers 1983), 715ff;

Focarelli C, 'State Immunity and Serious Violations of Human Rights: Judgment No. 238 of 2014 of the Italian Constitutional Court Seven Years on' (2021) 1 The Italian Review of International and Comparative Law 29ff;

Shelton D (ed), *International Law and Domestic Legal Systems: Incorporation, Transformation, and Persuasion* (OUP 2011);

Tanzi A, *Introduzione al diritto internazionale contemporaneo* (7th edn, CEDAM 2022).

Chapter 5

Breaching international law and its consequences

1. Introduction

The participatory character of international law-making as we have seen it above in Chapter 2, should in principle be conducive to **spontaneous** compliance with international law. One is to stress once more how states and intergovernmental organisations take part in the production of rules of which they are also addressees. As we have seen, this occurs directly through giving consent to treaties and, indirectly, by repeatedly adopting conduct through its officials which evolves into general practice and/or alternatively, recognising such practice as conforming to custom (*opinio juris*) or to what they believe ought to be regarded as custom (*opinio necessitatis*). This is different from domestic legal systems where the legislative organs or the courts of last resort operate above the recipients of the rules they produce, next to the rules created by contracts.

Even if the large majority of international rules are generally complied with as a matter of course every day, the above reasoning is only partly true, and, indeed, apparent breaches of international law are not infrequent.

In fact, the above assumption of the spontaneous compliance with international law relies on the legal **fiction of the unitary continuity of the legal personality of states**. On the one hand, it is only logical, and appropriate, that the same state that, one day, finds it useful to create reciprocal rights and obligations with other states and organisations, the next day consistently invokes such rights and complies with their reciprocal obligations. However, the ever-increasing international relevance of issues traditionally falling purely within the domestic competence of states – *e.g.* from health to judicial and police cooperation – has multiplied the **legal and administrative strains** on the contemporary state machine in most countries, to the detriment of the quality and consistency of their functioning *i.e.*, of the exercise of their sovereignty. That accounts for the not infrequent cases of infringements of international law by **inadvertence**.

The bureaucratic machinery of a state is crucial in engaging the latter's accountability under international law, no less than under domestic public law. Accordingly, one is not to lose sight of the fact that the state **officials in charge of the preparation and adoption of international rules are different from those responsible for their implementation and application**.

Whilst the state officials taking part in international law-making are assumed to be more knowledgeable and aware of both the advantages and constraints of international law, this is less so when it comes to those officials who are in charge of domestic affairs and frequently also responsible for the execution of many international rules. The lack of knowledge of international law and the consequent concerns regarding compliance with it, is often also to be found among state organs in charge of legal matters, as well as among practicing lawyers. [1]

The **separation of powers** between the legislative, executive and judicial branches of the state under most domestic Constitutions, whilst in perfect conformity with the principle of the rule of law, may add to the complexity of the matter. The *Jurisdictional Immunities of the State* case between Germany and Italy, addressed above in Chapter 4, is illustrative of the point at issue. We saw the Italian Government and parliament engaging in taking all necessary measures to bring the domestic legal system into conformity with the international custom on sovereign immunity and the ruling of the ICJ, whilst the domestic judiciary has repeatedly taken the opposite direction.

The policy considerations carried out so far pertain to circumstances which, in strict international law terms, fall within the scope

---

[1] See the quotation from Judge Higgins made in Chapter 4, Section 7.

of the **law of the responsibility of states for internationally wrongful acts**. Such rules may be relied upon by states when engaging in diplomatic exchanges no less, if not even more, than in international litigation. It is therefore important that politicians and state officials are appropriately knowledgeable of such rules. Those rules will be explained in Section 2, below.

Having special regard to the international obligations for states not to use, and not to allow to use, their territory in a way that may cause significant harm to other states (*sic utere tuo, ut alienum non laedas*), infringements of international law also occur as a consequence of damage caused by activities carried out by private subjects. If such damage is caused as a result of **negligence** by the state authorities in charge of the implementation of the international obligation of prevention, the rules of state responsibility apply, in the sense that the state would be internationally responsible for its **omissive conduct**.

If damage is caused nonetheless, the rules of so-called **state liability for lawful activity** apply. In order to avoid the engagement of state responsibility and state liability under similar circumstances, practice demonstrates the inclination of states to allow legal action by the victims of transboundary damage in order to pursue the **civil liability** of the private operators before the domestic courts either of the country where the damage was caused, or where it was suffered. Both issues concerning **state liability** and **civil liability** will be addressed below in Section 3.

2. International wrongs and state responsibility

As we have seen, states generally comply with international law. Sometimes, they may depart from international law either inadvertently, or by political choice. In the former case, the organs of the state in question may simply be **unaware** of the existence of the rule producing the obligations they are infringing upon, or they may interpret it incorrectly.

The state who is the beneficiary of the rights which correspond to the obligations breached will usually lodge a protest invoking the international wrongfulness of the conduct complained of. The state invoking the responsibility of another state will have to prove *a*) the actual conduct complained of, as a matter of fact and *b*) the existence of an international rule producing one or more obligations alleged to have been infringed upon by the conduct in question, as a matter of law.[2] If the state entitled to invoke the responsibility of another state, does not do so for a significant period of time since becoming aware of the conduct in question, it is estopped from raising the issue, according to the principle of **estoppel**, or **acquiescence** (Article 45(b) of the ASR).

The law of international state responsibility provides the rules for assessing the occurrence of an internationally wrongful act and its consequences.

It follows from the introductory considerations carried out above in Section 1, and from those in Chapter 4 on the relationship between international law and municipal jurisdictions, that the responsibility of a state *vis-à-vis* another state for a breach of international law should not be confused with any responsibility (liability) which a state may incur before the courts of a foreign country for breach of its domestic legislation. Similarly, the peculiar situation in which a state has breached *vis-à-vis* another state an obligation **governed by a certain domestic legislation** should not be framed under the law of international state responsibility. This applied to a dispute decided in 2005 by an arbitration tribunal in a case between Brazil and Italy (their respective Ministries of Defence) over the performance of a sub-licence agreement governed by English law concerning a joint-venture for the construction of military aircrafts.[3]

---

[2] See Article 2 of the ASR.

[3] International Chamber of Commerce, *Italy v Brazil* (Award) [2005] Case No 12988/FM.

The rules on international state responsibility are also applied by international courts and tribunals in the exceptional cases where the applicant is not a state or an intergovernmental organisation, but an individual or a company, as with the cases before **human rights courts** or **investment arbitration tribunals**. As already alluded to above (Chapter 2, Section 4.1), in strictly formal international legal terms, in those cases the private applicants would be exercising procedural rights vindicating the material international rights of states, *i.e.*, all the states parties to a human rights treaty, or the state of nationality of the investor. These qualifications will be relevant for the study of the topic of international dispute settlement which will be addressed in the next Chapter 6.

The international law body of state responsibility consists of **a unitary regime** which does not provide for different forms of responsibility according to the **kind of sources** of the obligations breached. This marks a difference from municipal jurisdictions which generally contemplate different forms of liability either for breach of contract, for tort, delict or crime. This will be confirmed below by the considerations concerning the international rule providing for the so-called state liability for activities not prohibited under international law.

The customary rules making up the body of international law under consideration have been authoritatively codified by the ILC in its ASR,[4] already referred to above (Chapter 4, Section 3). Such rules are so-called ***secondary rules***, insofar as they are **not** of a primary or substantive law character, such as '**obligations of conduct**,' namely, obligations to do or not to do.[5] According to the

---

[4] ILC, 'Draft Articles on Responsibility of States or Internationally Wrongful Acts, with Commentaries' (2001) II(2) Yearbook of the International Law Commission 25.

[5] On 'primary' and 'secondary' rules see J Combacau and D Alland, '"Primary" and "Secondary" Rules in the Law of State Responsibility Categorizing International Obligations' (1985) 16 Netherlands Yearbook of International Law

secondary rules under consideration, the occurrence of an internationally wrongful act triggers an **international legal relationship of responsibility** between the state which has breached an international obligation and the state which has suffered the breach of the right corresponding to the obligation infringed.

As already alluded to, the rule equally applies to breaches of obligations stemming from treaty or customary rules, general principles of law, or unilateral declarations. The fact that a state may react to a breach of a treaty against it by suspending or terminating that treaty under Article 60 of the VCLT, as we have seen above in Chapter 3, Section 3.1.2, does not preclude its right to invoke the rules of state responsibility, with special regard to *reparation* or, if necessary, the adoption of *countermeasures* outside the scope of application of the treaty in question.

2.1. *Internationally wrongful act of states*

2.1.1. *Violation of an international obligation and attribution thereof*

An internationally wrongful act consists of conduct in **violation** of an international obligation binding on a state, which is **attributable** to that state, as a subject of international law (Article 2 of the ASR). Whilst this general statement may appear self-evident, it requires few qualifications.

The occurrence of **damage**, distinct from the breach of an international obligation, is not ***in itself*** a requirement for there to be an international wrong. That is to say that the very of a conduct in **breach of an international obligation** is sufficient for generating an international wrong to be redressed under the international rules under consideration. Certain international obligations do require conduct that should not be materially harmful, but here the fact of

---

81 and E David, 'Primary and Secondary Rules' in J Crawford et al (eds), *The Law of International Responsibility* (OUP 2010), 27.

causing damage is **precisely contemplated** by the obligation in question, in terms of ***prevention***.

By way of example, one may recall the obligation not to expropriate or treat aliens in an arbitrary or discriminatory way, or that to respect the immunity from jurisdiction of foreign states. The *Jurisdictional Immunities of the State* case between Germany and Italy illustrated above in Chapter 4 is exemplary of a situation of occurrence of an internationally wrongful act flowing from a breach of an international obligation without causing significant damage to the victim state. This, at least, in relation to the part of the dispute concerning the infringement of the obligation not to entertain **adjudicative** jurisdiction over foreign states, and not to the case in which – if ever – the **executive** jurisdiction would result in effective measures of constraint over German sovereign assets and property. The same would apply to violations of the airspace of one country by military aircrafts of another state. Practice shows how such situations do give rise by strong reactions by the victim states, including the invocation of the international responsibility of the state of nationality of the aircrafts in question, even where the wrongful overflight would cause no apparent material damage.

The above considerations explain the importance of so-called declaratory judgments, *i.e.*, those judgments declaring the wrongfulness of a given conduct, usually enjoining the wrongdoing state to provide assurances against the repetition of the wrongful conduct in the future.

Next to damage, not even **fault** is considered as a necessary constituent element of an international wrong. As a psychological element, it could not apply to the state as an abstract entity, but only to the **state of mind** of the individual organs that carry out the conduct in breach of the international obligation. Were the international law of state responsibility to require fault on the part of the state organs that engage in conduct at variance with international law for there to be an international wrong, states could very rarely be held internationally responsible. Indeed, more often than not, state organs, when acting in contrast with an international obligation, are far from intending to breach the law. On the contrary, they usually assume to be acting in conformity with the law, even if they do so with municipal law in mind, be it the Constitution, statutory law or administrative instructions.

A short example can be taken from the *Norstar* dispute between Panama and Italy, in which the ITLOS found Italy internationally responsible for a breach of the UNCLOS, with special regard to Article 87 on freedom of navigation on the high seas.[6] Italy's conduct which was found in breach of international law originated from a Decree of seizure ordered in 1998 by the public prosecutor at the Tribunal of Savona against the motor vessel 'Norstar,' which was flying the flag of Panama. The Decree was issued based on Article 253 of the Italian Code of Criminal Procedure, according to which:

> '1. The judicial authority adopts, with motivated order, the seizure of the *corpus delicti* and of any other thing related to the crime and necessary to the assessment of the factual background of the case.'

The alleged crime to which the Decree was related pertained to avoidance of payment of excise duties, smuggling and other fraudulent behaviour under Italian tax law. The international law basis for the adoption of the Decree, according to the Italian public prosecutor, was Article 33 of the UNCLOS which would afford coastal states jurisdiction powers over the so-called '**contiguous zone**,' which ranges from the territorial sea up to 24 miles from the coastline. Indeed, for the relevant part, Article 33 reads as follows:

> 'In a zone contiguous to its territorial sea, described as the contiguous zone, the coastal State may exercise the control necessary to:
> *a*) prevent infringement of its customs, fiscal, immigration or sanitary laws and regulations within its territory or territorial sea;

---

[6] *The M/V "Norstar" Case* (Panama v Italy) (Judgment) [2019] ITLOS Rep 10, 76.

b) punish infringement of the above laws and regulations committed within its territory or territorial sea (…).'

Under the joint reading of Articles 33 and 77(3) of the UNCLOS,[7] however, the jurisdictional powers in question are subject to the proclamation of the contiguous zone by adoption of legislation to that effect by the coastal state. Since Italy, at that time, had not proclaimed its contiguous zone, the key disputed facts in the case, according to the ITLOS, had taken place on the high seas.[8]

Be that as it may, for the purposes of the issue of **fault**, it is worth noting that the ITLOS did not consider whether the Italian judiciary had the intention to breach international law, nor did it find that, in order for it to assess the commission of an internationally wrongful act by Italy, it had to prove that the Italian judiciary had fallen short of some kind of due diligence. It simply assessed that the disputed conduct was in contrast with an international obligation, without looking at subjective factors relating to how and why the conduct had been performed.

There are also international rules that may be breached by **negligence**. But this depends on the contents of the individual primary rules in question providing for **due diligence obligations** with regard to specific cases, rather than on the existence of a general secondary rule concerning international state responsibility which is applicable to the breach of **any** international obligation. That is simply to say that, in such cases, negligence is not a separate condition for the existence of an internationally wrongful act, but it coincides with what the obligation in question is meant to prevent. The same applies with respect to the existence of some sort of 'qualified' psychological status. This means that, albeit rarely, for the vi-

---

[7] Which reads as follows: 'The rights of the coastal State over the continental shelf do not depend on occupation, effective or notional, or on any express proclamation.'

[8] *The M/V "Norstar" Case* (Panama v Italy) (Preliminary Objections) (Judgment) [2016] ITLOS Rep 44, 73.

olation to occur, the primary rule may require that the conduct be carried out with a specific intent (so-called *dolus specialis*), as is the case, for example, for the commission of genocide, whereby for the violation to happen and the corresponding international responsibility to arise, the state is supposed to act with the specific intent 'to destroy th[at] [ethnic] group in whole or in part.' [9]

For there to be an internationally wrongful act, alongside the requirement of **conduct in breach of an international obligation**, it is necessary that such conduct be **attributed to a state**. Since states are abstract entities, they act through their organs either formally, or *de facto*, within the scope of their official functions, or irrespective of whether they are acting in compliance with their domestic law or instructions, or beyond them (*ultra vires*). A state may breach international law through **any of its organs**, be it the parliament, the central Government, a branch of central or local administration, the police, courts and tribunals, as clearly corroborated by Article 4(1) of the ASR. [10]

In the past, some states have invoked the independence of the judiciary under their Constitution as a justification in order to avoid international responsibility for judicial decisions in violation of an international obligation. The same has occurred with regard to conduct by local administrative authorities under Constitutions providing for a federalist organisation of the state or decentralised public administration. As we have seen above (Chapter 4, Section 3), however, a state may not invoke its municipal law to justify conduct in breach of international law.

According to the *chapeau* of Article 2 of the ASR, the relevant

---

[9] *Application of the Convention on the Prevention and Punishment of the Crime of Genocide* (Croatia v Serbia) (Judgment) [2015] ICJ Rep 3, 66.

[10] 'The conduct of any State organ shall be considered an act of that State under international law, whether the organ exercises legislative, executive, judicial or any other functions, whatever position it holds in the organisation of the State, and whatever its character as an organ of the central Government or of a territorial unit of the State.'

conduct by state organs may consist of **action or omission**, depending on the contents of the international rules relevant to any given case. When the latter provides for **negative obligations** (such as those of abstention or, more generally, '**obligations not to do**') active conduct at variance with any such obligation, which is usually easily detectable, amounts to a **commissive** wrongful act. That would be the case, for instance, with an act of expropriation without compensation, or with the conduct of police investigations carried out in the premises of a foreign embassy, or consulate, or a denial of justice, not to mention the use of force against the territorial integrity of another state.

Circumstances pertaining to breaches of positive obligations – such as those of prevention or, more generally, '**obligations to do**' – may lead one to think that here the state is accountable for acts of individuals, directly attributable to it. That would be the case with the takeover by protesters of a foreign embassy. Another example would be that of a chemical factory owned by a private corporation operating within state A, which – because of a malfunctioning of its plants – were to significantly pollute the air or soil of state B, adversely affecting the health of some of its population. Here, again, state A would not be internationally responsible because of the possibility of attributing to it the activities of the private corporation in question, but only to the extent that its competent authorities did not act diligently, that is taking all the appropriate measures required by international law to prevent significant transboundary harm. Such measures would range from the existence of a permit regime for the industrial activity in question requiring an EIA to monitoring that appropriate plant maintenance measures regularly carried out.

It would be wrong to assume that, under such circumstances, the state would be responsible for conduct of non-state authorities – *i.e.*, the protesters or the private corporation in question – but because of ***omissive conduct*** by its state organs. Though that would be so only if, and to the extent that, it is proved that its police, its central or local authorities had not taken all the possible preventive measures to prevent the takeover of the embassy or the pollution in question, respectively.

As already alluded to, conduct by state organs acting while on duty is attributed to the state even when they act beyond, or ***even against***, the scope of their mandate and instructions (*i.e.* acting *ultra vires*), provided they are not acting in their private capacity (Article 7 of the ASR). [11] By way of example, the conduct of a custom officer abusing his authority and dispossessing foreign visitors of their goods while performing his/her official functions at the custom control station at the airport, would be attributable to the state; if the same individual, when off duty and in lay clothing, engages in pickpocketing of foreigners, that would not be attributable to the state.

This proceeds from the principle of good faith and reliance by third states that the state in question diligently exercises control over its own officials. By the same principle, if the same official engaged in the same activity with police officers beknowing and condescending, the state in question **would be internationally responsible**. That, again, would not flow from the attribution to the state of the conduct of the individual in question, but of that – omissive in nature – of its police officers failing to comply with their official duties. This confirms the general statement anticipated above, whereby states cannot be **directly** responsible for the conduct of private individuals or non-state entities.

Finally, it is worth stressing the existence of at least two exceptions to this general regime.

First, according to Article 8 of the ASR, 'the conduct of a person or group of persons shall be considered an act of a State under international law if the person or group of persons is in fact acting

---

[11] Article 7 reads as follows: 'The conduct of an organ of a State or of a person or entity empowered to exercise elements of the governmental authority shall be considered an act of the State under international law if the organ, person or entity acts in that capacity, even if it exceeds its authority or contravenes instructions.'

on the instructions of, or under the direction or control of, that State in carrying out the conduct.' While this quick introduction does not allow to deepen into the thorny problem of the practical application of this rule on attribution, one should note that the ICJ has set the bar high for the possibility of 'transposing' the conduct of individuals to states under an effective 'direction and control' test. [12]

Second, according to Article 11 of the ASR, a conduct which is not generally attributable to a state 'shall nevertheless be considered an act of that State under international law if and to the extent that the State acknowledges and adopts the conduct in question as its own.' This is what happened, for example, in the *Tehran Hostages* case between the US and Iran, where the ICJ found the latter guilty of breaching a number of international obligations, both conventional and customary in nature, on diplomatic and consular relations on a twofold level: **firstly**, because, by incurring in an **omissive wrongful act directly attributable to it**, Iran did nothing to prevent the assault by an enraged mob against the embassy of the US in Teheran – allegedly motivated by the freezing of certain Iranian assets in the US –; and, **secondly**, because, by the repeated and express endorsement to the violent protests carried out against the US embassy given by the then *de facto* Head of state, the Ayatollah Khomeini, the ICJ ascertained that Iran had 'adopted as its own' the wrongful conduct. [13]

2.1.2. *Circumstances precluding wrongfulness*

The wrongfulness of state conduct in breach of an international obligation is precluded on the basis of a number of exceptional cir-

---

[12] See *Military and Paramilitary Activities in and against Nicaragua* (Nicaragua v United States of America) (Judgment) [1986] ICJ Rep 14, 64 and *Application of the Convention on the Prevention and Punishment of the Crime of Genocide* (Bosnia and Herzegovina v Serbia and Montenegro) (Judgment) [2007] ICJ Rep 43, 208-209.

[13] *United States Diplomatic and Consular Staff in Teheran* (United States of America v Iran) (Judgment) [1980] ICJ Rep 3, 45-46.

cumstances, so-called **circumstances precluding wrongfulness**, codified under Articles 20-25 of the ASR.

One such circumstance is **consent** (Article 20).[14] That is the consent by state A to another state's conduct in breach of a given obligation of the corresponding right, which would otherwise amount to an international wrong. Such consent is given ***prior*** to the occurrence of conduct consented to, and should not be confused with ***acquiescence subsequent to the conduct in question*** (Article 45(b) of the ASR). Consent precludes wrongfulness, **acquiescence** precludes the right to invoke responsibility: thus, the former has material effects, as it 'precludes' the existence of the breach, while the latter has only procedural effects, as it does not affect the existence of the breach, *per se*.

A typical example of consent occurs when state A authorises state B, upon request, to send its police, or intelligence agents, or to conduct investigations over or arrest individuals, on its territory. If such conduct is carried out without consent it amounts to an internationally wrongful act of state A. However, if the local authorities of state B gave no consent and, after the breach occurred, could be considered as having, by reason of their conduct, validly acquiesced in the lapse of the claim, then state B would be precluded, or **estopped**, from invoking the responsibility of the wrongdoing state.

Another such circumstance is when the otherwise wrongful conduct is adopted by way of a **countermeasure** (Article 22),[15] adopted unilaterally, or jointly, by states in response to an international wrong previously suffered. Such a circumstance operates as a preclusion of wrongfulness when the measures in breach of an international rule, usually in the field of trade, are adopted in conformity

---

[14] 'Valid consent by a State to the commission of a given act by another State precludes the wrongfulness of that act in relation to the former State to the extent that the act remains within the limits of that consent.'

[15] 'The wrongfulness of an act of a State not in conformity with an international obligation towards another State is precluded if and to the extent that the act constitutes a countermeasure taken against the latter State (…).'

with the requirement of **proportionality** and are subject to the requirement that the infringed obligation does not flow from an imperative norm of international law (see above Chapter 3, Section 3.1.2 on *jus cogens*), such as those prohibiting on the use of armed force, torture, slavery or genocide.

In this vein, Article 26 of the ASR also recalls more in general that the circumstances precluding wrongfulness do not operate in respect of any act of state not in conformity with an obligation arising under a peremptory norm of general international law.

A similar circumstance precluding wrongfulness applies when conduct in breach of certain international rules is authorised or requested in conformity with the *UN Charter*. That is the case when an arms or economic embargo against a certain country is demanded by a Security Council resolution under Chapter VII of the *UN Charter*, as a reaction to a serious breach of international law regarded as a threat to international peace and security. Such collective responsive conduct is called a **sanction**. Since the heinous 9/11 terrorist attack against the Twin Towers in 2001, the Security Council has developed the practice of adopting resolutions targeting individuals (so-called **targeted sanctions**), for example, providing the freezing of their bank accounts or withdrawing their passport.

With the renewed international tensions between some of the five **permanent Members of the Security Council** – PRC, France, Russia, US and UK – to an extent and degree which was unimaginable until their very occurrence, it is obvious that, in the foreseeable future, no Security Council Chapter VII resolution will be adopted as, under the *UN Charter*, their adoption requires the reaching of a common agreement between them, at least in the sense that none is going to vote ***against*** the adoption of the resolution (whereas, from the 1960s, *abstention* is admitted and does not translate into a veto).[16]

---

[16] As was clarified by the ICJ in its famous interpretation (arguably *contra litteram*) of Article 27(3) of the *UN Charter* in *Legal Consequences for States of the Continued Presence of South Africa in Namibia (South West Africa) not-*

Regional organisations may also adopt sanctions which are then implemented by their Member states. That was the case of the EU sanctions adopted in 2014 against Russia and Russian nationals deemed to be influential in its policy-making realisation, following the Crimean crisis. The same sanctions have been revived and increased after Russia's aggression on Ukraine in February 2022. Obviously, differently from the case of Security Council resolutions binding on all states parties of the organisation, thus of the international society, sanctions adopted by regional organisations would remain subject to assessment of international lawfulness on a case-by-case basis. For clearer understanding of the point at issue, it will be taken up again below in more systemic terms.

Consistent with Article 51 of the *UN Charter*, Article 21 of the ASR provide that, when the international wrongful act against which a response is taken consists of an act of aggression or armed attack, the response may well involve the use of armed force, as a **legitimate self-defence**, provided it be proportionate and carried out in compliance with international humanitarian law. That shows how self-defence represents a circumstance precluding wrongfulness. [17]

A highly controversial type of circumstance which precludes wrongfulness is that of **necessity**. International case-law shows that, whenever invoked by the respondent state to justify allegations of wrongfulness by the applicant, it has hardly ever been upheld by an international court, or tribunal. It is noteworthy, however, that the invocation of necessity has never been rejected as a matter of law, in the sense of denying the existence of the rule, or principle, in question, but as a matter of fact. Namely, by assessing that the fac-

---

withstanding Security Council Resolution 276 (1970) (Advisory Opinion) [1971] ICJ Rep 16, 22. On Article 27(3) of the *UN Charter* see also below, Section 2.2.

[17] Article 21 of the ASR reads as follows: 'The wrongfulness of an act of a State is precluded if the act constitutes a lawful measure of self-defence taken in conformity with the Charter of the United Nations.'

tual circumstances of the case were deemed to fall short of the requirements of the rule, or principle, in question.

That explains why this rule has been codified by the ILC in very restrictive terms under Article 25 of the ASR, according to which a situation of necessity may be validly invoked only exceptionally in order to preclude conduct in violation of international law. Namely, when such conduct was 'the only way for the state to safeguard an essential interest against a grave and imminent peril.' Also, necessity may not constitute a valid ground justifying conduct at variance with an international rule when the invoking state has contributed to the occurrence of the circumstances invoked. [18]

In recent international investment arbitration case-law, Argentina has repeatedly invoked its financial collapse in 2001 as a ground for justifying the breach of a number of international contractual and financial obligations *vis-à-vis* foreign investors in contrast with international investment protection treaties and parallel customs. In the overwhelming majority of such cases the awards rejected such defence, either because the wrongful conduct in dispute was not considered to have been the only way by which the Argentinian authorities could 'safeguard an essential interest against a grave and imminent peril,' or because it was found that Argentina had contributed through its economic and financial policy to the occurrence of the circumstances invoked to ground necessity. [19]

---

[18] Article 25 of the ASR reads, in full, as follows: '1. Necessity may not be invoked by a State as a ground for precluding the wrongfulness of an act not in conformity with an international obligation of that State unless the act: *a*) is the only way for the State to safeguard an essential interest against a grave and imminent peril; and *b*) does not seriously impair an essential interest of the State or States towards which the obligation exists, or of the international community as a whole. 2. In any case, necessity may not be invoked by a State as a ground for precluding wrongfulness if: *a*) the international obligation in question excludes the possibility of invoking necessity; or *b*) the State has contributed to the situation of necessity.'

[19] See, for instance, *LG&E Energy Corp, LG&E Capital Corp, and LG&E*

Preclusion of wrongfulness is of a transitory character, that is, until the circumstances in question persist. Furthermore, even where one of the grounds for justification of an international wrong in question is upheld, this does not dispense the 'justified' state from having to pay compensation for the damage caused by its 'lawful breach of law.' In this regard, Article 27(b) of the ASR reads as follows:

> 'The invocation of a circumstance precluding wrongfulness in accordance with this chapter is without prejudice to the question of compensation for any material loss caused by the act in question.'

The amount of compensation due should possibly be lower than that due as a form of reparation for an internationally wrongful act.

2.2. *The legal relationship of responsibility*

The occurrence of an international wrong triggers an **international legal relationship** which arises between the **wrongdoing state** and the **victim state**, *i.e.*, the state who has suffered the infringement of the right corresponding to the obligation breached. The generally bilateral nature of the secondary legal relationship of responsibility corresponds to the traditionally bilateral nature of the legal relationships stemming from the primary, or material, rules of international law based on reciprocity. This consideration will be further qualified with regard to breaches of the relatively new category of

---

International, Inc v Argentine Republic, ICSID Case No ARB/02/1, Award (25 July 2007). On virtually identical facts, however, other arbitration tribunals did find state of necessity applicable, see *CMS Gas Transmission Company v The Republic of Argentina*, ICSID Case No ARB/01/8, Award (12 May 2005). For an in-depth analysis of the 'Argentinian bond saga' see A Carlevaris and R Digón, 'The Argentinian Bond Saga: An International Investment Law Perspective' in A Tanzi et al (eds), *International Law Investment Law in Latin America* (Brill-Nijhoff 2016), 605.

erga omnes obligations stemming from peremptory rules of international law, or *jus cogens*.[20]

Reparation constitutes **the main object of the legal relationship** of responsibility or, to put it more plainly, it represents the ***principal legal consequence*** of an internationally wrongful act. As stated in the landmark judgment by the PCIJ in the *Factory at Chorzów* case, reparation is to be intended in the following wide terms:

> 'Reparation must, as far as possible, wipe out all the consequences of the illegal act and re-establish the situation which would, in all probability, have existed if that act had not been committed.'[21]

As restated by the ILC under Article 31 of the ASR, '[t]he responsible State is under an obligation to make full reparation for the injury caused by the internationally wrongful act [including] any damage, whether material or moral, caused by the internationally wrongful act of a State.' The forms of reparation consist of 'restitution, compensation and satisfaction, either singly or in combination.'[22]

The re-establishment of the situation existing prior to the wrongful act (*status quo ante*) may consist, apart from the material restitution of a given good when materially possible (restitution in kind), in a legal form of **restitution**, such as the obligation for the wrongdoing state to repeal a given statute, reconsider an administrative measure, or annul a judicial decision. In the case of a breach having a continuing character – as with the case of an ongoing unlawful seizure of a foreign vessel, or arbitrary detention – the obligation of restitution encompasses that of **cessation** of the wrongful conduct, in the sense that putting an end to the unlawful conduct

---

[20] See Section 2.2.1.

[21] *Factory at Chorzów* (Germany v Poland) [1928] PCIJ Series A/No 17, 47.

[22] See Article 34 of the ASR.

will automatically result in the re-establishment of the *status quo ante* (that is, the release of the foreign vessel or of the detainee, respectively).

When restitution in kind is not possible, the obligation to pay proportionate **compensation** applies. It may be noted that, under the WTO framework, differently from investment law arbitration, international trade dispute settlement panels generally conform to the rule whereby the obligation of restitution **comes first**, by usually ordering the lifting, or reconsideration, of certain custom duties, including by adopting amending legislation where necessary. Such practice reinforces the obligation breached, enhancing the legal relationship stemming therefrom.

Conversely, international investment arbitration tribunals tend to uphold the request for compensation made by the foreign investors, irrespective of the feasibility of restitution in kind. This attitude tends to undermine the continuation of the foreign investment relationship with the authorities of the state hosting the investment. However, it also protects the economic interests of foreign investors who may have lost confidence in those authorities and have no interest in continuing investing in that state. Not only that, it may also benefit the host state with regard to the freedom of choice pertaining to its sovereign regulatory power.

Another element of the contents of the **legal relationship of international responsibility** between the wrongdoing state and the state, or states, whose rights have been infringed, is the right of the latter to take **countermeasures**, as illustrated above under Section 2.1.2. on the circumstances precluding wrongfulness. For present purposes, it is to be stressed that the right of the victim state to take countermeasures is to be confined to the aim of exerting pressure on the wrongdoer in order for it to cease the unlawful conduct and redress the situation produced, including, restitution and/or compensation.

More generally, it is also worth noting that countermeasures constitute a form of **self-help** as the main feature of law **enforcement in the decentralised international law system**. Sanctions by the

UN Security Council do represent a tentative form of **centralised law enforcement** system. However, as anticipated, the functioning of the enforcement role of the Security Council is subject to some kind of 'restricted form of sovereign equality,' namely, one operating only as between its above-mentioned five permanent Members. In this regard, Articles 27(2) and 27(3) of the *UN Charter*, for the relevant part for our purposes, read as follows:

> '2. Decisions of the Security Council on procedural matters shall be made by an affirmative vote of nine members.
> 3. Decisions of the Security Council on all other matters shall be made by an affirmative vote of nine members including the concurring votes of the permanent members (…).'

That accounts for the fact that during the Cold War the Security Council has been blocked by the vetoes (or the prospect thereof) of Members belonging to either the Western or the Soviet bloc. After a few years of harmony amongst the five permanent Members further to the fall of the Berlin Wall, new divisions have arisen following the Kosovo crisis at the end of the 1990s, which have further deepened in connection with the Syrian Civil War (2012) and the Crimean crisis of 2014 and would render the functioning of the Security Council, again, a highly difficult political task to be achieved. The Russian aggression on Ukraine, in combination with the strong reaction by three of the other four permanent Members, has turned such difficulty into impossibility for years to come.

2.2.1. *Violation of* erga omnes *obligations*

Reverting to the structural aspects of the international law of state responsibility, the above referred consequences of an internationally wrongful act operate relatively easily in relation to **breaches of traditional bilateral international legal obligations based on reciprocity**. Namely, such breaches give rise to an international legal relationship responsibility between the victim State and the wrongdoing State, where the former is entitled to invoke the responsibility of the latter to claim redress from the latter and adopt countermeasures against it if it does not comply with its obligation of reparation.

However, as we have repeatedly indicated, international law has developed new rules aimed to the protection of collective interests of the international community as a whole. Within the framework of treaty law, such rules are meant to operate as *jus cogens*, or a set of *peremptory rules*, in the sense of rules derogation from which is not permitted, to the extent that, pursuant to Article 53 of the VCLT, a treaty in contrast with any of such rules would fall under a cause of invalidity. However, the same disposition falls short of identifying the rules in question, even in non-exhaustive exemplary terms.[23] On the contrary, it confines itself to merely define the concept of peremptory rules in purely abstract and somewhat circular terms by referring to rules regarded by the international community as a whole as rules from which derogation is not permitted.

However, the year following the adoption of the VCLT, in the *Barcelona Traction* case between Belgium and Spain, the ICJ addressed the matter in jurisprudentially useful terms for the purposes of identifying such rules, as well as the **states entitled to invoke the international responsibility for breaches of so-called *erga omnes* obligations** stemming from the ***jus cogens*** rules in question. In its most famous *obiter dictum*, the ICJ observed that:

> '[A]n essential distinction should be drawn between the obligations of a State towards the international community as a whole, and those vis-à-vis another State in the field of diplomatic protection. By their very nature the former are the concern of all States. In view of the importance of the rights involved, all States can be held to have a legal interest in their protection; they are obligations *erga omnes*. Such obligations derive, for example, in contemporary international law, from the outlawing of acts of aggression, and of genocide, as also from the principles and rules concerning the basic

[23] See also Chapter 3, Section 3.1.2.

> rights of the human person, including protection from slavery and racial discrimination.' [24]

Later, when codifying the international law of state responsibility, the ILC 'operationalised' the above concepts by recognising also for states other than those (materially) injured by an international wrong the right to invoke the international responsibility of the wrongdoer. In particular, Article 48(1) of the ASR allows for the invocation of responsibility by a state other than the (materially) injured state when: '*a*) the obligation breached is owed to a group of states including that state, and is established for the protection of a collective interest of the group; or *b*) the obligation breached is owed to the international community as a whole.'

An exemplary case under letter *a*) would be found in the breach of an obligation stemming from a human rights treaty or a MEA containing obligations *erga omnes partes* (towards all the states parties). Letter *b*) clearly envisages breaches of obligations stemming from peremptory norms of international law, such as the obligations to prevent and punish the crime of genocide, which equally stem from the 1948 *Genocide Convention* and the corresponding customary rule of a *jus cogens* nature.

Not only would, a state who is not materially injured, be **entitled to invoke at the diplomatic level** a breach of international law in such cases, or be recognised as having the necessary **legal interest to sue** the wrongdoing state before an international competent court or tribunal (*locus standi*), but it would also be entitled to take **countermeasures** against the wrongdoing state for the benefit of the state that has been materially injured by wrong. [25] A recent example

---

[24] *Barcelona Traction, Light and Power Company, Limited* (Belgium v Spain) (Judgment) [1970] ICJ Rep 3, 33.

[25] Article 54 of the ASR recognises 'the right of any State, entitled under article 48, paragraph 1, to invoke the responsibility of another State, to take lawful measures against that State to ensure cessation of the breach and reparation in the interest of the injured State or of the beneficiaries of the obligation breached.'

of this is represented by the economic measures adopted by the EU and its Member states in the interest of Ukraine against Russia for its occupation of Crimea in 2014 and military aggression in 2022.

There is a potential downside in this adjustment of the law of state responsibility to the emergence of the material international rules introducing an element of multilateralism to the traditional international rules protecting bilateral interests. It consists of the concern that the power to take countermeasures by states who are not directly injured may be **abused** as a means of economic and political coercion by the few states that have the economic and financial capacity to take such measures, the latter being burdensome also for the states adopting them. This concern depends on the still highly decentralised character of the international community.

3. State liability and civil liability

The term 'liability' in municipal jurisdictions, is a synonym with 'legal responsibility.' There are different kinds of liability, or liability doctrines, according to the kind of infringed rules, such as civil liability, *e.g.* for breach of contract, liability in tort law – *i.e.*, outside breaches of contract, such as claims for damages cause by an accident –, or criminal liability. A special kind of liability doctrine under domestic law, which is of particular interest in comparative terms for the purposes of international law, is that of **strict liability** in common law systems, which finds a comparator in the civil law

---

Reference to 'lawful measures' instead of 'countermeasures' is somewhat misleading, and has sparked a debate on whether third states are actually entitled to adopt countermeasures or whether this disposition should be read in the sense of only allowing for the adoption of 'unfriendly,' though 'legal,' measures (so-called 'reprisals') – such as the suspension of diplomatic relations. International practice, however, seems to show that third states usually believe and feel entitled to adopt full-fledged countermeasure to react against the violation of an *erga omnes* obligation not directly affecting them.

systems with the **objective liability** doctrine. Strict liability applies in both tort law and criminal law. Its distinguishing feature is that of making a legal person liable for damage caused irrespective of negligence or intention in tort law, or fault in criminal law.

Under general international law, there is no such regime as strict or objective liability of the kind we find in domestic jurisdictions. Such a strict liability regime can be exceptionally found under the 1972 *Convention on International Liability for Damage Caused by Space Objects*, whose Article II provides that a state is 'absolutely liable to pay compensation for damage caused by its space object on the surface of the earth or to aircraft in flight.' The provision in point provides the absolute obligation of compensation for the damage caused irrespective of any breach of the law.

When the international society of states started addressing environmental concerns, the idea was pursued of codifying the general obligation of prevention of transboundary harm. This was based on the already mentioned Roman law principle of *sic utere tuo ut alienum non laedas*. The latter was translated into the so-called '**no-harm rule**' and recognised under international law in a number of authoritative cases of international judicial and diplomatic practice of the 20th century. In 1996, in its advisory opinion on the *Legality of the Threat or Use of Nuclear Weapons*, the ICJ stated that:

> 'The existence of the general obligation of States to ensure that activities within their jurisdiction and control respect the environment of other States or of areas beyond national control is now part of the corpus of international law relating to the environment.' [26]

In the early stages of the codification exercise in question, through the 1980s, consideration was given to the consolidation of the obligation of **transboundary harm prevention** with specific regard to

---

[26] *Legality of the Threat or Use of Nuclear Weapons* (Advisory Opinion) [1996] ICJ Rep 226, 241-242.

hazardous activities, such as the operation of chemical plants, or mining, as an **absolute obligation**. That is, one which would be automatically breached by the sheer occurrence of transboundary harm originating from the territory under the jurisdiction of the origin state.

While continuing to study the subject in point for the purposes of codification, the ILC, complemented by the regular comments provided by the governmental delegations sitting in the Sixth Committee of the General Assembly, swerved the trend towards the codification of the prevention obligation in question in relative terms as one of **due diligence**. Namely, as an obligation for states through their competent authorities to take all the appropriate measures – proportionate to the administrative, scientific and financial capacity of the state in question – to prevent transboundary harm being caused by activities carried out on the state's territory.

The rules articulating the no-harm principle in question as one of due diligence has eventually been codified by the ILC in the 2001 *Draft Articles on Prevention of Significant Transboundary Harm from Hazardous Activities*,[27] as also endorsed by the General Assembly in 2001 and 2006.[28]

Clearly, the occurrence of transboundary harm in combination with evidence of significant lack of care would fall within the legal framework of state responsibility for omission in breach of an international obligation of prevention (of due diligence), in terms illustrated previously. The question remains as to which legal regime should apply when transboundary harm occurs in the absence of conduct in breach of the international obligation for the state authorities to adopt all the appropriate preventive measures.

State liability comes into play as complementary to the general

[27] (2001) II(2) Yearbook of the International Law Commission 148.

[28] See UN General Assembly, Res 56/82 of 12 December 2001 and Res 61/36 of 8 December 2006.

no-harm rule (couched as a due diligence obligation of prevention), precisely when harm occurs despite all the appropriate preventive measures having been taken. It consists of a set of new primary obligations, set in motion by the occurrence of harm, which, themselves, are of a due diligence nature. Such obligations require the adoption of appropriate measures to eliminate, when possible, or to mitigate the harm, individually and in consultation with the affected state. Such a legal regime may involve forms of compensation to be negotiated by the states involved, usually falling short of the full reparation required as a consequence of an internationally wrongful act under the law of state responsibility. These rules and principles have also been codified by the ILC in the 2006 *Draft Principles on the Allocation of Loss in the Case of Transboundary Harm arising out of Hazardous Activities*[29] commended to the UN Member states by the General Assembly in 2006.[30]

One is to note that only a relatively low number of disputes have been brought at the interstate level over transboundary harm involving personal injuries and damage to property. This is so even if the international rules on state liability and state responsibility provide solid legal ground for the judicial or negotiated settlement of disputes of the kind in question. Practice shows a prevailing trend towards the **internalisation of liability for transboundary damage**, focusing on the position before domestic courts of the private operators from whose activity the damage has occurred.

First, this trend avoids the uncertainty of leaving the possibility of gaining a remedy – for the individual and corporate victims – at the hands of the inherently discretionary **diplomatic protection** of the state where the harm was suffered. Second, even when the state of nationality of the victims of transboundary harm is willing to invoke the international responsibility, or liability, of the origin state on behalf of its nationals, this may not necessarily lead to a judicial

---

[29] (2006) II(2) Yearbook of the International Law Commission 59.

[30] See UN General Assembly Res 61/36 of 8 December 2006.

assessment of the case, since the jurisdiction of the ICJ, as well as that of any international arbitral tribunal, is not compulsory.[31]

The chances of diplomatic settlement, particularly over the amount of compensation are also uncertain. This point prompts a third consideration in favour of leaving the interstate mechanisms for the settlement of disputes over transboundary harm subservient to the vindication of the civil liability of the private operators in question before domestic courts. Namely, one of economic justice within the origin state, which would otherwise have to pay compensation out of the public budget for damage caused by a private operator arising from its profit-making activity. In this case, the state and its taxpayers would be covering the commercial risks of both national and foreign investors. Such considerations underlie the rationale of Principle 13 of the *Rio Declaration* adopted at the end of the landmark 1992 UN Conference on Environment and Development:

> 'States shall develop national law regarding liability and compensation for the victims of pollution and other environmental damage. States shall also cooperate in an expeditious and more determined manner to develop further international law regarding liability and compensation for adverse effects of environmental damage caused by activities within their jurisdiction or control to areas beyond their jurisdiction.'[32]

Further reading

Cannizzaro E, 'On the Special Consequences of a Serious Breach of Obligations Arising Out of Peremptory Rules of International Law' in Id (ed), *The Present and Future of* Jus Cogens (Sapienza Università Editrice 2015), 133ff,

---

[31] See Chapter 7.

[32] UN Conference on Environment and Development, 'Rio Declaration on Environment and Development' (1992) 4 ILM 874, 876.

Crawford J, *State Responsibility: The General Part* (CUP 2013);

Crawford J and Olleson S, 'The Character and Forms of International Responsibility' in M Evans (ed), *International Law* (5th edn, OUP 2018), 415ff;

Crawford J et al (eds), *The Law of International Responsibility* (OUP 2010);

Creutz K, State *Responsibility in the International Legal Order* (CUP 2020);

Dominicé C, 'The Responsibility of States for Breaches of Multilateral Obligations' (1999) 10 European Journal of International Law 353;

Galvão Teles P and Bodeau-Livinec P (eds), *The Articles on Responsibility of States for Internationally Wrongful Acts: A Commentary* (OUP forthcoming);

Gattini A, 'Breach of International Obligations' in A Nollkaemper and I Plakokefalos (eds), *Principles of Shared Responsibility in International Law: An Appraisal of the State of the Art* (CUP 2014), 25ff;

Jiménez de Aréchaga E and Tanzi A, 'International State Responsibility' in M Bedjaoui (ed), *International Law: Achievement and Prospects* (Martinus Nijhoff Publishers 1991), 347ff;

Kurtz J, 'Delineating Primary and Secondary Rules on Necessity in International Law' in T Broude and Y Shany (eds), *Multi-Sourced Equivalent Norms in International Law* (Hart Publishing 2011), 231ff;

Paddeu FI, 'Circumstances Precluding Wrongfulness' in A Peters (ed), *Max Planck Encyclopaedia of Public International Law* (online edn, OUP 2014);

Scalese G, *La rilevanza delle scusanti nella teoria dell'illecito internazionale* (Editoriale Scientifica 2008);

Tams CJ, 'Identifying Obligations *Erga Omnes*' in Id, *Enforcing Obligations* Erga Omnes *in International Law* (CUP 2009), 117ff;

Tanzi A, *Introduzione al diritto internazionale contemporaneo* (7th edn, CEDAM 2022);

Tanzi A, 'Is Damage a Distinct Condition for the Existence of an Internationally Wrongful Act?' in B Simma and M Spinedi (eds), *United Nations Codification of State Responsibility* (Oceana 1987), 3ff;

Tanzi A, 'Liability for Lawful Acts' in A Peters (ed), *Max Planck Encyclopaedia of Public International Law* (online edn, OUP 2021);

Tanzi A, 'Restitution' in A Peters (ed), *Max Planck Encyclopaedia of Public International Law* (online edn, OUP 2021).

Chapter 6

The international means of dispute settlement

1. Introduction

Article 2(3) of the *UN Charter* provides that '[all Members] shall settle their international disputes by *peaceful* means in such a manner that international peace and security, and justice, are not endangered.' [1] Chapter VI of the *UN Charter* is entitled 'Pacific Settlement of Disputes.' [2]

Nowadays, the qualification that the international means of dispute settlement must be *peaceful* or *pacific* may appear obvious. However, this qualification must be appreciated in light of the fact that, until the first part of the 20th century, the use, or threat, of force in inter-state relations – also called ***gunboat diplomacy*** – has constituted a lawful means of dispute settlement for centuries. That freedom lasted until it became objected to by an increasing number of states, particularly those that were more frequently under the threat or the use of force – such as the Latin American countries, also supported by the US for geopolitical reasons –, and certainly after the combined horrors of the First and the Second World War.

This state of affairs was epitomised by the naval blockade imposed by the UK, Germany and Italy on Venezuela between 1902 and 1903 for the recovery of credit from unpaid public bonds and for the payment of compensation for the damages incurred by their nationals during the civil war in Venezuela (1859-1863). This episode deserves attention also in consideration of its impact on the gradual change of the law, eventually leading to the outright ban on the use of force in international relations. In fact, that crisis

---

[1] Emphasis added.

[2] Emphasis added.

prompted the convening of the Second Hague Peace Conference in 1907, which was promoted by the then US President Theodore Roosevelt.

For the purposes of the present Chapter, it is worth emphasising how the Second Hague Conference, *inter alia*, expanded the 1899 *Hague Convention for the Pacific Settlement of International Disputes*, whilst marking the adoption of the *Convention Respecting the Limitation of the Employment of Force for Recovery of Contract Debts*.

That accounts for the *UN Charter* provisions on dispute settlement quoted above being ancillary to the ban on the use of force under Article 2(4).[3] Consequently, under Article 33(1) of the *UN Charter*:

> 'The parties to any dispute, the continuance of which is likely to endanger the maintenance of international peace and security, shall, first of all, seek a solution by negotiation, enquiry, mediation, conciliation, judicial settlement, resort to regional agencies or arrangements, or other special means of their own choice, resort to regional agencies or arrangements, or other peaceful means of their own choice.'

The above obligation for the disputing parties to pursue the settlement of their disputes *peacefully*, that is through one of the means listed above is generally recognised to be part of international customary law. It has been authoritatively restated and developed by the General Assembly, first, through the 1970 *Declaration on Principles of international Law concerning Friendly Relations and Co-operation among States*,[4] and, second, through the

---

[3] Which reads as follows: 'All Members shall refrain in their international relations from the threat or use of force against the territorial integrity or political independence of any state, or in any other manner inconsistent with the Purposes of the United Nations.'

[4] UN General Assembly, Res 2625(XXV) of 24 October 1970.

1982 *Manila Declaration on the Peaceful Declaration of International Disputes*.[5]

Because good faith is the governing principle in this matter – like in most, if not all, areas of international law – the disputing parties are under an obligation to genuinely pursue the peaceful settlement of a dispute. Additionally, if a first attempt to agree on one of the available means of peaceful dispute settlement ends in failure, the obligation remains to continue to seek a peaceful resolution of the dispute avoiding its aggravation.

The present Chapter will first set out the constituent elements of an international dispute from a legal standpoint. Second, it will illustrate the diplomatic means of dispute settlement listed under Article 33(1) of the *UN Charter*, with special emphasis on the overarching role of negotiation. Third, adjudication will be explained stressing its increasingly complementary relation to negotiation. Lastly, the slow trends towards the institutionalisation of management of breaches of the international obligations for the protection of collective interests introduced after the end of the Second World War will be discussed.

2. The existence of a legal dispute

Under public international law, an **international legal dispute** is one between states (or states and intergovernmental organisations) governed by international law. This obvious statement is not to be taken for granted. As already alluded, states may engage in a dispute about their commercial rights governed by the **municipal law** of one of them, or of a third state if they choose so, either before a domestic court or an international arbitration tribunal.

Human rights disputes – between individuals and states before international human rights courts –, as well as those between pri-

[5] UN General Assembly, Res 37/10 of 15 November 1982.

vate investors and the state in which the investment was made, pertain to special bodies of public international law as described in Chapter 7.

There is no codified definition of the concept of international dispute. However, because the existence of a 'legal dispute' is a **jurisdictional requirement** for international courts and tribunals to entertain their jurisdiction over a given dispute, international case-law offers a significant number of authoritative statements that are useful in determining the existence of an international legal dispute and its constituent elements.

The first landmark judicial statement on the point in hand is to be found in the decision of the PCIJ, the predecessor to the ICJ, rendered in 1924 in the *Mavrommatis Palestine Concessions* case, between Greece and the UK, where the PCIJ plainly stated that '[a] dispute is a disagreement on a point of law or fact, a conflict of legal views or of interests between two persons.'[6] This oft-quoted passage requires some qualifications, corroborated by subsequent case-law.

First, for the purposes of a public international law dispute, as anticipated, the two disputing 'persons' or 'legal persons' are in principle states and international organisations. Furthermore, the above quoted passage may seem to identify the individual elements of a dispute as if each of them could be sufficient to constitute an international dispute on their own, whereas they are to be considered cumulatively.

Indeed, a shear 'conflict of legal views,' or a mere 'conflict of interests,' is not **on its own** sufficient for there to be a 'legal dispute.' There may very often be conflicts of interests between states, or states may have different legal views on matters of mutual interest, fortunately, without this implying the existence of a dispute between them.

---

[6] *The Mavrommatis Palestine Concessions* (Greece v Great Britain) (Judgment) [1924] PCIJ Series A/No 2, 11.

The ICJ, in its first judgment in the *South West Africa* cases, in 1962, had to decide, *inter alia*, whether there existed a legal dispute between Ethiopia and Liberia against South Africa as a requirement for its jurisdictional competence over the case. The ICJ stressed that, for there to be a dispute, 'it [is not] adequate to show that the interests of the two parties to such a case are in conflict. It must be shown that the claim of one party is positively opposed by the other.' [7]

In line with the latter statement, in the judgment rendered in 2005 between Germany and Liechtenstein (so-called *Certain Property* case), the ICJ noted that the 'complaints of fact and law formulated by Liechtenstein against Germany [we]re denied by the latter' in order to conclude that '[b]y virtue of this denial, there is a legal dispute' between Liechtenstein and Germany.' [8]

One may wonder what consequences are to be drawn from lack of objection, or denial, in response to a prior claim, or protest. Namely, whether **opposition** as a requirement for the existence of a dispute must be express, such that lack of response were to be taken as an expression of **acquiescence**. The short answer is no. Otherwise, any state could set at naught the general obligation to make a good faith attempt at amicable, *i.e.* negotiated, settlement of a dispute once arisen. International case-law has consistently maintained that 'the existence of a dispute may be inferred from the failure of a State to respond to a claim in circumstances where a response is called for.' [9]

In sum, two elements, or sets of elements, appear to be required for there to be an international legal dispute. First, a **disagreement**

---

[7] *South West Africa* (Ethiopia v South Africa) (Liberia v South Africa) (Preliminary Objections) (Judgment) [1962] ICJ Rep 319, 328.

[8] *Certain Property* (Liechtenstein v Germany) (Preliminary Objections) (Judgment) [2005] ICJ Rep 6, 18.

[9] *Application of the International Convention on the Elimination of All Forms of Racial Discrimination* (Georgia v Russian Federation) (Preliminary Objections) (Judgment) [2011] ICJ Rep 70, 84.

which must be based on **a claim** by a state that another state has breached, or is breaching, an international obligation owed to the former state. Second, such claim must be **opposed, or resisted**, by the latter state.

Usually, opposition or resistance are expressed through diplomatic exchanges (*notes verbales*), basically denying the charges, or may be inferred from a lack of response. Having regard to claims, or protests, against alleged continuing breaches, resistance can be inferred from a lack of response and/or continuation of the conduct complained of.

Now, the disagreement may be about the existence or the interpretation of the contents of the **legal obligation** claimed to have been breached and its relevance to the facts of the case, or whether a certain circumstance precluded wrongfulness. Also, disagreement may be about the actual occurrence and contours of the **conduct** alleged to have been committed and claimed to be in breach of the obligation in question. In the first case, the dispute would be on a **question of law** while, in the second, it would be on a **question of fact**. Under either such circumstances, a **legal dispute** would equally be considered to have arisen, also taking into account that the legal and factual elements of disputes are often difficult to separate, if only because the disputed issues of interpretation of a rule inevitably arise in relation to factual situations. That is to say that, with respect to any given dispute, there is no neat dividing line between **law** and **facts**, nor between **interpretation** and **application of law**.

The fact that a given legal dispute has political aspects to it, or that it is part of a wider **political dispute**, does not affect its existence as a legal dispute as such. As famously observed by the ICJ:

> 'The fact that [a] question also has political aspects, as, in the nature of things, is the case with so many questions which arise in international life, does not suffice to deprive it of its character as a 'legal question.' [10]

---

[10] *Legality of the Threat or Use of Nuclear Weapons* (Advisory Opinion)

This is an important point for jurisdictional purposes, since international courts and tribunals are only competent to decide legal disputes, but it is also important from a political standpoint in order to facilitate the settlement of political disputes. Since political disputes are often complex – as they are made up of various disputed aspects, including technical legal ones –, the decoupling of singular disputed issues from the wider political conflict may increase the chances of settlement of such individual disputes separately. This approach would reduce the overall political tension between the countries involved, or **depoliticize the dispute**. Be that as it may, such a piecemeal approach would often benefit specific constituencies which are less involved than central Governments in the political dimension of the conflict in question.

The often-composite character of inter-state disputes accounts for the fact that different means of dispute settlement may be cumulatively applied to the same dispute, including with regard to diplomatic and adjudicative means.

A legal dispute has been defined above as one arising from a claim combined with an objection to it which pertains to an alleged breach of a legal obligation and hence, of the corresponding right. This suggests that the means of dispute settlement are normally geared towards the pursuit of **reparative justice** based on restitution or compensation. However, practice shows that, when it comes to disputes over the allocation of shared natural resources, such as transboundary water or oil fields, or about territorial or maritime boundaries, the parties tend to pursue **distributive justice** through declaratory statements and/or terms of reference for the negotiation of an agreement.

It is to be stressed also that the latter category of disputes is about rights or, rather, the **allocation of rights**. Usually such dis-

---

[1996] ICJ Rep 226, 234. The ICJ was here referring to the possibility of giving an advisory opinion on a 'legal question' with clear political implications, but the principle also applies to the exercise of its contentious jurisdiction when solving 'legal disputes.'

putes also involve, at the same time, breaches of law, in which case the appropriate means of settlement would pursue **both** distributive and reparative justice. If, for instance, a state issues a permit for exploitation in an area which is not subject to its jurisdiction, inevitably, it infringes the rights inherent in the exclusive territorial sovereignty of another state. The same would occur if a state allowed water works on its territory that significantly reduced the flow of water to which a co-riparian were entitled. In such cases, dispute settlement should be geared towards the delimitation of the boundaries involving the disputed area, as well as the cessation of, or compensation for, the exploitation of natural resources subject to the jurisdiction of another state.

As already alluded, a dispute may arise exclusively over the entitlement of a right, without any such right having been (yet) infringed upon. In such a case, the settlement of the dispute through an agreement about the allocation of the rights involved would, at the same time, serve the purpose of **dispute prevention** concerning potential breaches of the same rights.

3. Diplomatic means of dispute settlement

Negotiation is the principal diplomatic means of dispute settlement amongst those set out in Article 33(1) of the *UN Charter*, and it is overarching with respect to all of them. On the one hand, good offices, mediation, enquiry and conciliation are all geared towards facilitation of a **negotiated settlement** of a dispute. The same can be said of adjudication, especially when the dispute in question is of a kind requiring the application of distributive justice. We will return to this point when dealing with adjudication in the following Section.

On the other hand, negotiation is also necessary in order to agree to set in place any other means of dispute settlement – *e.g.*, a special agreement, or *compromise*, to submit a dispute to adjudication or arbitration – except for the rare cases in which third-party involvement is compulsory under some form of consent given before the dispute has arisen.

Negotiations over the choice and operation of a third-party mechanism is not to be confused with negotiations over the merits of the dispute in question. However, as stressed by the arbitration tribunal in the 2015 decision on jurisdiction in the *Philippines v China* case, 'diplomatic communications and exchanges do not divide neatly between procedural and substantive matters,' adding that:

> 'With rare exceptions, States in the midst of a pressing dispute will not separate their communications between the two. Correspondence elaborating the Parties' views on the substantive matters between them may well shed a great deal of light on their respective views on how the dispute may – or may not – be settled. Proposals on the mode of settlement will necessarily involve some discussion of substance.' [11]

Even though we have emphasised that basically all methods of international dispute settlement aim to facilitate negotiations, it is worth recalling that negotiations constitute a means for the settlement of disputes and **not a goal in themselves**. The main goal of diplomatic means of settlement is the **agreement** between the disputing parties over the object of the dispute. When this cannot be achieved because the positions of the disputing parties remain far apart, the fall-back aim of negotiations is the reaching of an agreement over the choice of a third-party means of dispute settlement.

Reverting to the general obligation to negotiate on the merits of a dispute before resorting to adjudication, when available, this does not imply an obligation to reach agreement, but only to pursue it in good faith. As stated by the ICJ *North Sea Continental Shelf* case

---

[11] *The South China Sea Arbitration* (The Republic of Philippines v The People's Republic of China) (Jurisdiction and Admissibility) (Award) [2015] PCA Case No 2013-19, 115.

between the Federal Republic of Germany against The Netherlands and Denmark:

> 'The Parties are under an obligation to enter into negotiations with a view to arriving at an agreement, and not merely to go through a formal process of negotiation (...); they are under an obligation so to conduct themselves that the negotiations are meaningful, which will not be the case when either of them insists upon its own position without contemplating any modification of it.' [12]

Good offices consist of the involvement of a third party trying simply to **promote communication** and diplomatic exchanges between the disputing parties on the subject-matter of the dispute, without any direct involvement over the **contents** of the communications. The latter would be the case with **mediation**. Mediators usually present each party's proposal to the other, highlighting the elements of common ground between the differing stands of the disputing parties, obviously when possible. The mediator may even advance proposals to each party, adjusting such proposals according to the initial reaction by the parties.

Sometimes, the role of the third party may initially be confined to good offices and later evolve into mediation, if the third party increasingly gains the **trust** of both disputing parties. Good offices and mediation may be performed **by an individual**, such as a highly-respected statesman, or a **state**, or even an **institution**.

An instance of **good offices** can be found in the role played through the 1980s by King Fahd Ben Abdul Aziz of Saudi Arabia in a dispute between Qatar and Bahrain over maritime and territorial conflicting claims. His role was confined to convening and hosting meetings between the parties. After years of negotiations on the merits of the case, to no avail, in 1991 the dispute was submitted by Qatar to the ICJ based on the minutes of a meeting between the

---

[12] *North Sea Continental Shelf* (Federal Republic of Germany v The Netherlands and Denmark) (Judgment) [1969] ICJ Rep 42, 47.

three parties mentioning referral to the Court. The ICJ affirmed its jurisdiction over the case in a judgment of 1994,[13] deciding on the merits in 2001.[14]

The Government of Algeria brokered an articulated agreement between Iran and the US in connection with a major crisis between the two countries, initially under the framework of good offices and later as a mediator. At the end of the Khomeini Revolution – which ousted the then US supported Persian Shah Reza Pahlavi –, in 1979 Iranian student-militants seized US diplomatic and consular premises in Teheran, holding hostage some fifty US diplomats for more than one year. This blatant breach of international law was aimed at pressuring the US into returning the former Shah's family and their financial assets (which had been transferred to the US) to the new Iranian Government.

The **mediation** by the Government of Algeria was crowned with success. Namely, the conclusion of the *Algiers Agreement* that put the dispute to an end in 1981. The terms of the Agreement provided that: *a*) Iran would set the US diplomats free; *b*) the US would abstain from interfering with Iranian domestic, political and military affairs, lift the trade sanctions against Iran and the freeze of Iranian assets in US banks; *c*) the US would allow the recovery of the property of the former Shah through civil suits in the US, removing any procedural shield based on immunity from jurisdiction and execution; and *d*) Iran would pay US agencies outstanding debts.

Another important term of the Agreement (*e*)) provided that the lawsuits pending in both countries between the two Governments, as well as those instituted by their respective nationals against the other Government for contract and expropriation claims, were ended and referred to international arbitration. To that end, the **Iran-**

---

[13] *Maritime Delimitation and Territorial Questions between Qatar and Bahrain* (Qatar v Bahrain) (Preliminary Objections) (Judgment) [1994] ICJ Rep 112.

[14] *Maritime Delimitation and Territorial Questions between Qatar and Bahrain* (Qatar v Bahrain) (Judgment) [2001] ICJ Rep 40.

US Claims Tribunal was established in The Hague, backed by a billion-dollar escrow account in the Central Bank of England. As of today, whilst all private claims (nearly 5,000) have been decided by the Claims Tribunal, few intergovernmental claims are still pending before it.

When the alleged facts at the origin of a dispute are characterised by technical aspects – be them chemical, ballistic, engineering, hydrological, naval, etc. – a commission of **inquiry**, possibly composed of experts, may clarify the terms of the dispute to the political level of the disputing parties, therefore easing the task of reaching a negotiated settlement of the dispute.

Whilst the setting up of inquiry commissions, like with any third-party mechanism, is usually based on the agreement of the disputing parties after a certain dispute has arisen, multilateral conventions may provide for its establishment for future disputes arising out of the interpretation and application of the same convention. Similar formulas are usually set out in optional terms. The outcomes of an inquiry, or of fact-finding procedures, are generally non-binding, but they inevitably represent **authoritative terms of reference** for the future negotiations of the parties aimed to the settlement of the dispute. The agreement establishing the inquiry, or fact-finding, commission may also provide for the binding character of the findings of the commission.

The **PCA** in The Hague, or in the countries with which it has entered into *Host Country Agreements*, may provide administrative and logistic support to a commission of inquiry. This was the case with the so-called ''Red Crusader' Incident,' which involved a British vessel that was arrested within the waters of the Faroe Islands (Denmark). The inquiry commission was created by agreement on 15 November 1961, and rendered its decision a few months later, on 23 March 1962. [15] In 1997, the PCA updated its rules in this field

[15] See XH Oyarce, 'Red Crusader Incident (1961)' in A Peters (ed), *Max Planck Encyclopaedia of Public International Law* (online edn, OUP 2007).

with the adoption of the *Optional Rules for Fact-Finding Commissions of Inquiry* offered to states that may want to adopt and/or adjust to any given dispute by agreement with the other disputing party, or parties.

Conciliation replicates some characteristic features of inquiry, to the effect that it is usually entrusted by agreement by the disputing parties – hence, on a **non-compulsory basis** –, to a commission whose outcomes are generally **non-binding**. The additional value of conciliation with respect to an inquiry is that the competence of a conciliation commission is not confined to the factual or technical assessment of the circumstances of the case, but can also address the **legal arguments** advanced by the disputing parties.

Here, again, the PCA makes available to the disputing parties its bureau for the efficient administration of the procedure and offers its *Optional Conciliation Rules*, in general, and, more specifically, the *Optional Rules for Conciliation of Disputes Relating to Natural Resources and/or the Environment*. Both sets of rules are inspired by the UNCITRAL *Conciliation Rules*.

Another set of rules on conciliation is provided under Annex V of the UNCLOS. These rules have been applied in the dispute over maritime boundaries between Timor-Leste and Australia before a conciliation commission established under the auspices of the PCA.[16] The conciliation process was conducted in consultation with the parties, who appeared committed to follow the indication gradually emerging from the commission towards a newly agreed maritime boundary, that would supersede a previous agreement on the matter.

[16] *Timor Sea Conciliation* (Timor-Leste v Australia) (Report and Recommendations of the Compulsory Conciliation Commission) [2018] PCA Case No 2016-10.

4. Adjudicative means

The picture of the low confidence in international justice until the late 1970s, with special regard to little, or no resort to the ICJ by disputing states, was depicted with his usual witty eloquence by Sir Christopher Greenwood – former Judge of the ICJ, a former Professor of international law, experienced international law practitioner and currently one of the nine members of the above-mentioned Iran-US Claims Tribunal in The Hague – at a conference he gave in 2020 at Middle Temple, provocatively entitled *The Highways, Byways and Dark Alleys of International Law*, as follows:

> 'At the time that I was Called to the Bar, public international law scarcely seemed a promising field for practice. The clerk in my first chambers told me that it might bring in a case every four or five years but that I was better off focusing on personal injury. The International Court of Justice could scarcely have been described as busy in those years. In 1977-78, it had one case on its books which it did not have jurisdiction to hear. When I became a judge of the International Court 30 years later, my office contained a handsome bound set of the Court's reports. The volume for 1977 contained only four pages; two pages in English and two pages in French on the same point. The inside cover of the volume stated rather sadly that "this volume contains neither an index nor a table of contents". Underneath, someone had written in pencil 'nor anything else!' [17]

As pointed out in the same speech, however, since then the picture has soon changed, and most significantly as of the 1980s. Suffice to recall that, since the beginning of the life of the ICJ, in 1947, to date, 181 cases have been brought before it. [18]

---

[17] C Greenwood, 'The Highways, Byways and Dark Alleys of International Law' in *The Honourable Society of the Middle Temple* (October 2020), available at: <www.middletemplar.org.uk>.

[18] The full list is available at: <www.icj-cij.org/en/list-of-all-cases>.

It is noteworthy that, amongst the most recent cases initiated before the ICJ, features the Ukrainian application filed on 27 February 2022 in which Ukraine sued Russia under the 1948 *Genocide Convention*, arguing that the latter has 'abused' this legal instrument when grounding its military aggression on allegations of genocide being carried out against Russian minorities in Eastern Ukraine.[19] It should also be recalled here[20] that, on 13 July 2022, a *Joint statement on supporting Ukraine's ICJ proceedings* was made by 43 states, plus the EU, also stating their intention to avail themselves of the right, under Article 63 of the *ICJ Statute*, to intervene in the proceedings, so as to provide their interpretation of the *Genocide Convention.*[21]

In international law the distinction is often made between **adjudication** and **arbitration**. **Adjudication** is performed by pre-established permanent adjudicative bodies, the principal international judicial body being the ICJ established in 1945 under its Statute which is an integral part of the *UN Charter*. More recently, in 1996, the ITLOS was established under UNCLOS.

International human rights courts of a regional nature will be addressed separately in connection with an overview of human rights law in Chapter 7. The same applies to international criminal tribunals and the ICC, as they do not address inter-state disputes, but are

---

[19] *Allegations of Genocide under the Convention on the Prevention and Punishment of the Crime of Genocide* (Ukraine v Russian Federation) (Application Instituting Proceedings) [2022], 8.

[20] See also Chapter 1, Section 5.

[21] The statement was made by Albania, Andorra, Australia, Austria, Belgium, Bulgaria, Canada, Croatia, Cyprus, Czech Republic, Denmark, Estonia, Finland, France, Germany, Greece, Iceland, Ireland, Italy, Japan, Latvia, Lithuania, Luxembourg, Malta, Marshall Islands, Moldova, Monaco, Montenegro, Netherlands, New Zealand, North Macedonia, Norway, Palau, Poland, Portugal, Romania, San Marino, Slovakia, Slovenia, Spain, Sweden, the UK, the US and the EU. The statement is available on the webpage of the UK Government (<www.gov.uk>).

there to try individuals accused of international crimes. Investor-state arbitration also deserves separate treatment in connection with international investment law.

Arbitration is performed by *ad hoc* arbitration tribunals established either by agreement – so-called *compromis* – between the disputing parties after a dispute has arisen, or on the basis of an arbitration clause contained in a treaty with regard to disputes that may arise on the interpretation and application of the treaty in question. In this respect, international inter-state arbitration faithfully reflects arbitration as we know it in national jurisdictions, with the only difference that the former is established by international agreements instead of contracts and the arbitral tribunals so established are competent to decide inter-state disputes and not those between individuals or companies.

A recent inter-state arbitration, which has made the headlines, is the *Enrica Lexie* arbitration between Italy and India.[22] The case, decided in 2020, was triggered by Italy over the arrest and detention of two Italian marines accused of killing two Indian fishermen from aboard the 'Enrica Lexie,' a tanker flying the Italian flag, where they were conducting what appeared to be an anti-piracy operation.

Resort to arbitration in this case – which ended with the arbitration tribunal finding that the Italian judiciary had jurisdiction to try the accused marines – led to the **depoliticization** of a kind of dispute which, like many inter-state disputes, cannot be compromised, since domestic popular opinion would not lightly accept any bit of concession, something inevitable when settling a dispute by agreement.

In public international law, the distinction between arbitration and adjudication is less sharp than in domestic jurisdictions, since **international adjudication** as administered by permanent courts

---

[22] *The 'Enrica Lexie' Incident* (Italy v India) (Award) [2020] PCA Case No 2015-28.

and tribunals like the ICJ and ITLOS, is largely **arbitral in nature**. That flows from the fact that the jurisdiction of international courts and tribunals is based **on the consent** of the disputing parties.

That is to say that, a state that has been sued before the ICJ would not be bound by its jurisdiction, thus, by its decision – otherwise legally binding on the parties of a dispute – unless it has consented to its jurisdictional competence over a certain case by a **jurisdictional clause** in a treaty (also called *compromissory clause*), or by a separate agreement. A special means of expression of consent to the jurisdiction of the ICJ is provided for under **Article 36(2) of the *ICJ Statute***. It reads as follows:

> 'The states parties to the present Statute may at any time declare that they recognize as compulsory ipso facto and without special agreement, in relation to any other state accepting the same obligation, the jurisdiction of the Court in all legal disputes concerning:
> *a*) the interpretation of a treaty;
> *b*) any question of international law;
> *c*) the existence of any fact which, if established, would constitute a breach of an international obligation;
> *d*) the nature or extent of the reparation to be made for the breach of an international obligation.'

As indicated in the above provision, the legal effect of declarations of the kind in question is subject to reciprocity. That is to say that a state which has issued a declaration would be bound by the ICJ's jurisdiction only when sued by a state which, in turn, had previously made a similar declaration. By way of example, the UK revised its declaration of acceptance of 2017 as follows:

> '1) The Government of the United Kingdom of Great Britain and Northern Ireland accepts as compulsory ipso facto and without special convention, on condition of reciprocity, the jurisdiction of the International Court of Justice, ln conformity with paragraph 2 of Article 36 of the Statute of the Court, until such time as notice may be given to terminate the acceptance, over all disputes arising after

1 January 1987, with regard to situations or facts subsequent to the same date, other than:
i) any dispute which the United Kingdom has agreed with the other Party or Parties thereto to settle by some other method of peaceful settlement;
ii) any dispute with the Government of any other country which is or has been a Member of the Commonwealth;
iii) any dispute in respect of which any other Party to the dispute has accepted the compulsory jurisdiction of the International Court of Justice only in relation to or for the purpose of the dispute; or where the acceptance of the Court's compulsory jurisdiction on behalf of any other Party to the dispute was deposited or ratified less than twelve months prior to the filing of the application bringing the dispute before the Court;
iv) any claim or dispute which is substantially the same as a claim or dispute previously submitted to the Court by the same or another Party;
v) any claim or dispute in respect of which the claim or dispute in question has not been notified to the United Kingdom by the State or States concerned in writing, including of an Intention to submit the claim or dispute to the Court failing an amicable settlement, at least six months in advance of the submission of the claim or dispute to the Court;
vi) any claim or dispute that arises from or is connected with or related to nuclear disarmament and/or nuclear weapons, unless all of the other nuclear-weapon States Party to the Treaty on the Non-Proliferation of Nuclear Weapons have also consented to the jurisdiction of the Court and are party to the proceedings in question.
2) The Government of the United Kingdom also reserves the right at any time, by means of a notification addressed to the Secretary-General of the United Nations, and with effect as from the moment of such notification, either to add to, amend or withdraw any of the foregoing reservations, or any that may hereafter be added.'

As it emerges from this declaration of acceptance, each state may make a declaration that covers a different scope of potential disputes with respect to which it accepts the jurisdiction of the ICJ.

Therefore, a state will be bound by the jurisdiction of the ICJ under its declaration only with regard to issues which have not been excluded by it and by that of the other disputing party or parties.

There are currently about 70 such declarations in force. Italy has filed its declaration in November 2014, whereas the US withdrew theirs in 1985, after the ICJ decided to uphold its jurisdiction over a case brought by Nicaragua that the US argued would fall outside the scope of the ICJ's jurisdiction.[23] That does not mean that the US cannot be a party in international litigation before the ICJ, as it has often happened, under compromissory clauses in international treaties.

The **UNCLOS** peculiarly provides for a form of **compulsory jurisdiction by default** in the sense that, under Article 287(1), its parties are free to choose to settle their disputes over its application, either before the ITLOS, the ICJ, or different forms of arbitration, but, if a party makes no such choice, it will be considered to be bound by arbitration under Annex VII of the UNCLOS. That was the ground upon which Italy started the *Enrica Lexie* arbitration with India, mentioned above.

The **rules and principles governing international proceedings** make up a highly specialised field of international law. For the purposes of the present treatise, it will suffice to briefly address a few policy considerations emphasising the often **integrated relationship between adjudicative and non-adjudicative means of dispute settlement**. Such an integrated approach is possible *a*) when the legal dispute in question is part of a wider complex dispute, and/or *b*) when such a dispute requires, partly, or exclusively, the application of rules pertaining to distributive justice, such as resources allocation or boundaries delimitations.

As to legal disputes of the kind under *a*), it is worth recalling that the ICJ, when seized by the US against Iran in the middle of the al-

---

[23] That case being *Military and Paramilitary Activities in and against Nicaragua* (Nicaragua v United States of America) (Preliminary Objections) (Judgment) [1984] ICJ Rep 392.

ready recalled hostages crisis during the Islamic Revolution of 1979,[24] stressed that:

> 'It is for the Court, the principal judicial organ of the United Nations, to resolve the legal questions that may be in issue between parties to a dispute; and the resolution of such legal questions by the Court may be an important, and sometime decisive, factor in promoting the peaceful settlement of the dispute.'[25]

The complementary relationship between the adjudicative and diplomatic means of dispute settlement has been stressed further by the ICJ in the *Military and Paramilitary Activities* case between Nicaragua and the US, as follows:

> '[T]he Court is of the view that the fact that a matter is before the Security Council should not prevent it being dealt with by the Court and that both proceedings could be pursued *pari passu*. (…) The Council has functions of a political nature assigned to it, whereas the Court exercises purely judicial functions. Both organs can therefore perform their separate but complementary functions with respect to the same events.'[26]

This *pari passu* approach between adjudication and mediation has been successfully pursued in exemplary terms on the occasion of the US-Iran dispute leading to the *Algiers Agreement* illustrated in the previous Section.

As to legal disputes of the kind under *b*), recent case-law shows examples of the joint application of elements of retributive law and justice geared towards the assessment of the lawfulness (*vel non*) of the disputed conduct, together with the application of elements of distributive law and justice. This way, the adjudicative bodies in-

---

[24] See Chapter 5, Section 2.1.1 and above, Section 3.

[25] *United States Diplomatic and Consular Staff in Tehran* (United States of America v Iran) (Judgment) [1980] ICJ Rep 3, 22.

[26] *Military and Paramilitary Activities in and against Nicaragua* (n 23) 433.

volved have been, expressly or implicitly, promoting cooperation and, eventually, agreement between the disputing parties.

In that respect, it is worth recalling the ICJ judgment in the *Gabčíkovo-Nagymaros Project* case between Slovakia and Hungary over water works on the Danube River.[27] After deciding over the lawfulness, and unlawfulness, of the conduct of both disputing parties, the ICJ required them to 'find an agreed solution that takes account of the objective of the [disputed] Treaty,' which was precisely one of cooperation.[28]

Also illustrative of the point in issue here is the *Pulp Mills* case between Argentina and Uruguay over the transboundary environmental impact of two industrial plants (pulp mills) on Uruguayan territory.[29] It is worth stressing that, three months after the ICJ judgment which mostly found for Uruguay, the two disputing parties signed a MoU by which they resumed water cooperation also by means of a joint water body.

A third example is the 2013 case between India and Pakistan over the diversion on Indian territory of the Kishanganga River for hydropower purposes, initiated under the 1960 *Indus Waters Treaty* before the PCA. The final award, after deciding, *inter alia*, the minimum flow of the river to be ensured, states that:

> '[I]f, beginning seven years after the diversion of the Kishanganga (...), either Party considers that reconsideration of the Court's determination of the minimum flow is necessary, it will be entitled to seek such reconsideration through the Permanent Indus Commission and the mechanisms of the Treaty.'[30]

---

[27] *Gabčíkovo-Nagymaros Project* (Hungary/Slovakia) (Judgment) [1997] ICJ Rep 7.

[28] *Ibidem*, 78.

[29] *Pulp Mills on the River Uruguay* (Argentina v Uruguay) (Judgment) [2010] ICJ Rep 14.

[30] *Indus Waters Kishanganga Arbitration* (Pakistan v India) (Final Award) [2013] PCA Case No 2011-01, 41.

In light of the above, it is fair to say that the relationship between non-adjudicative dispute settlement and adjudication may result to be, not only one of full compatibility with one another, but also of mutual complementarity. As stated by Sir Robert Jennings, former President of the ICJ, in 1993:

> '[R]esort to an international court or to an arbitration is no longer regarded as something outside and different from the ordinary context of relations between Governments, but as a device, a tool, which can be used in the course of diplomatic negotiations.' [31]

This point has been developed most clearly by another former President of the ICJ, Stephen Schwebel, in his address to the UN General Assembly in 1998, as follows:

> 'The Court is no longer seen solely as 'the last resort' in the resolution of disputes. Rather, States may have recourse to the Court in parallel with other methods of dispute resolution, appreciating that such recourse may complement the work of the Security Council and the General Assembly, as well as bilateral negotiations (...). The result is that, in some cases, political negotiations have resumed and succeeded before the Court rendered judgement. In other cases, the Court's decision has provided the parties with legal conclusions which they may use in framing further negotiations and in achieving settlement of the dispute.' [32]

Finally, a short reference should be made to the **advisory jurisdiction** of the ICJ under the *UN Charter* (Article 96) and the *ICJ Statute* itself (Article 65). Whilst the ICJ is vested with the competence to give advisory opinions 'on any legal question,' its political relevance is, however, self-evident.

---

[31] See PCA, *First Conference of the Members of the Court, Peace Palace, The Hague, 10 and 11 September 1993* (TMC Asser 1993), 31.

[32] The full speech is available on the webpage of the ICJ at: <www.icj-cij.org>.

The advisory jurisdiction of the ICJ can be set in motion only through a highly complex multilateral diplomatic exercise consisting in the cajoling of the support, and vote, for the request to the ICJ of an advisory opinion by the majority of the Member states in the General Assembly or the Security Council. One should consider the often highly political character of the subject-matter of requests for advice. Amongst such requests, one may recall, *inter alia*, the conditions for admission to membership of the UN and the competence of the General Assembly in the matter, submitted, respectively, in 1948 and 1950,[33] *i.e.*, at the beginning of the Cold War when admission in the UN as a Member state was highly politically controversial; the status of South West Africa and the legal consequences for the continued presence of the 'white' and colonial South Africa in Namibia, respectively in 1950 and 1971,[34] at the time of a conflictual and politicised process of decolonisation; the legality of the threat or use of nuclear weapons in 1996;[35] the legality of the construction of the wall in the occupied Palestinian territory by Israel in 2004;[36] the conformity with international law of the Kosovo declaration of independence in 2008,[37] discussed above in Chapter 2, Section 2.1.1; and, very recently, the legal consequences for the continued administration of the Chagos Archipela-

---

[33] *Admission of a State to the United Nations (Charter, Art. 4)* (Advisory Opinion) [1948] ICJ Rep 57 and *Competence of Assembly regarding Admission to the United Nations* (Advisory Opinion) [1950] ICJ Rep 4.

[34] *International Status of South-West Africa* (Advisory Opinion) [1950] ICJ Rep 128 and *Legal Consequences for States of the Continued Presence of South Africa in Namibia (South West Africa) notwithstanding Security Council Resolution 276 (1970)* (Advisory Opinion) [1971] ICJ Rep 16.

[35] *Legality of the Threat or Use of Nuclear Weapons* (n 10).

[36] *Legal Consequences of the Construction of a Wall in the Occupied Palestinian Territory* (Advisory Opinion) [2004] ICJ Rep 136.

[37] *Accordance with International Law of the Unilateral Declaration of Independence in Respect of Kosovo* (Advisory Opinion) [2010] ICJ Rep 403.

go by the UK as encroaching upon the right of self-determination of its previous colonial possession, Mauritius. [38]

Whilst the ICJ's advisory opinions are, by definition, non-legally binding, they represent significantly **persuasive**, if not **authoritative**, statements. Such statements are often quoted as evidentiary of the state of the law, so that conduct in conformity, or at variance, with a given ICJ's opinion are difficult to justify in the light of the overall 'international legal discourse' on that matter.

5. Institutional means for the settlement of disputes over collective interests and emerging cases of resort to adjudication

Traditional international rules establishing bilateral legal relationships based on reciprocity allow for the identification of the state entitled to lodge a complaint and to invoke the international responsibility of the wrongdoing state, both on the diplomatic and judicial levels. According to this feature of bilateralism, which still characterises most international legal rules to this day, a breach of an international obligation by a state results in the breach of the corresponding right of another state.

The **bilateral nature of inter-state legal relations** protecting the **individual interests** of states based on reciprocity, can also stem from a general customary rule, or a **multilateral convention**. Let us take the classical rules on the inviolability of diplomatic premises, or the freedom of navigation (and commerce) on the high seas. Every state is to comply with such obligations *vis-à-vis* any other state, but the violation of such kind of international obligations gives rise to a relationship of responsibility **solely between the wrongdoing state and the individual state materially affected by the breach in**

[38] *Legal Consequences of the Separation of the Chagos Archipelago from Mauritius in 1965* (Advisory Opinion) [2019] ICJ Rep 95.

question. Namely, between the state whose public authorities have entered the premises of a foreign embassy, or have illegally seized a foreign vessel, on the one hand, and the national state of the embassy or the flag state of the vessel in question, on the other.

On the basis of the international rules on the law of state responsibility addressed above in Chapter 5, the victim states can: **first**, assess the violation of an international legal right of theirs, occurred through the infringement of the material interest protected by the legal right in question, as well as the corresponding obligation in question; and, **second**, invoke (*uti singuli*) the responsibility of the wrongdoing state.

The means of dispute settlement illustrated above were devised and applied for centuries, when international law was made up only of this kind of reciprocity-based rules. As illustrated above in Chapter 3, Section 3.1.2, in relation to treaty law, and in Chapter 5, in connection with the law of state responsibility, since the Second World War, new rules have emerged that protect **collective rights**, either of all the states parties to a multilateral treaty, or of all the members of the international community as a whole. Breaches of legal obligations of this kind may give rise to international disputes no less than violations of traditional bilateral rules. Given the collective relevance of such disputes, special means of dispute settlement are often provided for in international treaties for their identification and resolution.

As already anticipated, formally, breaching an obligation owed towards all the states parties to a treaty (*erga omnes partes*), or to the international community as a whole (just *erga omnes*), amounts to a corresponding breach of a right **of all such states**. Each and all such states are therefore entitled to invoke (*uti universi*) the responsibility of the wrongdoer and ask for reparation for the benefit of those directly affected by the breach in question.

However, there is general awareness that, according to the specific circumstances of any give case, there may often be little political interest by states not directly affected to raise the matter. Also, the violation of certain obligations of the kind in question may be difficult to be identified due to the highly technical nature of the obligations.

It is on the basis of such awareness that the international community has envisaged different mechanisms of a permanent nature for the management and settlement of disputes which complement – in some cases, supplant – the traditional bilateral inter-state forms of dispute settlement. All such mechanisms contain elements of the traditional forms of dispute settlement, individually, or in combination. They range from the role of the General Assembly, or the Security Council, to human rights courts, or compliance review mechanisms.

Before addressing the institutional mechanisms in question, mention should be made of the rather exceptional case brought by The Gambia in November 2019 against Myanmar based on allegations of acts of genocide being committed against the Rohingya Muslim minority. In the incidental proceedings triggered by a request for provisional measures by The Gambia, Myanmar objected to the standing, or *locus standi*, of the applicant in the case, since The Gambia was not specially affected by the alleged violations.[39] In its order of provisional measures handed down in January 2020, the ICJ rejected the respondent's objection to the admissibility of the application, thus asserting its *prima facie* jurisdiction in the case. In this regard, the ICJ observed as follows:

> 'In view of their shared values, all the States parties to the Genocide Convention have a common interest to ensure that acts of genocide are prevented and that, if they occur, their authors do not enjoy impunity. That common interest implies that the obligations in question are owed by any State party to all the other States parties to the Convention. (…) It follows that any State party to the Genocide Convention, and not only a specially affected State, may invoke the responsibility of another State party with a view to ascer-

---

[39] *Application of the Convention on the Prevention and Punishment of the Crime of Genocide* (The Gambia v Myanmar) (Provisional Measures) (Order) [2020] ICJ Rep 3, 16.

> taining the alleged failure to comply with its obligations *erga omnes partes*, and to bring that failure to an end.' [40]

A marked turnaround from the earlier 1966 judgments in the *South West Africa* cases, in a time when the category of *erga omnes* obligations was still in its inception. Here, as Ethiopia and Liberia argued their *locus standi* to bring a claim against South Africa to expose the implementation of the systematic practice of apartheid in what is now Namibia on the basis of 'humanitarian considerations,' the ICJ replied that:

> 'The Court does not think so. It is a court of law, and can take account of moral principles only in so far as these are given a sufficient expression in legal form. Law exists, it is said, to serve a social need; but precisely for that reason it can do so only through and within the limits of its own discipline. Otherwise, it is not a legal service that would be rendered.' [41]

5.1. *The UN*

The UN was created primarily to pursue the maintenance of international peace and security and 'to bring about by peaceful means (…) adjustment or settlement of international disputes or situations that might lead to a breach of the peace.' [42] To that end, under the already mentioned **Chapter VI of the *UN Charter*** on the pacific settlement of dispute, the General Assembly or the Security Council, either upon request by a state concerned or *motu proprio*, may make recommendations on how to settle a certain dispute. [43]

---

[40] *Ibidem*, 17.

[41] *South West Africa* (Ethiopia v South Africa) (Liberia v South Africa) (Judgment) [1966] ICJ Rep 6, 34.

[42] Article 1(1) of the *UN Charter*.

[43] Articles 33, 34 and 35 of the *UN Charter*.

As already anticipated, under **Chapter VII** on action with respect to threats to the peace, breaches of the peace or acts of aggression, the Security Council may take enforcement action, first, of a kind non-involving the use of force, such as economic sanction banning trade with the targeted state (Article 41 of the *UN Charter*),[44] and, second, if such measures do not prove effective, it may authorise the use of force against that state (Article 42 of the *UN Charter*).[45] Again, it is to be stressed that any such decision must be taken by a Security Council resolution, adopted according to a peculiar voting procedure – illustrated above, in Chapter 5, Section 2.1.2 – affording the five permanent Members with the so-called 'right of veto,' as the adoption of such resolution can be blocked upon the mere initiative of any of them.

As already alluded to, this procedural rule accounts for the fact that during the Cold War the Security Council could not do much of what it was originally envisaged to do by the *UN Charter*. This was particularly the case with the threats to international peace and security deriving from both the East-West tensions between NATO and the states parties to the *Warsaw Pact*, and the dramatic acceleration of the North-South divide with the decolonisation process, especially with respect to the wars of national liberation in the 1960s and the 1970s in Africa and Asia.

---

[44] The Security Council may decide what measures not involving the use of armed force are to be employed to give effect to its decisions, and it may call upon the Members of the United Nations to apply such measures. These may include complete or partial interruption of economic relations and of rail, sea, air, postal, telegraphic, radio, and other means of communication, and the severance of diplomatic relations.'

[45] 'Should the Security Council consider that measures provided for in Article 41 would be inadequate or have proved to be inadequate, it may take such action by air, sea, or land forces as may be necessary to maintain or restore international peace and security. Such action may include demonstrations, blockade, and other operations by air, sea, or land forces of Members of the United Nations.'

Nonetheless, during those decades the UN, through its General Assembly, has served as an important **cooling-off forum** of a number of major international tensions (in certain cases less successfully than in others) and for the restatement, review, or adjustment, of the international 'rules of the game,' with special regard to the ban on the use of force, territorial integrity, the right to self-determination, the right to development, and to the rules on international economic relations.

To that end, it is worth recalling the above-mentioned landmark General Assembly Resolution 2625(XXV) of 24 October 1970 on the *Declaration on Principles of International Law concerning Friendly Relations and Co-operation among States in accordance with the Charter of the United Nations*. This document, carefully crafted through impassioned negotiations between delegations grouped in three factions – the first, made up by the Western liberal countries, the second by the Socialist block and the third one by developing countries, who, for the large part, sided with the second – bears witness to the confidence in international law as a common language able to restate and review the then existing rules, as well as to promote co-existence and co-operation, where possible.

Nowadays, against the background of the contemporary multipolar fragmentation, a similar approach to the international rule of law appears all the more needed. However, the increasing upsurge of nationalistic unilateralism of our times does not bode well for the rule of law in the present and coming years.

A significant revitalisation of the functions of the UN Security Council as they were envisaged in the *UN Charter* characterised the years immediately following the end of the Cold War in 1989. This revival was epitomised by the unanimous reaction of the Security Council against the invasion of Kuwait by Iraq under the dictatorship of Saddam Hussein in 1990.[46] The same was with the adoption

---

[46] UN Security Council, Res 678 of 29 November 1990.

of the unanimous reaction by the delegations in the Security Council to the 2001 terrorist attack of the Twin Towers. [47]

However, even a few years before, with the differences between the NATO countries and Russia over the independence of Kosovo, the golden days for the Security Council had started to fade. The Crimean crises of 2014 has deteriorated the situation further, while the Russian aggression on Ukraine, the ensuing war and new alliances have given a very serious **blow to institutional multilateralism**, paradoxically at a time when international institutions are most needed in order to counter global threats to the international society.

5.2. *Compliance review mechanisms*

One of the factors which accounts for state conduct at variance with international rules may lie in the fact that compliance with certain international rules may require high technological, administrative or financial capacities. This is often the case with international environmental obligations laid down in MEAs. Such obligations are usually owed to the community of the states parties to the agreements in question.

Having regard to conduct allegedly in violation of such obligations, the agreements in question usually establish **compliance review mechanisms** prior to the engagement in diplomatic exchanges, where the international rules on state responsibility would be invoked by the interested states. The procedures and tasks of such mechanisms usually resonate with the basic features of traditional means of dispute settlement, ranging from inquiry to conciliation. However, they certainly go beyond such traditional means, if only because they pre-exist the dispute that the parties are supposed to address and are of a permanent character. Such mechanisms are aimed primarily at providing states parties with assistance in com-

[47] UN Security Council, Res 1368 of 12 September 2001.

plying with treaty obligations of a highly legal, administrative, scientific and technological complexity.

To that end, such mechanisms may be resorted to by the very state that encounters a difficulty with complying with a given convention ('self-trigger'), even if this occurs very rarely. They usually operate in conjunction with a **reporting system**, whereby parties are to submit periodically, every two or three years, reports about their implementation of and compliance with the convention in question. On the basis of such reports, or information gathered elsewhere, the compliance review bodies in question may act upon their own motion. Some of them, such as those established under agreements whose direct beneficiaries are individuals, may be set in motion by referrals, or communications, from the public. This is the case with the 1998 *Aarhus Convention on Access to Information, Public Participation in Decision-making and Access to Justice in Environmental Matters*, or the 1999 *London Protocol on Water and Health*, both negotiated and adopted under the auspices of the UNECE.

The mechanisms in question are conceived as primarily non-adversarial and non-confrontational in nature. However, they may also be set in motion by a party having difficulties with another party, or even in conflict with it. The treaty bodies in hand usually recommend measures to be taken by the CoP or MoP. Such measures range from technical, scientific, legal, administrative, or financial advice to the issuance of caution or, even, the suspension from certain rights under the relevant legal instrument. Generally, in the worst-case scenario, such mechanisms may lead to the adoption of social sanctions of the kind epitomised by the expression 'name and shame,' based on the exposure of the record of non-compliance of a given state.

The degree of effectiveness of such mechanisms is proportional to the degree of consideration for reputation and social control. One has the impression that, regrettably, these days' consideration for social values, let alone conventional wisdom, features low on the list of priorities of an increasing number of states and individuals.

Further reading

Akande D, 'Selection of the International Court of Justice as a Forum for Contentious and Advisory Proceedings (Including Jurisdiction)' (2016) 7 Journal of International Dispute Settlement 320;

Clapham A, *Brierly's Law of Nations: An Introduction to the Role of International Law in International Relations* (7th edn, OUP 2012);

Forlati S, *The International Court of Justice: An Arbitral Tribunal or a Judicial Body?* (Springer 2014);

Gaja G, 'The Protection of General Interests in the International Community' (2013) 364 Collected Courses of the Hague Academy of International Law 110;

Jiménez de Aréchega E, 'International Law in the Past Third of a Century' (1978) 159 Collected Courses of the Hague Academy of International Law 143;

Kawano M, 'The Role of Judicial Procedures in the Process of the Pacific Settlement of International Disputes' (2011) 346 Collected Courses of the Hague Academy of International Law 19;

Lauterpacht E, 'Principles of Procedure in International Litigation' (2011) 345 Collected Courses of the Hague Academy of International Law 391;

Lowe V, 'The Function of Litigation in International Society' (2012) 61 International and Comparative Law Quarterly 209;

Mills A, 'Rethinking Jurisdiction in International Law' (2013) 84 British Yearbook of International Law 187;

Tanzi A and Pitea C, 'Non-Compliance Mechanisms: Lessons Learned and the Way Forward' in T Treves et al (eds), *Non-Compliance Procedures and Mechanisms and the Effectiveness of International Environmental Agreements* (TMC Asser 2009), 569ff;

Tanzi A, 'Adjudication at the Service of Diplomacy: The *Enrica Lexie* Case' (2021) 12 Journal of International Dispute Settlement 448;

Thirlway H, *The International Court of Justice* (OUP 2016).

Chapter 7

Select areas of substantive international law

1. Introduction

So far, we have seen a broad-brush picture of the international law structural feature. To that end, we have addressed its principal subjects (Chapter 2); how international rules are made and implemented within national jurisdictions (Chapters 3 and 4); how they may be breached, together with the legal consequences of their breaches (Chapter 5); and rules and means by which international disputes can be settled (Chapter 6).

In short, we have focused on the **secondary, but constitutional, rules of organisation** of the legal system of the international society. That is, the rules about the subjects of the system, about the making and changing of substantive rules, about assessment of compliance with or violation of such substantive rules, and, finally, about enforcement of international rules.

The broad picture is one structurally different from the way states exercise domestically their jurisdiction to prescribe, to adjudicate and enforce, *i.e.*, in a centralised, **hierarchical** and **compulsory** way. The **three key constitutional functions** in the international legal system are participatory (law-making), consensual (adjudication) and decentralised (enforcement), with few exceptions which work only when the Great Powers are aligned. Since the crisis in Ukraine, this looks like it is not going to happen for a long time.

Through the above illustration in the preceding Chapters, few indications, by way of example, have emerged of few international **rules of conduct** (or '**substantive**'), the so-called **primary rules**. To that end, we have referred to rules of conduct setting out negative obligations, so-called ***obligations not to do***, and positive obligations, also called ***obligations to do***, such as the obligations **of prevention** of a **due diligence** nature.

Having regard to the kind of legal relationship established by substantive international rules of conduct, the distinction has also been highlighted between those producing obligations that operate at the **bilateral** level, based on reciprocity, on the one hand, and those producing obligations owed towards all the states parties to a treaty (***erga omnes partes*** obligations), or the international community as a whole (just ***erga omnes*** obligations).

The present Chapter will illustrate in a summary fashion a few important areas of international law characterised by the subject matter of their regulation.

First, within the wider framework of international economic law, we will address **international investment law** as a development of the traditional branch pertaining to the treatment of aliens.

Second, the modern evolution of **international trade law**, since the Second World War, will be considered in relation to the impulse towards the introduction of the rule of law on the treatment of foreign products and services and liberalisation, also as a reaction against the preceding decades of discriminatory protectionism.

Third, the accelerated and complex developments of the **law of the sea**, which have occurred throughout the second half of the last century, will be briefly illustrated. A special focus will be placed on the evolving codification of this body of law, which marked a **dramatic shift** from a static set of few rules basically confined to the freedom of navigation and trade beyond the territorial sea of coastal states to a highly nuanced 'zonal approach' to the exercise of different degrees of jurisdiction, mostly of an economic nature, primarily by coastal states, but not exclusively.

Forth, **international human rights law** will be presented as a recent development in the international community as delayed by the old *domestic jurisdiction* principle, preventing external interference with the internal affairs of states. Special emphasis will be placed on the added value of international control over compliance as a necessary requirement for the respect of the *nemo judex in re sua* principle.

Fifth, the body of **international environmental law** will be introduced addressing the gist of its substantive principles and its specific dynamics concerning law-making and implementation.

Finally, the evolution of **international criminal law** will be described succinctly by describing the main pillars of the developments of its substantive law and adjudication, from *ad hoc* international criminal tribunals to the establishment of the ICC.

It is assumed that the following very broad-brush illustration of those bodies of international law will be complemented by supplementary readings, cases and materials to be discussed in class, or in specialised advance courses devoted to any such area of international law, separately.

2. International economic law

2.1. *International law on protection and promotion of foreign investment*

International investment law (IIL) represents an important development of the traditional branch of international law on the **treatment of aliens**, complemented by the **right to property** as enshrined in the *Declaration of the Right of Man and the Citizen* solemnly proclaimed in 1789, at the beginning of the French Revolution.

This body of international law ensures **protection to foreign investors** from arbitrary, discriminatory, or abusive interference by the legislative, administrative or judicial authorities of the state in which the foreign investment has been made (so-called 'host state'). At the same time, IIL pursues the promotion of the **economic development of the host country**, with special regard to infrastructure, technology, mining, oil extraction, public utility services and other key sectors.

The applicable rules and principles to be found in customary international law, as specified in international bilateral treaties on investment promotion and protection (BITs) and free trade agreements (FTAs), are few and of a general character. They include, first, the ***fair and equitable treatment*** *principle* (FET), consisting of the obligation not to adopt arbitrary or discriminatory conduct against a foreign investor, the obligation to comply with the engagements undertaken with the latter and with its legitimate expectations; second, the right of the foreign investor to ***full protection and security*** (FPS), both from physical and legal violence, either from private individuals or state authorities; third, the **prohibition of expropriation**, except for ***lawful*** **expropriation**, that is, one carried out in a non-discriminatory way, based on the pursuit of a public purpose and, according to the 'Hull formula,' accompanied by prompt, adequate and effective compensation.

It is to be noted that – also with a view to accommodating the recent criticisms against the body of law under consideration – recent international investment treaties, as well as arbitration case-law, present new indications – even though, still controversial – to the effect that domestic measures depriving foreign investors of the enjoyment of their rights are not to be considered as compensable expropriation if such measures are proportionate to the pursuit of the public purpose for which they have been adopted. Whether this trend has grown into an international customary rule, or has become part of a general principle of proportionality, is still open for debate.

For an investment to qualify as a '**foreign investment**' for the purposes of the protection under IIL, a number of requirements are to be met, depending on the variations contained in any given applicable investment agreement. Generally, such requirements include that of a **substantive investment** in the host state for a **significant period of time** involving a **commercial risk**. It may involve the financial engagement in such a local investment, such as a loan. Whilst purely portfolio investments, until recently, were generally considered as excluded, in some cases – such as those against Argentina – protection has been afforded to bondholders, whilst excluded in others. This shows that the question whether purely financial investment falls within the scope of IIL remains open for debate and, especially, for clarification in future investment agreements.

The assessment of the 'foreign' character of the investor has prevailingly been one of a formal character, *i.e.*, one recognising to the investing company the nationality of the country of incorporation, or of the main seat of business, without ***piercing the corporate veil*** which consists in looking at the nationality of the actual owners. This formal approach has encouraged the business practice so-called of *nationality planning*, whereby a company would be formally incorporated in a foreign country also to acquire the status of 'foreign' investor, or to benefit from a more advantageous investment agreement between the country of nationality and the host country.

It is worth emphasising that the interpretation and application of international investment agreements **is not made *in a vacuum***. On the contrary, it is made within the context of the customary law on the **law of treaties**, which governs the validity and interpretation of such agreements, on the one hand, and of the **customary law of state responsibility**, on the other, which governs the assessment of the wrongfulness (*vel non*) and attribution of conduct in breach of the treaties in question, and the legal consequences of such wrongful act.

IIL, together with other components of international economic law, represents one of the areas of international law whose foundations are currently most debated. That accounts for the importance of briefly sketching the **policy background** to the body of law in question, also in view of an in-depth study of the technicalities of the subject in a specialised course on international economic law.

IIL in its present shape was strongly boosted by the **revival of liberalism** worldwide prompted by the fall of the Berlin Wall in 1989. After the end of the Cold War, a significant number of developing countries – until then following a statist economic model and depending on the economic support of the Soviet Union – reintroduced a free-market economy, privatising their industrial structure and public utility services, that had previously been nationalised. This liberalisation process also involved the opening up of the domestic economies of the countries in question to foreign investment, until then prevented, or strongly restricted.

Through the 1990s, those countries massively entered into BITs and FTAs. This represented a form of fair legal competition in order to attract foreign direct investment with a view to promoting the development of their economy through the establishment of a reliable legal environment. This included accepting that **disputes between foreign investors and the host state** authorities could be brought to **international arbitration** directly by foreign investors, rather than before the domestic courts of the host state, or left to the unpredictability of diplomatic protection by the state of nationality of the foreign investor (see also Chapter 2, Sections 2.3.1 and 2.3.3).

Since recently, IIL has prompted an intense political critical debate, initially led by a number of left-leaning sovereigntist Latin American countries that have withdrawn from investment treaties, in the wake of their defeat in a few egregious arbitration cases. This is particularly the case with the so-called 'Bolivarian countries,' *i.e.*, Bolivia, Ecuador and Venezuela, while Brazil never ratified BITs providing for investor-state dispute settlement (ISDS). Similarly, for instance, also Indonesia has started withdrawing from a significant number of BITs.

Curiously, though, those countries are rigorously complying with the awards which stem from arbitrations based on treaties from which they have withdrawn, but which remain in force for longer periods of time based on the so-called ***sunset clauses*** provided in such treaties, which will be illustrated immediately below. Such 'virtuosity' simply corroborates the original rationale of IIL and arbitration, in the sense that the promotion of foreign direct investments, through a predictable international legal environment, serves the interests of foreign investors as much as those of host states in attracting foreign investment.

Somewhat surprisingly, since recently, critical trends against IIL and ISDS are to be found in traditionally investment exporting countries, not only by activists, but also by those Governments who are sharing protectionist trends, as will be illustrated below. Fact is that, in an increasingly interdependent world, also those states have happened to be sued before investment arbitration tribunals by foreign investors, and the 'duty side' has revealed itself of a body of international law from which their companies have benefitted for decades. This has occurred, for instance, when the US have been sued by a Canadian company, or Germany by a Swedish one, or with the many intra-EU arbitration cases in which European companies have sued many other European states, particularly for legislative changes, removing subsidies for investment in solar energy in compliance with EU law banning state-aid.

It is worth stressing that the **unilateral termination** of a BIT usually does not leave deprived of legal protection nationals and national companies of the states parties who had made an investment prior to the denunciation in point. Generally, such treaties contain provisions that extend the operation of the treaty in question for a period ranging **between ten and twenty years since the denunciation**. Such provisions are colourfully called '**sunset clauses**.'

The main **criticism**, initially voiced by developing investment-importing countries, was that this body of law and its arbitral application would be vitiated by a **pro-investor bias**. This would be to the detriment of the legislative and regulatory power of host states in areas of general interest, such as the protection of the environment, health, and human rights. However, the statistics show that, by and large, international investment tribunals have found for foreign investors **no more frequently than** for host states, while often proving conducive to negotiated settlements. [1]

Until recently, with a certain degree of optimism, one could believe that economic development and adjustments in the production of wealth worldwide would create in the medium-term a new level playing field that would naturally dispel the legitimacy concerns over the body of law in question. It was arguable that, with the achievement of a higher level of development by the so-called

---

[1] According to the UNCTAD, investment tribunals have found for states in roughly 35% of cases, for investors in 28% of cases, whilst about 23% of cases have been settled through negotiation as of 2018. See the graphics available at: <www.investmentpolicyhub.unctad.org/ISDS>.

emerging countries, the economic relationship between investment-importing and investment-exporting countries would be balanced enough for states to equally realise the benefits produced by IIL for their economy by promoting foreign investment and protecting the national companies investing abroad, at the same time. In domestic constitutional systems, where the cardinal principle of 'equal treatment of equal situations' applies, one would expect that improved standards of protection for foreign investors would improve the principle of legality also for domestic investors.

Still, as anticipated above, recent practice shows a different scenario, where traditionally **investment exporting countries** are now also expressing concerns and criticisms over IIL and arbitration.

This change of attitude confirms the pendulum-like nature of the way in which the international legal process evolves, insofar as it is subject to the expansions and contractions of the international community of states, swinging between liberalism and protectionism, as much as between cooperation and conflict.

Following this attitude, Western countries would be turning their back on their companies investing abroad. This is an example of the **Janus-faced** attitude of states *vis-à-vis* international law in general, repeatedly referred to in the present book. That is, initially Governments speak with the face of those policy-makers and officials that engage in the creation of new international rights for their country and its nationals – in the instant case, those rights benefitting the national companies investing abroad; later, they speak with the face of those statesmen and officials that are to comply with the obligations corresponding to the rights in question.

Particularly in times of economic crises, it appears that, in the area of international law under consideration, even industrialised countries are more concerned with the risk of being sued before investment arbitration tribunals than with the benefits for their national companies abroad, even if their profits accrued abroad contribute to the state budget.

It is worth noting how, also in response to the above-mentioned criticisms over the ISDS system, states, often based on public debate with the involvement of civil society, have produced 'Model BITs,' or have actually entered into new generation investment agreements which have increased the attention to public interest concerns, including protection of the environment, health and human rights in general. At the same time, international investment arbitration institutions, such as **ICSID** and **UNCITRAL**, have introduced procedural adaptations that may enhance attention for public interest concerns, such as new forms of transparency or the participation in the proceedings by third parties representing public interests under the status of *amici curiae*. The possibility for defendant host states to file counterclaims not only to fend off the foreign investors' demands but also to invoke, in turn, a violation of international law, is also gradually developing.

No less importantly, international investment tribunals have gradually developed case-law which is ever more sensitive to public interest concerns, even by way of 'systemic interpretation' of BITs which would not contain explicit provisions to that effect. Such case-law developments are best illustrated by comparing the language of two awards expressing a radical change in rationale, within a span of eighteen years, on issues pertaining to the protection of the environment, both involving Costa Rica as defendant.

In the 2000 award in *Compañia del Desarrollo de Santa Elena SA v Republic of Costa Rica*, the arbitration tribunal stated as follows:

> 'While an expropriation or taking for environmental reasons may be classified as a taking for a public purpose, and thus may be legitimate, the fact that the Property was taken for this reason does not affect either the nature or the measure of the compensation to be paid for the taking. That is, the purpose of protecting the environment for which the Property was taken does not alter the legal character of the taking for which adequate compensation must be paid. The international source of the obligation to protect the environment makes no difference. (…) Expropriatory environmental measures – no matter how laudable and beneficial to society as a

whole – are, in this respect, similar to any other expropriatory measures that a state may take in order to implement its policies: where property is expropriated, even for environmental purposes, whether domestic or international, the state's obligation to pay compensation remains.' [2]

In 2018, in *Aven v Costa Rica* case, the Tribunal held that:

'Although the express terms of Article 10.11 [of the DR-CAFTA] essentially subordinate the rights of investors under Chapter Ten to the right of Costa Rica to ensure that the investments are carried out "in a matter sensitive to environmental concerns", this subordination is not absolute in the view of the Tribunal. It requires that the actions to be taken by the States Parties to DR-CAFTA act in line with principles of international law, which require acting in good faith. It is not a question of "not-applying" those provisions under Chapter Ten, but rather giving preference to the standards of environmental protection that were stated to be of interest to the Treaty Parties at the time it was signed.' [3]

It is also to be noted that, while in *Santa Elena* the arbitration tribunal awarded 16 million US dollars to the company – who, though, had claimed more than 40 million US dollars – in *Aven* the arbitration tribunal rejected the company's claim for damages on the merits. That shows how in litigation, aside from the applicable rules and principles, any contentious case is absolutely fact-specific and it is the disputed facts that lead the application of the law. Therefore, one is not necessarily suggesting that, had the *Santa Elena* claim been filed in 2018, it would have been treated in the same conclusion as in the *Aven* case. Be that as it may, the comparison

[2] *Compañia del Desarrollo de Santa Elena SA v Republic of Costa Rica*, ICSID Case No ARB/96/1, Award (17 February 2000), paras 71-72.

[3] *David R Aven and Others v Republic of Costa Rica*, ICSID Case No UNCT/15/3, Award (18 September 2018), para 412.

just sketched certainly emphasises a formidable change in adjudicative sensitivity.

One would remark by way of conclusion that, if the cross-fire currently targeting ISDS were to lead to its demise, the above-mentioned developments towards the protection of public interest concerns might risk to go wasted with it. However, foreign investment would continue worldwide under the framework of long duration **commercial contracts**, such as concession agreements, which would contain arbitral clauses referring disputes over their interpretation and application to **commercial arbitration**. Within that arbitration context, public interest concerns provisions of the kind increasingly laid down in IIL instruments might not apply.

This does not mean that commercial arbitrators may not address public interest concerns under some form of public policy, or *ordre public*, considerations to be inferred from domestic applicable law, even though this would be best for the domestic judge to do where execution of the award is sought.

2.2. *WTO law*

Since time immemorial, the peoples' survival, first, and economic well-being, later, have depended on **trade between** them. Since the formation of the modern international society until the mid-20th century, international trade has been carried out bilaterally between the nation-states across the customs at their borders.

Against the experience of the dramatic world economic depression in the decades between the two World Wars – associated with protectionist or highly selective international trade relations – the need for a shift towards the 'multilateralisation' of international trade was generally perceived as essential to economic development – even though it was ideologically rejected by nationalistic Soviet countries.

Further to the engagement by the parties to the August 1941 *Atlantic Charter* to 'further the enjoyment of all states (…) of access on equal terms to the trade and the raw materials of the world,'[4] in 1948 the *Havana Charter* provided the basis for the establishment of the International Trade Organisation (ITO). Meanwhile, in 1947, the ECOSOC adopted the GATT, that was meant to serve as a provisional framework for the liberalisation of the world market until the ITO would be established.

Since the ITO project was torpedoed by a new protectionist majority in the US Congress which would not ratify the *Havana Charter*, the GATT – without the participation by the socialist countries – provided an initial legal framework within which, through a number of 'rounds' of negotiations, a series of multilateral agreements were entered into to regulate the imports and treatment of specific sectors of goods, with a view to promoting their circulation.

After the end of the Cold War, in a new pro-multilateral internalisation environment, in 1994, the **WTO** was established. It incorporated a review version of the GATT, together with the agreements concluded under its framework and related 'rounds,' and with the new, fundamental trade-related treaties, that is the *General Agreement on Trade in Services* (**GATS**) and the *Agreement on Trade-Related Aspects of Intellectual Property Rights* (**TRIPS**).

A new compulsory and binding dispute settlement mechanism was established by the so-called *Dispute Settlement Understanding* (**DSU**) which even provides for an appeal procedure. Namely, when a trade dispute arises between two, or more, WTO Members, the Dispute Settlement Body (DSB), composed of all WTO states parties, sets up a dispute settlement panel. A panel's ruling may be appealed by either party before the **Appellate Body**. The reports of the panels or of the Appellate Body are adopted by the DSB which supervises their compliance.

In 1994, 128 states had already joined the GATT, whereas today 164 states are parties to the WTO, including the PRC (since 2001)

---

[4] See 'The Atlantic Charter: Declaration of Principles issued by the President of the United States and the Prime Minister of the United Kingdom' (14 August 1941), available at: <www.nato.int>.

and Russia (since 2012). India and the US have been parties to it to its very origin.

Contrary to what may be guessed by the layman, the WTO does not aim to achieve a fully-fledged liberalised world market with no custom duties. It basically pursues the introduction of the rule of law in international trade – having special regard to administrative procedures, their transparency and impartiality, and access to justice – based on the principle of non-discrimination through the standards of **national treatment** of foreign products and services, on the one hand, and of the **most favourite nation**, on the other.

According to the **national treatment standard**, the foreign products, services and intellectual property rights from countries that are parties to the agreements in force within the WTO system cannot be subjected to treatment less favourable than that accorded to domestic equivalent items. Under the **most favourite nation treatment**, the above items coming into a party to those agreements from another party cannot be treated less favourably than the like items coming from **any other party to the same agreements**. Accordingly, as provided for by Article I of the GATT:

> 'Any advantage, favour, privilege or immunity granted by any contracting party to any product originating in or destined for any other country shall be accorded immediately and unconditionally to the like product originating in or destined for the territories of all other contracting parties.'

The above primary trade aims are associated with the pursuit of **public policy aims** within the states parties to the system, which in modern times are ancillary to trade and economic development, such as sustainable development, the improvement of the standard of living, employment or equality of payment. In line with this rationale, restrictions to foreign trade are **admissible when justified** by need to protect human, animal, plant life or health (Article XX(b) of the GATT). The same applies in relation to the need to protect the public order and public morals.

Another tangible sign of the crisis of multilateralism these days is given by the blocking, since 2016, of the functioning of the Appellate Body through the refusal by the US to propose a candidate for it. [5]

3. The law of the sea

This body of international law addresses the legal relationships between states, hence, their rights and obligations, pertaining to the sea and the use thereof. In that sense, it is not to be confused with **maritime law** which is a branch of **domestic law**, hence, addressing the legal relationships in maritime matters between individuals and companies, such as insurance and transport contracts, or the liability of ship-owners or carriers. International conventions on the matter do not belong to the law of the sea proper, but aim to **harmonise domestic legislations** on such private law matters.

The law of the sea is one of the areas of international law that has undergone most developments since the Second World War. Until then, this body of law consisted of very few rules and principles that were developed at the beginning of the modern international community of nations at the end of the 16th century, after ocean exploration led to major discoveries overseas.

Such rules consisted of the recognition of the exclusive sovereignty of coastal states up to three nautical miles (nm) from the coast – being that the reach of cannons at the time – of their so-called **territorial sea**, on the one hand. On the other, beyond those waters – *i.e.*, in the **high seas** – the principle of the freedom of the seas applied, basically for the purposes of recognising the **freedom of navigation** and **trade**. In sum, those two basic principles divided up the

[5] On this topic see E Baroncini, 'Preserving the Appellate Stage in the WTO Dispute Settlement Mechanism: The EU and the Multi-Party Interim Appeal Arbitration Arrangement' (2020) 29 Italian Yearbook of International Law 33.

sea into the territorial sea, which fell under the jurisdiction of coastal states, and the high seas, which was open to navigation and utilisation by all. Such most liberal and minimalistic legal regime governed the subject for nearly four centuries.

With the accelerated technological developments of the last century, the state of the law in this area became problematic. Following the principle of freedom of the high seas, originally conceived with regard to navigation and trade as the only conceivable uses, any financially and technologically capable state could grab all the available resources, including on the seabed and in the subsoil. At the same time, such increased technological capacity rendered the limits of the territorial sea zone much more stringent a constraint than when originally conceived, particularly when confined to three nm.

Such urge for change and development in the law were reflected by the four exercises of law codification on the subject throughout the 20th century. A first attempt in that direction failed at the 1930 Hague Codification Conference, which was held under the auspices of the League of Nations (the predecessor to the UN). However, the work done in that context was treasured by the ILC for the elaboration of a draft-text[6] which was largely endorsed by the delegations participating in the **First** UN Conference on the Law of the Sea, held in Geneva, which in 1958 produced four conventions: respectively, the *Convention on the Territorial Sea and Contiguous Zone*, the *Convention on the High Seas*, the *Convention on the Continental Shelf* and the *Convention on Fisheries and Conservation of the Living Resources on the High Seas*.

The last two conventions reflected a **new normative approach** to the law of the sea which goes way beyond the redefinition of the territorial sea and the high seas. They introduced a much more articulated 'zonal' approach *in functional terms*, *i.e.*, calibrating the forms and degree of the jurisdiction of states which applies to the

---

[6] ILC, 'Articles concerning the Law of the Sea, with Commentaries' (1956) II Yearbook of the International Law Commission 265.

newly defined zones. The *Convention on Fisheries and Conservation of the Living Resources on the High Seas* also shows awareness that the need to regulate new technological capacity to utilise and exploit sea natural resources for economic development purposes should be accompanied by law making attention also to the conservation of such resources and protection of the marine environment.

The diplomatic attempt to go further down that law-making route with the **Second** UN Conference on the Law of Sea, again in Geneva, in 1960 did not work. The need for further refinement of the international law of the sea remained pressing, so much so that the international law of the sea diplomacy managed to trigger anew another codification exercise in 1974 (Third UN Conference on the Law of the Sea) which, in 1982, eventually led to the adoption in Montego Bay (Jamaica) of a comprehensive convention on the subject, the (already often mentioned) **UNCLOS**. It consists of 320 Articles, 9 Annexes and a Final Act, and as of today 168 states are parties to it. As illustrated above (Chapter 6, Section 4), it provides for an articulated dispute settlement procedure and the establishment of a permanent tribunal (ITLOS).

The UNCLOS develops the zonal approach alluded to which determines the kinds of activities that are allowed in certain **maritime zones**, but not in others. Such zones are: *a*) the territorial sea (extending to twelve nm from the baseline); *b*) the contiguous zone (extending up to twenty-four nm); *c*) the exclusive economic zone (EEZ, extending up to two hundreds nm); *d*) archipelagic waters; *e*) the continental shelf; *f*) the high seas; and *g*) the 'International Seabed Area' (or 'Area').

In its **internal waters**, such as its ports, the coastal state may exercise its jurisdiction in the same way, and under the same international law restrictions, as it may **on its land territory**. Therefore, no foreign vessel may be entitled to enter such waters, unless under circumstances of *force majeure* or distress. Similar considerations apply to the **territorial waters** – whose scope of application includes the seabed and subsoil beneath, as well as the airspace above – where the coastal state may expressly exercise under the UN-

CLOS its 'rights of sovereignty,' except that it is under the obligation to allow the right of 'innocent passage' to 'ships of all States.' '**Innocent passage**' consists of 'continuous and expeditious' travelling, [7] also from a port of the same coastal state, that 'is not prejudicial to the peace, good order or security of the coastal state.' [8] Apart from activities, even covertly, of a military nature, also smuggling, or 'any (...) activity not having a direct bearing on passage' are considered as 'prejudicial' to the coastal state. [9]

In the contiguous zone, the coastal state may only exercise limited sovereignty, to the extent necessary to control compliance with, punish and 'prevent infringement of its customs, fiscal, immigration or sanitary laws and regulations.' [10]

In the **EEZ** – which encompasses the contiguous zone – the coastal state is entitled, in exclusive terms, to exercise 'sovereign rights' to exploit 'living and non-living natural resources,' from fisheries to 'the production of energy from the water, currents and winds.' [11] The UNCLOS explicitly stresses that in the exclusive exercise of such rights the coastal state 'shall have due regard to the rights and duties of other States.' [12] This qualification aims to prevent abuses of the specific rights in question which, for instance, should not be taken to restrict the freedom of navigation of states other than the coastal state in the EEZ.

Frequently, almost invariably, the EEZ partly overlaps with the **continental shelf**, intended as 'the seabed and subsoil of the submarine areas that extend beyond [the] territorial sea throughout the natural prolongation of [the] land territory to the outer edge of the continental margin, or to a distance of 200 nautical miles from the

---

[7] Article 18(2) of the UNCLOS.

[8] Article 19(1) of the UNCLOS.

[9] Article 19(2)(l) of the UNCLOS.

[10] Article 33(1)(a) of the UNCLOS.

[11] Article 56(1)(a) of the UNCLOS.

[12] Article 56(2) of the UNCLOS.

baselines.'[13] In fact, in some cases, the land territory prolongation up to the point where it plunges into the abyss ('the edge of the continental margin'),[14] may go beyond two hundreds nm. However, it is to be stressed that, given the physical scope of the continental platform – *i.e.*, only the seabed and subsoil – where the latter reaches beyond two hundreds nm, it does not extend the rights pertaining to the EEZ applicable to the water column beyond that limit. Here, again, the coastal state is entitled, in exclusive terms, to exercise 'sovereign rights' of exploration and exploitation over the seabed and subsoil resources, such as minerals or sedentary species of living organisms. Such rights for the coastal state are without prejudice to the rights of other states in super adjacent waters, such as the rights of exploration and exploitation of the water column above it beyond two hundreds nm, where the platform reaches beyond that limit, or the right of navigation from beyond the limit of the territorial waters.

It is to be noted that claims by coastal states based on the provisions concerning the ***contiguous zone***, the EEZ and the archipelagic waters are subject to prior explicit declarations, or '**proclamations**,' by the coastal states establishing such zones. Proclamations are usually made by statutory law. Even though, 'express proclamation' is not required by the UNCLOS concerning the continental platform for the coastal state to be entitled to invoke the rights attached thereto, domestic legislation determining the extent of the continental platform is necessary where the latter reaches beyond two hundreds nm.

One of the most complex aspects of the application of UNCLOS pertains to the delimitation of maritime zones between **adjacent** or **opposite** states. This is especially the case where the coasts around the boundaries between two adjacent states are irregular, or where the distance between the coasts (better, baselines) of opposing states

[13] Article 76(1) of the UNCLOS.

[14] *Ibidem.*

is less than **twenty-four** nm, concerning their territorial waters, less than **eighty-four** nm, concerning their contiguous zones, or less than **two hundreds** nm, concerning their EEZs and continental platforms. Many disputes have arisen out of overlapping claims in such areas giving rise to an abundant international case-law focusing on the general principles – swinging between equidistance and equity – which are applicable to the varying specific circumstances of any given case.

As already alluded to above, there are increasing concerns in the international society of states that cannot be satisfactorily accommodated only through bilateral legal relations based on reciprocal rights and duties. The sea and its resources are exemplary of this, with specific regard to the finite character of its resources – living and non-living – and their vulnerability to pollution. Such issues are of an indivisible character and, therefore, are the concern of all. To that end, having regard to the conservation of marine living resources, Part VII of the UNCLOS on the high seas, devotes a whole Section to the regulation of the matter.

As to non-living resources, UNCLOS affirms that seabed and subsoil beyond the zones under the jurisdiction of coastal states belong to the **common heritage of the mankind** (Article 136). It also establishes an institution, the 'Seabed Authority,' as a form of trustee in charge of the administration of the Area for the benefit of mankind, land-locked states and those which, anyhow, do not have the technological or financial capacity of exploration and exploitation of the Area.

4. International human rights law

After illustrating two traditional areas of international law embedded in the international community since its inception, we shall now address the relatively recent branch of international human rights law.

The recent formation of this body of law in international law may appear to be in stark contrast with the fact that the progressive elaboration and recognition of human rights law marks the foundations and development of **constitutional law in certain national jurisdictions** since the *Magna Charta* (1215), through the *Liber Paradisus* by the Commune of Bologna (1256), the *Bill of Rights* in England (1689), the *Declaration of the Rights of Man and the Citizen* in France (1789), the *Bill of Rights* in the US Constitution (1791), the *Slavery Abolition Act* in the UK (1833), the 13th Amendment to the US Constitution which criminalised slavery (1865), up to the modern Constitutions as we know them today.

In fact, that is not a contradiction, insofar as until sometime after the end of the Second World War the way states dealt with their nationals fell outside the scope of international law. This has been considered for three centuries as a corollary of the principle of sovereign equality and independence of states, under the label of ***domestic jurisdiction*** or ***domain réservé*** doctrine. It is worth recalling that this doctrine used to be raised during the Cold War by Soviet countries and the PRC when **human rights issues** were argued and/or invoked by Western countries in diplomatic contexts.

This principle was dismantled by the widespread participation, including from Russia and the PRC, in international, regional and universal, human rights conventions, to the extent that the core of human rights is now part of customary international law.[15] In recent times, the record of compliance with international human rights has increasingly lowered, but one would argue that this has not affected the customary nature of the core of human rights law.

As observed by Dame Rosalyn Higgins, former President of the ICJ,

> 'The reason that the prohibition on torture continues to be a requirement of customary international law, even though widely abused, is not because it has a higher normative status that allows us to ig-

[15] See the classic T Meron, *The Humanization of International Law* (Martinus Nijhoff Publishers 2005).

> nore the abuse, but because *opinio juris* as to its normative status continues to exist. No state, not even a state that tortures, believes that the international law prohibition is undesirable and that it is not bound by the prohibition. A new norm cannot emerge without both practice and *opinio juris*; and an existing norm does not die without the great majority of states engaging in both a contrary practice and withdrawing their *opinio juris*.' [16]

As already illustrated, international human rights law epitomises the shift associating **international legal protection to collective interests** and solidarity legal relationships to the **traditional protection** of individual state interests through international legal rules establishing bilateral inter-state legal relationships. With the introduction of this type of new rules, **individuals** no longer matter for international law only insofar as nationals of a given state abroad under the body of law on the treatment of aliens, **but as individuals as such**, irrespective of their nationality. That implies that a state party to a human rights treaty, or under customary law, is duty bound to comply with the international human rights standards **also *vis-à-vis* its *own nationals***.

Article 1 of the ECHR reads as follows:

> 'The High Contracting Parties shall secure ***to everyone within their jurisdiction*** the rights and freedoms defined in Section I of this Convention.'

It is worth recalling that Article 1(3) of the *UN Charter*, in setting out the aims of the UN spells out that 'to achieve international co-operation (…) in promoting and encouraging respect for human rights and for fundamental freedoms for all without distinction as to race, sex, language, or religion.' Article 55(c) also engages the UN and its Members to promote 'universal respect for, and ob-

[16] R Higgins, *Problems and Process: International Law and How We Use It* (Clarendon Press 1994), 22.

servance of, human rights and fundamental freedoms for all without distinction as to race, sex, language, or religion.'

The *UN Charter* does not go on to spell out a **catalogue** of basic human rights, as we may find in most domestic Constitutions, but has enabled the UN to provide the forum for the developments of a generally agreed series of authoritative and legally binding instruments of human rights, complemented by the institutional framework for monitoring compliance.

In 1946, the ECOSOC established the **UN Commission on Human Rights** (CHR), replaced in 2006 by the **UN Human Rights Council** (HRC), composed of 47 Member states, vested with a so-called 'universal periodic review' focusing on periodic reports from states on the situation of human rights in their jurisdictions, resulting in recommendations by the HRC, where necessary.

The first task of the CHR was to draw up a catalogue of human rights which was then endorsed by the UN General Assembly by adopting it in 1948 in the form of a resolution solemnly entitled ***Universal Declaration of Human Rights***.[17] Revolving around the principles of **equality** and **non-discrimination**, it spelt out basic civil and political rights – such as the prohibition of slavery, cruel, inhuman and degrading treatment, arbitrary arrest and detention, the right to access to justice, or the freedom of opinion and expression – and economic, social and cultural rights – such as the right to education, social security, to form and join trade unions.

It took nearly twenty years of negotiations for the transformation of that soft-law instrument into two legally binding agreements at the universal level. Namely, **the two**, already mentioned,[18] **1966 *UN Covenants***, the *Covenant on Civil and Political Rights* (CCPR) and the *Covenant on Economic, Social and Cultural Rights* (CESCR). The length of such negotiations was due to the arm-twisting between the Western, then largely colonial countries, and the Socialist

---

[17] UN General Assembly, Res 217(A)(III) of 10 December 1948.

[18] See Chapter 3, Section 3.

delegations. The former insisted on the inclusion of the **right to property** – together with a number of political rights inspired by the principle of liberal democracy – which was resisted by the latter delegations, which in turn pressed for the recognition of the right to self-determination in support of the then national liberation movements. The compromise finally reached consisted in the exclusion of the right to property and the inclusion of the right to self-determination (as the opening provision to both Covenants) in exchange for the recognition of a significant number of rights and freedoms ancillary to the concept of liberal democracy. Both the CCPR and the CESCR entered into force in 1976.

The CCPR provides for the **Human Rights Committee** – not to be confused with the HRC – a body composed of independent experts and vested with compliance monitoring functions and recommendatory powers. According to the *Optional Protocol* attached to the CCPR, the Committee has the competence to be seized of complaints by individuals, subject to the prior exhaustion of local remedies. It exercises merely hortatory powers, however, hence short of issuing any retributive measures. The 'parallel' Committee established under the CESCR has been vested with the power to be seized of individual complaints only in 2013 with the entry into force of the 2008 *Optional Protocol* to that effect.

Further articulation and development of the fundamental rights enshrined in the 1966 *UN Covenants* was produced by the UN General Assembly over the years through a number of conventions addressing specific rights. To that end, it is worth recalling here the 1966 *Convention on the Elimination of All Forms of Racial Discrimination*, the 1979 *Convention on the Elimination of All Forms of Discrimination against Women*, the 1984 *Convention against Torture and Other Cruel, Inhuman or Degrading Treatment or Punishment*, the 1989 *Convention on the Rights of the Child*, and the 2006 *Convention on the Rights of Persons with Disabilities*. It is to be noted that all such instruments have entered into force and are also endowed with so-called 'treaty-based bodies' in charge with various forms of compliance review.

At the regional level in various continents – starting from Europe, which was most directly affected by the horrors of the Second World War – given the more intense cultural and political homogeneity in each of them, it has been easier to find the consensus necessary to establish permanent adjudicative bodies on the protection of human rights. This is the case of the 1950 ECHR which provides for the ECtHR, based in Strasburg (not to be confused with the Court of Justice of the EU, based in Luxemburg). One is to recall also the 1969 ACHR, adopted under the auspices of the OAS, which establishes the IACtHR. Whilst under the ECHR individuals may sue **directly** a state party for an alleged breach of it before the ECtHR, following an unsuccessful exhaustion of its local remedies, under the ACHR, individuals only enjoy an indirect access to international justice, as they will have to resort to the Inter-American Commission on Human Rights, in order for their case, after a first screening, to be submitted before the IACtHR.

In 1981 the then OAU (later the African Union) adopted the ACHPR. The latter was complemented by the African Commission on Human and Peoples' Rights, composed of eleven independent lawyers, charged with the review of periodical reports by states parties. In 1998, the ACtHPR was set up with a general advisory competence. Claims brought by individuals concerned and by NGOs can be entertained by the ACtHPR only if against a state party that has opted into its jurisdiction. It is worth noting that the scope of the competence of the ACtHPR is not confined to alleged breaches of the ACHPR, but extends to the interpretation and application of **any human rights convention to which a state party to the ACHPR is also a party**.

In 2000, the EU adopted the *Charter of Fundamental Rights of the European Union*, which is an instrument akin and parallel to the ECHR. The *EU Charter* has represented a persuasive authority, as a soft-law instrument, until it became legally binding by incorporation through reference under Article 6(1) of the TEU. It is to be noted that Poland and the UK opted out of the application of the *EU Charter* in their jurisdictions.

Under the auspices of the Arab League, in 2004 the ***Arab Charter on Human Rights*** was adopted, which provides for the Arab Human Rights Committee vested only with the power to review the periodical reports from states parties to the *Charter*. The ASEAN, in 2012, has adopted the ***ASEAN Declaration on Human Rights*** as a non-legally binding document.

Having regard to the conventional instruments in the area under consideration, formally, each and all states parties to them are entitled to the right that each and all the other states parties comply with the corresponding obligations to respect the fundamental rights spelt out in the treaty in question with regard to the individuals subject to their jurisdiction. As already illustrated in different parts of this textbook, such **obligations** are called ***erga omnes partes***, *i.e.*, obligations owed to all the other parties. Having regard to those fundamental human rights that are part of general customary law – such as the prohibition of genocide or torture and the related obligations of prevention and suppression thereto –, such obligations are owed towards the international community as a whole.

With a sufficient degree of realism, the drafters of international human rights treaties were aware that such a formal legal framework would apply with difficulty. Indeed, based on the old biblical quotation 'let him without sin cast the first stone,' as well as on consideration of **political comity**, it would be unlikely for a state to invoke the breach of a treaty for another state's conduct with regard to the way it treats its national or those of a third state. It is against this background that, under a number of human rights treaties, the individuals, or groups of individuals, concerned may vindicate breaches of such treaties before quasi-judicial or judicial treaty-bodies. Formally, the material beneficiaries of the international legal rights in question would be vindicating such rights on behalf of their holders, *i.e.*, the states parties.

The substantive human rights obligations spelt out under the treaties in question generally reflect, or duplicate, those enshrined in the Constitutions of the states parties to them. Therefore, it is arguable that **the true added value** of these conventions lies in the role of the above referred 'treaty-based bodies,' and especially of human rights courts. Such courts – once the applicant has exhausted the domestic remedies in the respondent state to no avail – represent the only means to ensure compliance with the principle ***nemo judex in re sua*** (nobody should be the judge of his own matter). This consideration accounts for the concerns expressed in Chapter 4, Section 8, over the impact that the increasing legal nationalism in many countries may have on the enforcement at the domestic level of international decisions, especially of those rendered by international human rights courts. The risk is high that the dialogue between domestic and international courts becomes a *dialogue de sourds* (a dialogue of the deaf).

Human rights are not interpreted and applied in isolation from other branches of international law and their mechanisms of dispute settlement, or compliance review. This is especially apparent **in relation to environmental law** whose evolution has been instrumental in the formation of the so-called 'green human rights,' with special regard to the right to health, but not exclusively. Similar considerations increasingly apply **in relation to IIL**.

5. International environmental law

This body of international law has made its appearance even more recently than that on the protection of human rights, whilst the two are now largely mutually entangled. This depends on the simple matter of fact that environmental concerns arose only with relatively recent scientific and technological developments that enhanced the capacity to detect the environmental impact of the evermore polluting industrial processes, transport, explorations and exploitation of finite natural resources. Awareness to that effect on the international plane only started at the end of the 1960s.

In order to appreciate the basics of international environmental law, it is necessary to have an idea of the scope of the legal concept of 'environment.' In fact, there is no general all-encompassing legal definition of the **environment**. However, by abstraction from the definition of the scope of protection provided in various international instruments, each addressing different parts and aspects of the **environment**, it is possible to infer a rather comprehensive concept. Namely, one ranging, from the air, sea, freshwater, living resources – intended as part of biodiversity, as animal endangered species or as an economic resource –, to human, plant life and health, or even cultural heritage.

This accounts for the fact that international environmental law is replete with acronyms and abbreviations often rendering the subject esoteric and obscure, and highly specialised with regard to many different elements of the environment and aspects of the international regulatory approaches thereto. This introductory presentation, being aimed to convey to the reader the gist of the subject, will try to avoid as much as possible its technicalities and details while keeping the acronyms and abbreviations to a minimum.

The definitional difficulty described above anticipates a key feature about the way international environmental law has evolved. Namely, through a **piecemeal approach** to the regulation of the utilisation, protection, conservation and management of specific parts and aspects of the environment through **specific treaties** – usually **MEA**s. This was the only choice. Given the extended and multifarious range of environmental issues, it would be unthinkable to engage in the codification of international environmental law within a single all-encompassing international agreement. Besides, since different groups of states have different interests over different areas and aspects of the environment, the wider the scope of the subject-matter under negotiation, the more complex the negotiation and the higher the bar for reaching a common denominator between delegations – something seen recently with respect to the fight against climate change.

Despite this inevitably fragmented picture, a number of overarching principles and concepts can be discerned from the different environmental instruments in place to date, *conventional and not*. Indeed, it is to be stressed how the international law-making process concerning the environment is especially characterised by **constructive interactions**, particularly **between municipal and international law**, and **between soft-law instruments, treaty law and customary law**.

One is to note how, since the last third of the 20th century, those countries with more advanced environmental legislations – mostly Scandinavians – promoted their environmental normative standards and principles on the international level according to some kind of an intergovernmental 'bottom up' approach. Once met with sufficient recognition internationally, such standards and principles have gradually trickled down onto less advanced domestic legal systems.

The promotion of such environmental standards and principles internationally was initially made through **soft-law instruments** of a general character that, as such, were easier to negotiate. Once an agreement could be reached on general but authoritative statements enshrining those standard and principles, the latter would be developed and articulated into legally-binding treaties in relation to individual specific areas and aspects of environmental law.

This international gradual 'top-down' approach is epitomised by the final *Declarations* of the 1972 **UN Conference on the Human Environment** (*Stockholm Declaration*) and of the 1992 **UN Conference on Environment and Development** (*Rio Declaration*), which produced the first general level of authoritative statements in the field. From the combination of such instruments, one may discern the general statements of the basic environmental principles that provided the impulse and guidance for their incorporation and development in specific MEAs.

For the sake of the records, the third major UN Conference in the field – the 2002 **Johannesburg World Summit on Sustainable Development** – did not go much further than: *a*) producing general statements on the engagement to implement and comply with the international standards in the field adopted until then, and *b*) promoting the corporate engagement in the environmental law process.

The most important of the overarching principles in question is undoubtedly that of **sustainable development**, which represents the ***rationale*** for most of the other environmental rules and principles that to a large extent are ancillary to it. One is to recall, *inter alia*, that of **no-harm**, equitable and reasonable utilization, **co-operation**, polluter-pays, **EIA**, the right to **access to information, participation and access to justice concerning decisions by the public authorities in environmental matters**. Particularly in this day and age, it is worth stressing the **intergenerational** reach of the principle of sustainable development, which was spelt out in Principle 2 of the *Stockholm Declaration*, as follows:

> 'The natural resources of the earth, including the air, water, land, flora and fauna and especially representative samples of natural ecosystems, must be safeguarded for the benefit of present and future generations through careful planning or management, as appropriate.'

The collective relevance of the environment is reflected in the extension of the scope of the no-harm rule – addressed earlier as the source of due diligence, rather than absolute, obligations [19] – from the environment subject to national jurisdictions to that beyond such limits. This is reflected in Principle 21 of the *Stockholm Declaration*, later reiterated in Principle 2 of the *Rio Declaration*, as follows:

> 'States have (…) the sovereign right to exploit their own resources pursuant to their own environmental policies, and the responsibility to ensure that activities within their jurisdiction or control do not cause damage to the environment of other States or of areas beyond the limits of national jurisdiction.'

The two UN environmental conferences just mentioned and the environmental diplomatic network with them gave a robust impulse to

---

[19] See Chapter 5, Section 3.

the negotiation and adoption of a significant number of **MEAs** which translated into specific treaty law the general environmental principles enshrined in the two *Declarations* in point. One may recall: the 1991 *Espoo Convention on Environmental Impact Assessment*; the 1992 *Helsinki Convention on the Protection and Use of Transboundary Watercourses and International Lakes*; the 1992 *Helsinki Convention on the Transboundary Effects of Industrial Accidents*; the 1992 *Convention on Biological Diversity*; the 1998 *Aarhus Convention on Access to Information, Public Participation in Decision-making and Access to Justice in Environmental Matters*, and the 1999 *London Protocol on Water and Health*.

The same progressive approach to law making applies also to individual MEAs. They are often envisaged in terms of **framework conventions** endowed with a MoP or CoP and subsidiary bodies devoted to compliance assistance, but also to the development and specification of the often very general provisions of the framework convention in point. As we have illustrated in Chapter 5, Section 3, substantive environmental obligations are generally couched in due diligence terms.

Accordingly, oftentimes the norm-development and specification exercises of such treaty bodies consist precisely of the elaboration and specification of due diligence standards pertaining to the subject-matter of the framework convention in point. Such normative processes within a given MEA produce sets of **guidelines** on any specific topic within the scope of the convention in point, or even **protocols**, as self-standing pieces of treaty law. For instance, one may recall the various Protocols to the 1992 *Convention on Biological Diversity* – namely, the 2000 *Cartagena Protocol on Biosafety* and the 2010 *Nagoya Protocol on Access and Benefit-Sharing of Genetic Resources* – amongst others of no less importance.

The normative force of the principles in question would lie in their translation into MEAs, as much as in their recognition through other unwritten sources of international law, including their reception in domestic practice, including case-law and statutory laws. Under both kinds of sources of international law, the principles in question would also be relevant for the purposes of the **contextual interpretation** of treaties previously stipulated.

In the *Gabčíkovo-Nagymaros Project* case between Hungary and Slovakia over the use of the Danube, mentioned earlier (Chapter 6, Section 4), the dispute in point arose out of the interpretation and application of a bilateral treaty on economic co-operation entered into by the disputing parties in 1977, against the background of the subsequent emergence of the concept of **sustainable development**. In fact, no reference to such principle appeared in the language of the 1977 treaty.

In 1997, however, the ICJ stated as follows:

> '[N]ew norms and standards have been developed, set forth in a great number of instruments over the last two decades. Such norms have to be taken into consideration, and such new standards given proper weight, not only when States contemplate new activities but also when continuing with activities begun in the past. This need to reconcile economic development with protection of the environment is aptly expressed in the concept of sustainable development.' [20]

Finally, the considerations made in the previous Section concerning the interpretation and application of human rights law in integrated terms with other bodies of international law also apply to international environmental law.

As to the relationship between environmental law and human rights law, this depends on the basic assumption set out in Principle 1 of the *Rio Declaration* to the effect that '[h]uman beings are at the centre of concerns for sustainable development. They are entitled to a healthy and productive life in harmony with nature.'

Whilst the right to a healthy environment is not expressly recognised under the ECHR, in *Hatton v United Kingdom*, the ECtHR

---

[20] *Gabčíkovo-Nagymaros Project* (Hungary/Slovakia) (Judgment) [1997] ICJ Rep 7, 78.

addressed the right to life under Article 2 and the right to respect for private and family life under Article 8, observing that a state party to the ECHR, not only has duties of abstention, but also 'has positive duties, [while] the right to a healthy environment is included in the concept of the right to respect for private and family life.'[21]

As to the relationship between international environmental law and **IIL**, one is to recall how international investment treaties and arbitration case-law increasingly conceive the host state obligations *vis-à-vis* foreign investors in combination with those on environmental protection. Reference should also be made to in relation to international trade law, particularly insofar as constraints on foreign products, services and rights are admissible when adopted in the pursuit of the need to protect human, animal and plant life or health (Article XX(*b*) of the GATT).

6. International criminal law and justice

International criminal law is confined to international rules whose obligations are addressed to individuals, and which, in turn, provide for **individual international criminal responsibility**.

Accordingly, those elements of municipal criminal law which, because of their extra-territorial application, may evoke 'international aspects' to it, will not be addressed. The same applies to inter-state judicial cooperation instrumental in the exercise of the national criminal jurisdiction of the co-operating states, such as through extradition treaties, or treaties on the gathering of evidence concerning facts occurred abroad.

The (core) crimes falling under international criminal law as it will be addressed in the present Section are **war crimes, crimes against humanity**, **genocide** and **aggression**. Based on the premise

[21] ECtHR, *Case of Hatton and Others v the United Kingdom*, App No 36022/97, Judgment (2 October 2001), Separate Opinion of Judge Costa.

that contemporary international law does not contemplate **state criminal responsibility**, the assessment of the individual responsibility for the crimes in question is **separate** and **independent** from the assessment of the international responsibility of a state arising out of the same circumstances. That is to say that an accused may be acquitted of a charge of genocide, or aggression (international crime), even where the state he/she was acting for may be found internationally responsible for a breach of the international prohibition of genocide or aggression (international wrongful act in violation of a *jus cogens* obligation).

This does not depend only on the fact that the international adjudicative bodies jurisdictionally competent to prosecute individuals for international crimes **are different** from those competent to decide on the responsibility of states cases. A certain military official may make an 'on the ground' decision that amounts to an act of genocide contravening all governmental instructions. Conversely, a certain military official may be acquitted of the charge of genocide, not having taken part in any way in the military operations decided by his/her Government with the aim of destroying an ethnic group, or parts of it.

It is worth recalling that, for instance, while the ICTY did convict for the crime of genocide a number of perpetrators belonging to the Serbian Army, including General Mladić,[22] for the 1995 Srebrenica massacre, the ICJ, in the 2007 judgment in the *Bosnia v Serbia* case, found that Serbia was not internationally responsible for the act of genocide in breach of the *Convention on the Prevention and Punishment of the Crime of Genocide.*[23] However, the ICJ found that Serbia had infringed the international obligations to pre-

---

[22] ICTY, *Prosecutor v Ratko Mladić*, Case No IT-09-92-T, Judgment (22 November 2017).

[23] *Application of the Convention on the Prevention and Punishment of the Crime of Genocide* (Bosnia and Herzegovina v Serbia and Montenegro) (Judgment) [2007] ICJ Rep 43, 215.

vent the acts of genocide in question, as well as to punish its perpetrators.[24]

International criminal law as we know it today originates from the customary rules providing criminal jurisdictional competence for states to arrest and try suspects of crimes that were considered the concern of the international community of nations, so-called ***crimina juris gentium***. Initially, such crimes comprised only **piracy** as a threat to international navigation and trade. By the end of the 19th century and through the 20th century, slavery and slave trade, torture and hijacking were, in different forms, added to the list.

Suspicion that an individual has committed an international crime affords states the power to exercise their criminal jurisdiction – *i.e.*, **universal jurisdiction** – also when lacking the traditional nationality or territoriality connections with the crime in question. The states under whose jurisdiction a suspect of such crimes is to be found are under an obligation either to prosecute or to extradite the suspect in question (***aut dedere***, ***aut judicare***).

Against the background of the horrors of the Second World War, during which most heinous crimes were committed against enemy armies and populations, but also against national civilians and ethnic groups, aggression, war crimes, genocide and crimes against humanity were added to the list of international crimes. The path for the codification of such core crimes within the UN has not been straight and smooth.

The Statutes of the Nuremberg and Tokyo Tribunals set the first stepping stone, but formally they lacked universal legal force, since they consisted of treaties concluded by the winning powers. That is why the UN General Assembly in 1946, in one of its first resolutions,[25] endorsed the principles set out in the Nuremberg and Tokyo Statutes. At the same time, it requested and set in motion the codification of the rules and principles in point. While the multilat-

---

[24] *Ibidem*, 237.

[25] UN General Assembly, Res 95(I) of 11 December 1946.

eral *Convention on the Prevention and Punishment of the Crime of Genocide* was successfully adopted in 1948, the ILC embarked on the preparation of a comprehensive code, which was blocked in the shallows of the Cold War mainly over the disagreements on the definition of aggression. Despite the adoption of UN General Assembly Resolution 3314(XXIX) of 14 December 1974 containing the definition of aggression, the project for the code in question did not make much of a headway.

Following the usual and dramatic pendulum way by which History proceeds, it was only in the midst of the horrors occurring in the Balkans and in Africa in the early 1990s that the codification process was revived. In 1993, the UN Security Council established the ICTY [26] and in 1994 the ICTR. [27] The resolutions setting up the two international criminal tribunals also contained the relative Statutes, which set out and defined the crimes falling under their jurisdictional competence. Those Statutes, together with the *Draft-Code of Crimes against the Peace and Security of Mankind*, which had been finalised by the ILC in 1996, [28] paved the way for the negotiations that led to the adoption of the *Rome Statute* and the establishment of the ICC in 1998.

The *Rome Statute* provides a carefully crafted set of definitions of the crimes falling under the jurisdiction of the ICC, the element of crimes, the preconditions to the exercise of jurisdiction and admissibility, the general principles of criminal law which it will apply, the penalties and its rules of procedure. It also establishes the Assembly of States Parties (Part 11) for review of the Rome Statute every seven years, next to the usual procedure for amendments.

---

[26] UN Security Council, Res 827 of 25 May 1993.

[27] UN Security Council, Res 955 of 8 October 1994.

[28] ILC, 'Draft-Code of Crimes against the Peace and Security of Mankind, with Commentaries' (1996) II(2) Yearbook of the International Law Commission 15.

It was within such legal-diplomatic context that later agreement on the thorny definition of the crime of aggression was reached (2010), but could not be found for the addition of important new crimes, such as terrorism.

The jurisdiction of the ICC is of a **complementary nature** (Article 17 of the *Rome Statute*). Namely, the ICC may proceed only when the state having otherwise (primary) jurisdictional competence over a suspect under the Statute is 'unwilling or unable' to prosecute.

It is to be noted that the *Rome Statute* has not been ratified by important states, such as the PRC, India, Russia and the US. As said, both the US and Russia had indeed signed the *Rome Statute*, but later, by issuing an *ad hoc* statement, denied their intention to ratify it, respectively in 2002 and 2016.[29]

As for Russia in particular, apart from the symbolic relevance of a similar statement,[30] under Article 18(a) of the VCLT, the latter implies that Russia is no longer bound under the principle of good faith not to undertake conduct that might frustrate the object and purpose of the *Rome Statute*, for instance as a permanent Member of the Security Council, or not cooperating with states that are parties to the Statute.

7. The law of jurisdictional immunities

International customary law on jurisdictional immunities of states and their officials is an integral part of contemporary international law. The relevant rules constitute the oldest core of international law, since they are ancillary to the horizontal legal setting which emerged from the Peace of Westphalia. The common rationale of

---

[29] Chapter 3, Section 3.1.1.

[30] 'Russia Withdraws Signature From International Criminal Court Statute' in *The Guardian* (16 November 2016).

these rules is expressed by the Latin tag *par in parem non habet judicium*, which means that entities on the same footing may not pass judgment over each other, even less so adopt enforcement measures.

The distinction between the rules which provide for **state immunity** and those on the **immunity of state officials** is a relatively recent one. At the origin of the international society, the absolutist and patrimonial conception of the state encompassed within the scope of one single customary rule the two kinds of immunity.

The need to differentiate such immunity into **separate rules and exceptions** with regard to foreign states, their highest-ranking officials, their diplomatic agents and the generality of their organs arose with the constitutionalist conception of the state involving the principles of the rule of law and the separation of powers. This brought to the distinction between the state as separate from the Head of state, the Head of Government and the Ministry for Foreign Affairs, diplomatic agents; and the rest of state officials.

Amongst the mentioned immunities, the one which has evolved most significantly as of its inception is **state immunity**. The major change dates back to the time of the Soviet revolution. The nationalization of the means of production and economic activities in the USSR and, later, in its allied countries, meant that Soviet international trade was carried out by state agencies. These would invoke sovereign immunity based on their public nature whenever sued before a domestic court in relation to a dispute which had arisen out of a commercial dispute abroad.

In order to circumvent this bar to remedies for the local commercial partners of Soviet agencies, thus avoiding the abuse of sovereign immunity, between 1920 and 1930, municipal courts in Italy and Belgium triggered a transformation of the rule, by rejecting claims of state immunity in relation to *acta jure gestionis*, *i.e.*, commercial activities, while upholding claims of immunity exclusively for *acta jure imperii*, *i.e.*, conduct carried out in the exercise of elements of governmental authority/public functions, such as military and police activities.

Notwithstanding the opposition by Soviet countries to the above case-law, the latter soon brought about a new configuration of the custom in hand, so-called ***restrictive immunity***, even before the Fall of the Berlin Wall in 1989. After an intensive preparatory work on the topic, the ILC substantiated the customary nature of the restrictive immunity rule,[31] which has been codified in the 2004 *United Nations Convention on Jurisdictional Immunities of States and Their Property*, which, though, has not yet entered into force at the time the present book is going to press.

The rule on state immunity, as codified by the 2004 *UN Convention*, excludes both the domestic courts' **jurisdiction to adjudge** and the **jurisdiction to enforce** over a foreign state. In fact, these are two distinct immunities under two distinct rules. A state may well be found liable for a breach of contract, or a tort claim, but its property used for public functions – such as the diplomatic premises or bank account, or military equipment – remains protected from enforcement jurisdiction.

In some legal literature and domestic case-law in certain countries pressure has emerged to the effect of widening the exception, or restriction, to **state immunity**, so as to encompass also **claims for damages caused by breaches of *jus cogens*** rules carried out by state officials, such as war crimes, crimes against humanity or genocide.

Having regard to the rules on state immunity, this trend has been supported by the Greek and Italian judiciaries, with specific regard respectively to the *Prefecture of Voiotia v Federal Republic of Germany*[32] and *Ferrini v Federal Republic of Germany* cases.[33] Both cases concerned claims for damages caused by war crimes committed by the Third Reich during the Second World War. It is important to stress that the above judicial context did not concern

[31] ILC, 'Draft Articles on Jurisdictional Immunities of States and Their Properties' (1991) II(2) Yearbook of the International Law Commission 12.

[32] Tribunal of Livadia, Judgment No 137 of 30 October 1997.

[33] Italian Court of Cassation, Judgment No 5044 of 11 March 2004.

criminal proceedings **against state officials** for international crimes – with respect to which the fact that immunity does not apply is undisputed – but ***civil*** **liability claims** before domestic courts against a state for damages related to such international crimes.

As referred above, in Chapter 4, Section 3.1, the Italian decision of the Court of Cassation denying the immunity of Germany in the ***Ferrini*** **case** led to a dispute between Germany and Italy which was decided by the ICJ in 2012 finding for Germany.[34] The ICJ referred to the 2004 *UN Convention* and its *travaux préparatoires* in order to hold that no sufficient evidence of state practice, nor *opinio juris*, exist which would substantiate the formation of an exception to state immunity for damage claims of the kind in question.[35] The ICJ also stressed that its decision concerned state immunity alone, without prejudice to the existence of an exception to immunity of state officials for international crimes.[36]

The ICJ judgment in the *Jurisdictional Immunities of the State* case would certainly undermine the progressive erosion of state immunity for cases of the kind in question. As already illustrated, this judgment was resoundingly rejected by the Italian Constitutional Court in 2014.[37] But it cannot be said that it paved the way to significantly widespread domestic case-law in the same direction.

The **diplomatic immunity** is codified by the 1961 *Vienna Convention on Diplomatic Relations*. Such immunity is of a twofold nature. On the one hand, diplomatic agents enjoy immunity *ratione materiae*, *i.e.*, for acts performed in the exercise of their official functions, and remains **after the end of the period of accreditation** to a foreign country. On the other hand, diplomatic agents enjoy also immunity *ratione personae*, that is, also for conduct carried

---

[34] *Jurisdictional Immunities of the State* (Germany v Italy: Greece intervening) (Judgment) [2012] ICJ Rep 99.

[35] *Ibidem*, 122.

[36] *Ibidem*, 143.

[37] Chapter 4, Section 3.1.

out in personal capacity. But once their period of accreditation comes to an end and they have had the time to leave the host country, **also the immunity expires**, and they may be sued or tried for their private acts carried out at the time they were on mission. The same rules apply to the **Heads of state**, **Heads of Government** and the **Ministries for Foreign Affairs**.

The absolute mandatory nature of the 1961 *Vienna Convention* was solemnly affirmed by the ICJ in the already recalled *Tehran Hostages* case between the US and Iran. The case prompted from the occupation of the US embassy in Teheran by Iranian activist students, and the subsequent taking of fifty US diplomats as hostages. The ICJ rejected the Iranian argument according to which the occupation of the embassy and the hostages taking was a **countermeasure** against espionage activities carried out by the US, as follows:

> 'Even if the alleged criminal activities of the United States in Iran could be considered as having been established, the question would remain whether they could be regarded by the Court as constituting a justification of Iran's conduct and thus a defence to the United States' claims in the present case. The Court, however, is unable to accept that they can be so regarded. This is because diplomatic law itself provides the necessary means of defence against, and sanction for, illicit activities by members of diplomatic or consular missions.' [38]

The rationale of the absolute nature of diplomatic immunity during the accreditation period, far from granting impunity, is based on the aim of avoiding impairment of the diplomatic function (*ne impediatur legatio*) from abuses of legal process in foreign countries, possibly politically motivated.

Another kind of jurisdictional immunity under international law

---

[38] *United States Diplomatic and Consular Staff in Tehran* (United States of America v Iran) (Judgment) [1980] ICJ Rep 3, 39.

concerns state officials in general when acting abroad, the so-called ***functional immunity*** or **immunity *ratione materiae***. It mostly applies to conduct relevant under criminal law, such as acts of sabotage or espionage. The immunity rule in question has been reduced so as to exclude its application to crimes against humanity, war crimes, acts of genocide and aggression. This immunity has been successfully argued by Italy in the *Enrica Lexie* case illustrated above in Chapter 6, Section 4.

The rationale of functional immunity is that a state official, while exercising its public function, is not acting as an individual but **on behalf of the state**. Thus, functional immunity would be substantive in nature, in the sense that under the circumstances in question an official may not be tried by the courts of the host state, not so much for a procedural bar, but because the conduct in question is attributed to the state for which the official was acting, even for *ultra vires* acts, *i.e.*, those which went outside the scope of the instructions received. It flows from this substantive law approach to the matter that functional immunity has **no time limit**, differently from personal immunity.

8. International law on migration

Migration is one of the most recent and complex challenges confronting the international society of states. From a European standpoint, both along the Mediterranean and the Balkan routes, migratory flows from Africa and the Middle-East raise significant social concern and legal questions. The phenomenon is acute also within Africa, in Latin America and Asia, for example with regard to the massive exodus of Venezuelans and Colombians to neighbouring States or of the Rohingya population from Myanmar to Bangladesh.

International legal rules pertaining to migrations are usually subsumed into some kind of so-called *migration law*. However, it is difficult to consider the international rules relevant to migration as making up an **autonomous body of international** law. Rather, under the concept of 'migration law' one finds a plurality of rules coming from different bodies of international law, all equally relevant to migration. This **composite legal regime** draws from international economic law, human rights law, refugee law and the law of the sea, to the extent that migrants cross the sea to reach their destination. **Environmental law** is also relevant in relation to the so-called *environmental migration* prompted by the desertification in the sub-Saharan continent, or by the gradual disappearance of small insular states due to sea-level rising and climate change.

Migratory matters belong in principle to the *domaine réservé* of states. That is to say that a state is allowed to regulate migration as it deems appropriate. Apart from human rights law generally applicable to all individuals, a state has specific obligations towards migrants only insofar as they are **asylum seekers refugees**. On the contrary, so-called '**economic migrants**' have no special status in international law. In sum, a state may adopt all the administrative procedures it deems necessary to manage inbound and outbound migratory flows, provided that it guarantees protection to asylum seekers and respects migrants' fundamental human rights. These administrative procedures will have to take into account other obligations incumbent upon a state under specific treaties, such as the 1949 *ILO Migration for Employment Convention*.

The most important instrument relevant to the international protection of migrants is the 1951 *Geneva Convention relating to the Status of Refugees* (*Refugee Convention*) and its subsequent 1967 *Protocol on the Status of Refugees* (*Refugee Protocol*). The *Refugee Convention* is managed by the Office of the United Nations High Commissioner for Refugees (UNHCR), established in 1950 in order to provide assistance to the European migrants who fled their country during the Second World War. Despite the UNHCR being meant to operate only for three years, it soon became clear that migration was not restricted to the European continent.

The *Refugee Convention* and *Protocol* boast 144 states parties. According to the former, a refugee is defined as an individual who:

> '[O]wing to a well-founded fear of being persecuted for reasons of race, religion, nationality, membership of a particular social group or political opinion, is outside the country of his nationality and is unable or, owing to such fear, is unwilling to avail himself of the protection of that country; or who, not having a nationality and being outside the country of his former habitual residence as a result of such events, is unable or, owing to such fear, is unwilling to return to it.' [39]

The concept of 'refugee' subsequently appeared in other international instruments, such as the 1954 *Convention on Diplomatic Asylum* and the 1954 *Convention on Territorial Asylum* within the OAS framework, or the 1977 *Geneva Conventions Additional Protocol I* in the field of humanitarian law. The widespread use of the definition of refugee makes it possible to consider it as part of customary international law.

According to Article 33 of the *Refugee Convention*, asylum seekers enjoy the **right to *non-refoulement***. Under this provision, generally recognised as evidentiary of international customary law, sometimes even of a *jus cogens* nature,[40] states are required to abstain from deporting or transferring a refugee to another state in which his/her personal safety is at risk, or where he/she risks suffering inhuman and degrading treatments. This rule does not apply to a refugee whenever he/she represents a danger for the host state. In addition to this right, the asylum seeker benefits from other fundamental rights, *e.g.*, the right to non-discrimination regarding access to essential services (Article 23) and regarding employment legislation (Article 24). Furthermore, he/she must benefit from the same treatment accorded to host state's nationals regarding economic rights.

The *Refugee Convention* leaves the host state free to establish and carry out its administrative procedures concerning the assess-

---

[39] Article 1(a).

[40] J Allain, 'The *Jus Cogens* Nature of *Non-Refoulement*' (2001) 13 International Journal of Refugee Law 533.

ment of the **refugee status**. It only requires that the asylum seeker is accorded the possibility to reside in the state's territory until the procedure is concluded. Once the refugee status has been recognised, he/she will enjoy the right to reside freely and legitimately in the state's territory, as well as all the other rights accorded to nationals, except for political rights.

The situation of '**irregular migrants**' – *i.e.*, those individuals who enter a country in breach of its customs and administrative rules procedures – is different from that of refugees. Irrespective of the reason why an 'irregular migrant' left his/her country of origin, he/she enjoys fundamental human rights. Needless to say, he/she cannot be subject to torture or to inhuman and degrading treatment. The right to *non-refoulement* also applies to 'irregular migrants,' but they do not benefit from the principle of non-discrimination or the right to national treatment.

In the Mediterranean region, where migration occurs also along maritime routes, though not predominantly, both human rights and ***rescue-at-sea* rules** apply.

Article 98 of UNCLOS on the duty to render assistance reads as follows:

> '1. Every State shall require the master of a ship flying its flag, in so far as he can do so without serious danger to the ship, the crew or the passengers:
> *a*) to render assistance to any person found at sea in danger of being lost;
> *b*) to proceed with all possible speed to the rescue of persons in distress, if informed of their need of assistance, in so far as such action may reasonably be expected of him;
> *c*) after a collision, to render assistance to the other ship, its crew and its passengers and, where possible, to inform the other ship of the name of his own ship, its port of registry and the nearest port at which it will call.'

This provision is generally recognised to reflect a customary rule already codified under Article 12 of the 1958 *Geneva Convention on the High Seas*. It is also considered to be interpreted and applied in combination with the 1974 *International Convention for the Safety of Life at Sea* (*SOLAS Convention*) and the 1979 *International Convention on Maritime Search and Rescue* (*SAR Convention*). The latter requires states to engage in co-operation, through exchange of information and coordination, in order to guarantee the maximum speed in rescue-at-sea operations. Pursuant to the SAR Convention, the IMO has divided the seas into search-and-rescue zones (SAR zones). Within each SAR zone, coastal states have joint and individual surveillance obligations.

As to 'environmental migrants,' also referred to 'environmental displaced persons,' since they do not fall within the definition of refugee provided by the *Refugee Convention* and *Protocol*, the UNHCR has been studying the issue. This study led in 2015 to a document, entitled *The Environment and Climate Change*,[41] which proposes to extend legal protection also to environmental migrants.

Finally, reference is to be made to the *Global Compact for Safe, Orderly and Regular Migration*, adopted in Marrakech in December 2018. Against often confused and imprecise information emerging from the media, it seems appropriate to single out from the document in question its objectives: 1) collect and utilize accurate and disaggregated data as a basis for evidence-based policies; 2) minimize the adverse drivers and structural factors that compel people to leave their country of origin; 3) provide accurate and timely information at all stages of migration; 4) ensure that all migrants have proof of legal identity and adequate documentation; 5) enhance availability and flexibility of pathways for regular migration; 6) facilitate fair and ethical recruitment and safeguard conditions that ensure decent work; 7) address and reduce vulnerabilities in migration; 8) save lives and establish coordinated international efforts on missing migrants; 9) strengthen the transnational response to smuggling of migrants; 10) prevent, combat and eradicate trafficking in

---

[41] V Türk et al, *UNHCR, the Environment & Climate Change* (UNHCR 2015).

persons in the context of international migration; and 11) manage borders in an integrated, secure and coordinated manner.

Further reading

Baroncini E, 'The EU Approach to Overcome the WTO Dispute Settlement Vacuum: Article 25 DSU Interim Appeal Arbitration as a Bridge Between Renovation and Innovation' in M Kolsky Lewis et al (eds), *A Post-WTO International Legal Order: Utopian, Dystopian and Others Scenarios* (Springer Law 2020), 115ff;

Baroncini E, 'L'approccio al contenzioso internazionale per il libero scambio dell'Unione europea' in E Baroncini et al (eds), *Enforcement & Law-Making of the EU Trade Policy* (AMS Acta 2022), 1ff;

Baroncini E, 'The EU and the Multi-Party Interim Appeal Arbitration Arrangement (MPIA) – A Contingency Tool to Save the WTO Appellate Stage' in B Barel and A Gattini (eds), *Le prospettive dell'export italiano in tempi di sfide e crisi globali. Rischi e opportunità* (Giappichelli 2021), 83ff;

Boyle A and Redgwell C, *Birnie, Boyle, and Redgwell's International Law and the Environment* (4th edn, OUP 2021);

Conforti B, 'The Specificity of Human Rights and International Law' in U Fastenrath et al (eds), *From Bilateralism to Community Interest: Essays in Honour of Judge Bruno Simma* (OUP 2011), 433ff;

De Schutter O, *International Human Rights Law: Cases, Materials, Commentary* (2nd edn, CUP 2014);

Fitzmaurice M, 'The Relationship between the Law of International Watercourses and Sustainable Development' in M Fitzmaurice et al (eds), *Research Handbook on International Environmental Law* (Edward Elgar 2010), 605ff;

Fox H and Webb Ph, *The Law of State Immunity* (3rd edn, OUP 2015);

Gaeta P, Viñuales JE and Zappalà S (eds), *Cassese's International Law* (3rd edn, OUP 2020);

Gilbert G and Rüsch AM, *International Refugee and Migration Law*, in M Evans (ed), *International Law* (5th edn, OUP 2018), 811ff;

Kreibaum U, Dolzer R and Schreuer C, *Principles of International Investment Law* (3rd edn, OUP 2022);

Schabas WA (ed), *The Cambridge Companion to International Criminal Law* (CUP 2016);

Tanaka Y, *The International Law of the Sea* (2nd edn, CUP 2015);

Tanzi A, *Introduzione al diritto internazionale contemporaneo* (7th edn, CEDAM 2022);

Tomuschat C, *Human Rights. Between Idealism and Realism* (3rd edn, OUP 2014).

Conclusions

Multilateralism v Unilateralism

In the previous Chapters it has repeatedly emerged how the functioning of the international legal system is fundamentally based on the **interplay between the national and international legal levels**. The more these two levels harmoniously and concertedly interact, the more streamlined the functioning of the international legal system will be. As already recalled, in the words of Judge Crawford, '[m]any of the things international law tries to do have to be done at the national level.' [1]

At a time when the international society is becoming increasingly split by war, the above considerations still hold for the countries who are conducting themselves in a peaceful manner and in the relations between themselves.

Following the 'dualist approach' analysed in Chapter 4, a long string of scholars, from de Vattel to Triepel, and beyond, have emphasised that the international and national legal systems, formally distinct from one another, needed to be coordinated through the **common will of states members of the international community**. [2] Such a voluntarist approach came to the fore at the time the in-

---

[1] J Crawford, 'Chance, Order, Change: The Course of International Law' (2013) 365 Collected Courses of the Hague Academy of International Law 13, 214.

[2] P Gragl, *Legal Monism: Law, Philosophy, and Politics* (OUP 2018), 34.

ternational society lost its Eurocentric homogeneity of interests and values. Needless to say, the more inhomogeneous and conflictual the relationship between states, the more difficult is to find a common denominator among them, and the rustier is the international legal process. This need for coordination and coherence was profoundly felt and addressed by the community of states in the 20th century, **after the Second World War**.

After hitting bottom during the latter conflict, with its horrors, genocide, destructions and fifty-four million deaths, the community of states – particularly in Europe, which had been the field of operation of that conflict, and later the major arena for the **Cold War** – engaged into a process of social, political, economic, legal and moral reconstruction. Winston Churchill's declarations relating to the need to 'build a kind of United States of Europe' [3] is to be considered through the lens of those efforts, particularly in consideration of the fact that the horrors of the Second World War, as much as those of the First one, had been triggered by the European rivalries. The same holds true for his conviction that:

> 'There is no reason why a regional organisation of Europe should in any way conflict with the world organisation of the United Nations. On the contrary, I believe that the larger synthesis will only survive if it is founded upon coherent natural groupings.' [4]

In a similar vein, the then US President Franklin D Roosevelt, abandoning the recurrent US isolationist policy, affirmed that

> 'We cannot live alone, at peace: (…) our own well-being is dependent on the well-being of other nations far away. (…) We have

---

[3] W Churchill, 'Speech Delivered at the University of Zurich, 19 September 1946', 1 available at: <https://rm.coe.int>.

[4] *Ibidem*.

learned to be citizens of the world, members of the human community.'[5]

This open approach and multilateralist inclination provided the incentive for the establishment of a number of international organisations. The **UN** were established with a view to making up the demise of the League of Nations, which had 'failed because [its founding] principles were deserted by those states who had brought it into being.'[6] To that end, the UN was set up with the primary aim to 'maintain international peace and security,' 'develop friendly relations among nations' and 'achieve international co-operation in solving international problems' (Article 1 of the *UN Charter*).

The establishment of the **CoE** in 1949 was geared towards the enhancement of the common European moral and human rights values. The setting up in 1950 of the building blocks of what later became the **EU** was meant to provide the institutional and legal space for internal economic and political stabilisation and cooperation that would replace the internal competition and conflict which had characterised the intra-European relations for centuries. Externally, a European integration organisation would constitute a larger economic, and possibly political, actor capable of competing on the global markets, while contributing to the promotion of international dialogue through the rule of law, as it did for decades.

This political impetus towards **multilateralism** and expansion through coordination and cooperation within Europe and between Europe and the US through harmonious economic, political and military transatlantic relations was enhanced by their participation in international institutions, such as the IMF, WB, OECD, GATT, first, and WTO, later, on the economic side, and NATO on the military level.

---

[5] 'FDR Inaugurated For Fourth Term, Jan 20, 1945' in *POLITICO* (20 January 2018).

[6] Churchill (n 3) 1.

Those alliances and institutions allowed primarily the Western countries to face the economic challenges of the post-War reconstruction, and the military ones stemming from the dramatic East-West divide characterising the Cold War. Meanwhile, the UN General Assembly – despite the block of the Security Council due to the criss-cross vetoes by the five permanent Members – served as a forum for shock-absorption, not only *vis-à-vis* the East-West divide, but also with regard to the North-South tensions deriving from decolonisation.

Against this background, we have seen how the **UN** has provided the framework for the **re-negotiation and consolidation of the rules of the game**, particularly due to the demands from the newly independent states stemming from the process of **decolonisation**, gathered under the so-called **G77** grouping and sided by the **Soviet Block**.

Other multilateral diplomatic forums, such as the **Conference on Security and Cooperation in Europe** (CSCE), from the preparations of the 1975 *Helsinki Final Act* onward,[7] have paved the way for the fall of the Soviet Union and, once evolved into the **OSCE**, provided the framework for supporting the newly independent states stemming from the former Soviet Union in their transition towards constitutional democracy and market economy through the rule of law. In this vein, mention is to be made to the European Commission for Democracy through Law ('Venice Commission') also tasked to

> 'Help states wishing to bring their legal and institutional structures into line with European standards and international experience in the fields of democracy, human rights and the rule of law.'[8]

---

[7] CSCE, 'Final Act' (1 August 1975), available at: <www.osce.org>.

[8] CoE, 'The Venice Commission of the Council of Europe' (Doc 121014RF of 2015), 1.

Meanwhile, multilateral negotiations addressing indivisible international community interests (***global commons***) produced since the 1970s the new body of **international environmental law**. The latter progressed throughout the 1990s through compromise between different approaches and interests between industrialised and developing countries around the generally agreeable **sustainable development** principle. The latter emerged from the **1992 UN Rio Conference on Environment and Development** and was consolidated by many subsequent MEAs that gave effect to the general principles enshrined in the Rio Declaration.[9] The winning feature of the sustainable development principle was and remains its flexible due diligence nature, whereby implementation and compliance with it are proportional to the financial, legal, administrative, scientific and technological capacity of any given state.

At the same time, a parallel expansive trend characterised the **human rights law process** through conventional and jurisprudential terms which formalised legal elements of the common denominator between the different social, cultural, religious, economic and political components of a highly diversified, but relatively organised, international community. In the 1990s, the human rights law process was complemented by new instruments for the **fight against impunity** for war crimes, crimes against humanity and genocide. As seen, this was marked by the establishment by the Security Council of the ICTY and the ICTR in 1993 and 1994, respectively, followed by the *Rome Statute* for the ICC adopted in 1998.[10]

Indeed, multilateralism reached its peak though the UN during the first part of the1990s, after the **Fall of the Berlin Wall** and on the occasion of the unprecedented cohesion among the five permanent Members in the Security Council. This cohesion was epito-

---

[9] See further M Fitzmaurice, A Tanzi and A Papantoniou (eds), *Multilateral Environmental Treaties* (Edward Elgar 2017).

[10] See Chapter 7, Section 6.

mised by the unanimous reaction against Iraq after its invasion of Kuwait in August 1990. [11]

This revival of the UN and international law suffered **the first blows** with the failures of the peace operations in the Balkans and in Somalia, Rwanda, and Sierra Leone, amongst others. The newly found cohesion among the five permanent Members in the Security Council started cracking when, in 1999, Russia rejected to support a resolution authorising NATO's use of force against Milošević's Serbia due to its cruel policy of repression against the Muslim minority in Kosovo, while NATO forces proceeded to the bombing of strategic targets in Serbia without the Security Council authorisation.

Unilateralist approaches to international affairs started coming significantly to the fore in the US with the George Bush Jr Presidency in 2001. On the other side of the Atlantic, over the first decade of the Millennium, European Governments retained a strongly internationalist, cooperative and rule-based approach to international affairs, while nationalist movements have been for a while contained within minority political parties. This led to political and ideological tensions in Transatlantic relations.

One may recall that an advisor to the George Bush Jr Administration (2001-2009), for a short period US Ambassador to the UN, John R Bolton – later, National Security Advisor in the Trump Administration –, back in 1994, maintained that:

> 'There is no such thing as the United Nations. There is an international community that occasionally can be led by the only real power left in the world and that is the United States when it suits our interest and we can get others to go along.' [12]

---

[11] Un Security Council, Res 660 of 2 August 1990.

[12] 'There Is No Such Things As the United Nations' in *The Times* (2 August 2005).

Indeed, the US, after a period of moderate engagement in the multilateral dialogue to tackle the challenges to the collective interests of the international community under the Obama Presidency (2009-2017), have reverted to its **isolationist** attitude to an unprecedented extent and hyperbolic degree, only softened during the current Biden Presidency.

This attitude is epitomised by the statement of the former US President, Donald J Trump, in his address to the UN General Assembly on 25 September 2018 announcing that the US 'reject the ideology of globalism and (…) embrace the doctrine of patriotism.' [13] Similarly illustrative is the explanation of the reason for the US withdrawal from the 2015 *Paris Agreement on Climate Change*, whereby 'our withdrawal from the agreement represents a reassertion of America's sovereignty.' [14]

What adds to the recent political novelties on the international scene that may have a significant impact on the course of the international law process is the swerving towards unilateralism among some EU Member states, such as Austria, Italy, Hungary, Poland and the UK. Others may be added to the list in the future.

It has been puzzling for a few years that, while the 'multilateralist' liberal approach to international relations is being challenged by the very same powers which sternly fought for it for 70 years since the end of the Second World War, it is now invoked and promoted by the PRC and Russia, even though in contradictory terms. In this sense, the curious 2016 *Joint Declaration by the Russian Federation and the People's Republic of China on Promotion of International law* reads as follows:

---

[13] 'Remarks by President Trump to the 73rd Session of the United Nations General Assembly' (25 September 2018), available at: <www.whitehouse.gov>.

[14] 'Statement by President Trump on the Paris Climate Accord' (1 June 2017), available at <www.whitehouse.gov>.

> 'The principles of international law are the cornerstone for just and equitable international relations featuring win-win cooperation, creating a community of shared future for mankind, and establishing common space of equal and indivisible security and economic cooperation.' [15]

In the same vein, it is also worthy to recall the statement of the Chinese President Xi during the 2017 WEF, as follows:

> '[W]e should pursue a well-coordinated and inter-connected approach to develop a model of open and win-win cooperation. Today, mankind has become a close-knit community of shared future. Countries have extensive converging interests and are mutually dependent. All countries enjoy the right to development. At the same time, they should view their own interests in a broader context and refrain from pursuing them at the expense of others. We should commit ourselves to growing an open global economy to share opportunities and interests through opening-up and achieve win-win outcomes. One should not just retreat to the harbour when encountering a storm, for this will never get us to the other shore of the ocean. We must redouble efforts to develop global connectivity to enable all countries to achieve inter-connected growth and share prosperity. We must remain committed to developing global free trade and investment, promote trade and investment liberalization and facilitation through opening-up and say no to protectionism. Pursuing protectionism is like locking oneself in a dark room. While wind and rain may be kept outside, that dark room will also block light and air. No one will emerge as a winner in a trade war.' [16]

---

[15] 'Declaration of the Russian Federation and the People's Republic of China on the Promotion of International Law' (25 June 2016), available at: <www.fmprc.gov.cn>.

[16] 'Xi Jinping Keynote Speech at the World Economic Forum' (17 January 2017), available at: <www.china.org.cn>.

After the Russian attack on Ukraine in February 2022, the picture is undergoing major and unfortunate adjustments. Obviously, Russia has abandoned international multilateral cooperation, while the PRC and India are turning inward retreating between nationalism and regionalism, while gradually moving closer to Russia. The unity of the Western countries is increasingly more fragile. Against this background, the multilateral platforms of intergovernmental organisations, especially, the UN and OSCE – which much had contributed during the Cold War to contain destructive impulses – are held increasingly less in consideration by those very Member states who might profit most from them.

Be that as it may, the developments of international law ahead of us will result from the combination of the currently turbulent social, political and legal developments in nation-states around the world. In this regard, and by way of conclusion, let me quote again the remarks expressed, more than a century ago, by the Russian diplomat and jurist Fredrich Martens, and which still hold true today:

> 'On doit nécessairement reconnaître que les défectuosités du droit international et le manque de précision de ses règles ne sont que la conséquence inévitable des imperfections et de l'instabilité qui caractérisent l'ordre intérieur ayant prévalu jusqu'à ce jour dans tous les Etats.' [17]

---

[17] F de Martens, *Traité de droit international* (Vol I, Libraire Marescq 1883), 287. The passage has been translated to English in Chapter 1, Section 8.

www.ingramcontent.com/pod-product-compliance
Lightning Source LLC
Chambersburg PA
CBHW080938240926
51849CB00004BA/490
* 9 7 8 9 4 6 2 3 6 3 3 9 7 *